NO OTHER NAME

RAMON BENNETT

JERUSALEM

All *italics* within the text are Scripture quotations. Those in *heavier italics*, except for ***bold italics*** used for emphasis, are Scripture quotations from the Old Testament.

Written permission must be secured from the author to use or reproduce, ***by any means***, any part of this book, except for brief quotations in reviews or articles.

Copyright © 2016 Ramon Bennett
All Rights Reserved
First printed July 2016

ISBN 978-1-943423-18-7

Published in the United States by Shekinah Books LLC

Distributed in Israel by: Ramon Bennett,
P. O. Box 37111, Jerusalem 91370.
eMail: armofsalvation@mac.com

Shekinah Books LLC
A division of *Arm of Salvation Ministries*, Jerusalem.

This paperback is subject to discounts for orders of 10 or more copies when purchased through Shekinah Books. *No Other Name* is also available as a Kindle e-Book or in PDF form. Further information can be obtained, and purchases of multiple hard copies or single PDF purchases may be made, by logging onto: *http://www.shekinahbooks.com*. All titles are available for purchase on Amazon.com

*There is **No Other Name** under heaven given among men by which we must be saved*

(Acts 4:12).

God, who at various times and in various ways spoke in time past to the fathers by the prophets, has in these last days spoken to us by His Son, whom He has appointed heir of all things, through whom also He made the worlds

(Hebrews 1:1–2a).

Wherefore God has highly exalted Him and given Him the name which is above every name, that at the name of Jesus every knee should bow, of those in heaven, and of those on earth, and of those under the earth, and that every tongue should confess that Jesus Christ is Lord, to the glory of God the Father

(Philippians 2:9–11).

Contents

Introduction	7
Luke's Preamble	15
The Gospel of the Grace of God	17
Endnotes	221
Newsletter	289
Other Titles by Ramon Bennett	290
Book & Music Titles by Zipporah Bennett	292

Introduction

My purpose in blending the gospel accounts together is to produce a single, continuous narrative of *the Gospel of the Grace of God*, an uninterrupted story of the nativity, life, death, resurrection, and ascension of Jesus Christ as presented throughout the four gospels. This is not another translation of the Scriptures, the purposeful omitting of all chapter and verse numbers reflect this—there were no chapter and verse divisions in the original writings. I have, however, indicated in fine print the home of the passages from the Old Testament.

This work is meant to be read and reread as a book. I have included Endnotes (aka comments and short Bible studies) on words, expressions, and passages in the gospels that have either been passed over too lightly, misunderstood, or not understood at all. I trust readers will find these informative and edifying. Having a Bible near at hand could be helpful to the reader. I purposely stayed away from including a running commentary throughout because the book could easily have morphed into a thousand-page tome.

No two of our gospels are the same; each contains events not recorded in the others and each gospel contains richer detail on certain events that are not found in either of the other three. I have attempted to produce the fullest account of each event by the weaving of sections together.

Apparently, in the three years that Jesus preached throughout the length and breadth of the land of Israel—despite what many "scholars" and Bible publishers would have us believe, there was no such place or entity called

"Palestine" in Christ's time—he would use variations of certain stories and the reader should be aware of the existence of variations, they are not mistakes.

The gospels were presented to us in ages past by four different writers. They gave us, over intervals of years and for posterity, their personal eyewitness accounts of the memorable, often earth-shattering events that took place during Jesus Christ's thirty-three-year sojourn on earth. Obviously, when different people recall the same happenings from memory there must, of necessity, be some variances in their recollections.

The word "gospel" means "good news." Jesus is, therefore, the *Gospel of God* (Romans 1:1). He is the personification of *the gospel of the grace of God* (Acts 20:24), and He brought *the gospel of the kingdom* (Matthew 4:23) to us—a kingdom to which everyone becomes a part should they choose to truly believe Jesus is God's Son who came in the flesh, died, and rose again. Jesus is *the gospel of your salvation* (Ephesians 1:13), and Jesus is *the gospel of peace* (Ephesians 6:15)—peace with God and peace with our own self.

Jesus was God incarnate. He was God acting like God in the body of a man. All the power of *God Almighty* was available to him, but he came expressly to give his life in order that men might live. Jesus felt all the pain a man in the flesh could possibly feel, together with the pain felt in God's heart because of man's lack of faith and his rejection of him.

In our present day and age Jesus, God, repentance, and salvation are not exactly the flavors of the month. I long

Introduction

ago chose to believe the "good news" and have since walked and talked with God for more than fifty years. I can testify to God's mercy, love and faithfulness and have witnessed the clear manifestation of God's mighty power on numerous occasions.

Those who spent time with Jesus, following his mind-boggling resurrection after having lain three days in a tomb in scorching Middle East temperatures, and who later wrote the gospels and epistles, were not a bunch of crazies suffering from dementia. These people knew that they knew that they knew what they had seen, heard and experienced—and were prepared to die for the privilege of testifying to it, which most of them did. John, wrote:

> *That which was from the beginning, which we have heard, which we have seen with our eyes, which we have looked upon, and our hands have handled, concerning the Word of life—the life was manifested, and we have seen, and bear witness, and declare to you that eternal life which was with the Father and was manifested to us—that which we have seen and heard we declare to you, that you also may have fellowship with us; and truly our fellowship is with the Father and with His Son Jesus Christ. And these things we write to you that your joy may be complete* (1John 1:1-4).

John is saying that they not only heard Jesus, but they saw and touched him. John passionately wants his readers to understand that he is not being ridiculous, but that they heard Jesus, saw Jesus—before and after the resurrection—

and they had touched and handled him. Jesus was not a ghost, rather he was the harbinger of life to all who believe.

The Apostle Paul began as an ultra-religious Pharisee who persecuted those believing Jesus was *the only begotten Son* of God and claiming he had been resurrected. After a personal encounter with Jesus on the road to Damascus, where he was heading with letters in hand to take back to Jerusalem and imprison those believing in Jesus, Paul became transformed. Subsequently Paul became largely responsible for the proclamation of the gospel to the entire non-Jewish world. He writes to the Christians in Corinth:

> *I delivered to you first of all that which I also received: that Christ died for our sins according to the Scriptures, and that he was buried, and that he rose again the third day according to the Scriptures, and that he was seen by Cephas [Peter], then by the twelve [disciples].* **After that he was seen by over five hundred brethren at once**, *of whom the greater part remain to the present, but some have fallen asleep [died]. After that he was seen by James, then by all the apostles. Then last of all he was seen by me also, as by one born out of due time*
> (1Corinthians 15:4–8).

Jesus was seen by over five hundred followers at one time. It was a public confirmation. Obviously, the death and resurrection of Jesus was not something that was done in a corner out of sight. And if the testimony of five hundred people did not prove the resurrection of Jesus, no number of witnesses could.

Introduction

Working daily for months among the gospels has been a singularly wonderful blessing for me—never before had I seen with such clarity the majesty, divinity, love, compassion, strength, and fervor of our Lord Jesus Christ. Often it was necessary for me to pause and allow the enormity of this "man" to wash afresh over my soul. Obviously, the acclaimed physicist Albert Einstein must also have been captivated with the person of Jesus. In a quotation published in the *Saturday Evening Post*, on 26 October 1929, Einstein said:

> I am a Jew, but I am enthralled by the luminous figure of the Nazarene. Jesus is too colossal for the pen of phrase-mongers, however artful. No man can dispose of Christianity with a *bon mot*.
>
> No man can read the Gospels without feeling the actual presence of Jesus. His personality pulsates in every word.

I have used Luke's gospel to set the pace for this book because Luke's gospel is by far the longest of the gospels (forty-two percent longer than Mark, twenty-five percent longer than John, and nine percent longer than Matthew), which simply means that Luke's gospel narrative contains significantly more text and recorded events.

Many short extracts, which added clarity and depth to a particular passage contained in Luke's gospel, have been interpolated from the other gospels. (For an indication to where each passage of scripture has been taken, the reader would need to either purchase or borrow a copy of my book HI*STORY*.) Only direct duplications have been omitted. The sole instance of a seemingly true duplication of an event is the passage in Matthew's gospel where two blind men are reported to have been healed outside of Jericho (20:29–34), whereas the narratives of Luke (18:35–43) and Mark (10:46–50) tell of only one blind man being healed, and Mark supplies the name of that man. Some believe that two blind men were actually healed and Mark's naming of the lone man may have been due to him being well known in the area where it took place, which may have captured Mark's attention.

I based the text on the *King James Authorized* text because it is in the public domain, which precludes possible battles with Bible publishers over perceived copyright infringements. I have minimally modernized the *Authorized* text by replacing archaic usage with more modern usage to make a slightly more colloquial narrative without removing the nuances of the original. The Middle English word "behold" has but few appropriate synonyms in colloquial English. The word is still found in modern writings and I chose to retain it in a number of instances. No attempt was made to put events in chronological order, they strictly follow Luke's order.

Only rarely did I feel it necessary to add a word or two for the sake of clarity, so readers may rest assured the text is 99.85 percent true to the original, and throughly checked against the Greek *Textus Receptus* text.

I have corrected what tradition has long ensconced into almost all English translations through its use of the two Greek words *agapao* and *phileo*, which are both

Introduction

traditionally rendered "love" in John 21:15–17. The Greek words have subtle differences in meaning and giving them identical meanings in English distorts the reason for the discourse and confuses those who do not have a proper understanding of the point of the interchange between Jesus and Peter. I have used better, more appropriate equivalents of those Greek words, and these reflect themselves in the passage. There is also my explanatory Endnote for those wishing to better understand what was taking place at that moment.

It is my fervent hope and prayer that my labor of love among the gospels will bring delight, edification, and revelation to many. I believe this work will enrich the spiritual life of those who already have an intimate relationship with the Lord Jesus Christ, and it is my fervent prayer that it will be a source of spiritual blessing for many who do not as yet have a personal relationship with him.

Ramon Bennett
Jerusalem
8 July 2016

Luke's Preamble

*S*ince many have attempted to set out an orderly account of those things that are most surely believed among us, just as they, who from the beginning were eye-witnesses and ministers of the word, gave them to us. It also seemed good to me, having had a perfect understanding of everything from the very beginning, to write to you, most excellent Theophilus [which, being interpreted means, "Friend of God"], that you may know the certainty of those things in which you have been instructed.

The Gospel of the Grace of God

In the beginning was the Word, and the Word was with God, and the Word was God. He was in the beginning with God. Everything was made through him, and apart from him nothing was made that was made.[1] In him was life, and the life was the light of men. The light shines in the darkness, and the darkness does not comprehend it. He was in the world, and the world was made through him, and the world did not know him. He came to his own, and his own did not receive him. But for all those who did receive Him, he gave them the prerogative of becoming the sons of God, even to those who believe in his name; who were born, not of blood, nor by the will of the flesh, nor by the will of man, but of God. The Word was made flesh, and lived among us; and we beheld his glory, the glory as of the only begotten of the Father, full of grace and truth. Of his fullness we have all received, and grace for grace. For the Law was given by Moses, but grace and truth came by Jesus Christ. No man has seen God at any time; the only begotten Son, who is in the bosom of the Father, he has declared him.

There was in the days of Herod, the king of Judea, a certain priest named Zacharias, of the division of Abijah, and his wife was of the lineage of Aaron, and her name was Elisabeth. They were both righteous before God, walking in all the commandments and ordinances of the Lord, blameless. They had no child because Elisabeth was barren, and they were both then well advanced in years.

It came about that while he carried out his priestly duties before God in the order of his division, according to the custom of the priesthood, he was chosen by lot to burn incense when he went into the temple of the Lord. The whole multitude of the people were praying outside at the time of incense, and there appeared to him an angel of the Lord standing on the right side of the altar of incense.

When Zacharias saw him, he was troubled, and fear came upon him. The angel said to him, "Do not be afraid, Zacharias, for your prayer has been heard and your wife Elisabeth will bear you a son, and you will call his name John. You will have joy and happiness, and many will rejoice at his birth. For he will be great in the sight of the Lord and will drink neither wine nor strong drink; he will be filled with the Holy Spirit even in his mother's womb. He will turn many of the children of Israel to the Lord their God, and will go before him in the spirit and power of Elijah, to turn the hearts of the fathers to the children, and the disobedient to the wisdom of the righteous; to make ready a people prepared for the Lord. As it is written in the prophets:

> *Behold, I send my messenger before your face, who will prepare your way before you. The voice of one crying in the wilderness, "Prepare the way of the Lord, make his paths straight"* (Isaiah 40:3).

Zacharias said to the angel, "How will I know this? For I am an old man and my wife is well advanced in years." Answering, the angel said to him, "I am Gabriel who stands in the presence of God, and have been sent to speak to you, to bring you these glad tidings. And, indeed, you will be mute and not able to speak until the day that these things will be fulfilled, because you did not believe my words, which will be fulfilled in their own time."

The people waited for Zacharias, and marveled that he remained so long in the temple. When he came out he could not speak to them, and they understood that he had seen a vision in the temple; for he beckoned to them, and remained speechless.

It happened that as soon as the days of his priestly duties were completed, he went to his own house. After some days his wife Elisabeth conceived, and she hid herself for five months, saying, "This is how the Lord has dealt with me in the days when he looked upon me, and took away my reproach before men."

In the sixth month the angel Gabriel was sent by God to a city of Galilee, called Nazareth, to a virgin betrothed to a man whose name was Joseph, of the house of David; and the virgin's name was Mary. The angel came in to her and said, "Greetings! You are highly favored; the Lord is with you; blessed are you among women!" When she saw him she was troubled at his words, and wondered in her mind what manner of greeting it could be.

The angel said to her, "Do not be afraid, Mary, for you have found favor with God, and, surely, you will conceive in your womb and bring forth a son, and will call his name Jesus. He will be great, and will be called the Son of the Most High, and the Lord God will give him the throne of his father David, and he will reign over the house of Jacob forever; and of his kingdom there will be no end."

Then Mary said to the angel, "How will this be, seeing I do not know a man?" The angel answered and said to her, "The Holy Spirit will come upon you and the power of the Highest will overshadow you, therefore the holy child you will bear will be called the Son of God. Look, your cousin Elisabeth has also conceived a son in her old age; and this is the sixth month for her who was called barren. For with God nothing will be impossible." Mary said, "See, the handmaid of the Lord; let it be to me according to your word."[2] And the angel left her.

Mary arose in those days and went quickly into the hill country, into a city of Judah, and entered the house of Zacharias and greeted Elisabeth. It came to pass, that when Elisabeth heard Mary's greeting, the baby leaped in her womb and Elisabeth was filled with the Holy Spirit; and she spoke out with a loud voice and said, "Blessed are you among women, and blessed is the fruit of your womb. How is it that the mother of my Lord should come to me? For, lo, as soon as the sound of your greeting came to my ears the baby leaped in my womb for joy. Blessed is she who believed; for there will be a fulfillment of those things that were told her by the Lord.

Mary said: "My soul magnifies the Lord, and my spirit has rejoiced in God my Savior. For he has regarded the humble state of his handmaid: for, surely, from henceforth every generation will call me blessed.

"For he who is mighty has done great things for me; and holy is his name. His mercy is on those who fear him from generation to generation.

"He has shown strength with his arm; he has scattered the proud in the imagination of their hearts. He has pulled down the mighty from their lofty seats, and exalted those of low estate. He has filled the hungry with good things; and the rich he has sent away empty-handed.

"He has helped his servant Israel, in remembrance of his mercy, as he spoke to our fathers, to Abraham, and to his descendants for ever."

Mary stayed with her about three months, and then returned to her own house.

Now Elisabeth's time came that she should deliver; and she brought forth a son. Her neighbors and her cousins heard how the Lord had shown great mercy to her, and they rejoiced with her.

It came about on the eighth day, when they came to circumcise the child, they called him Zacharias, after the name of his father. His mother responded and said, "Not so! He shall be called John." They said to her, "There is no one among your relatives who is called by that name." And they made signs to his father, what name he would have him called. He asked for a writing tablet, and wrote, "His name is John," and they all marveled. His mouth was immediately opened and his tongue loosed, and he spoke and praised God.

Fear came on all that lived around about them; and all these sayings were talked about throughout all the hill country of Judea. All those who heard them kept them in their hearts, saying, "What manner of child will this be!" And the hand of the Lord was with him.

His father Zacharias was filled with the Holy Spirit and prophesied, saying:

> Blessed is the Lord God of Israel, for he has visited and redeemed[3a] his people. He has raised up a horn of salvation[3b] for us in the house of his servant David, as he foretold by the mouth of

his holy prophets who have been since the world began, that we should be saved from our enemies, and from the hand of all those who hate us; to perform the mercy promised to our fathers and to remember his holy covenant; the oath that he swore to our father Abraham, that he would grant to us deliverance out of the hand of our enemies, that we may worship before him without fear, in holiness and righteousness all the days of our life.

And you, child, will be called the prophet of the Most High; for you will go before the face of the Lord to prepare his ways; to give knowledge of salvation to his people by the forgiveness of their sins through the tender mercy of our God. Whereby the Dayspring from on high has visited us, to give light to those that dwell in darkness and in the shadow of death; to guide our feet in the way of peace.

And the child John grew, and increased in strength of spirit, and was in the deserts until the day he began his ministry to Israel.

The birth of Jesus Christ was like this: When his mother Mary was betrothed to Joseph, before they came together, she was found to be with child by the Holy Spirit. Then Joseph her husband, being a righteous man and not willing to make a public example of her, was of the mind to send her away quietly. While he thought on these things, behold, the angel of the Lord appeared to him in a dream, saying, "Joseph, son of David, do not be afraid to take Mary as your wife, for that which is conceived in her is by the Holy Spirit. She will bear a son and you will call his name JESUS, for he shall save his people from their sins."

All this was done that what was spoken by the Lord through the prophet might be fulfilled:

Observe, a virgin will be with child, and will bring forth a son and they will call his name Immanuel
(Isaiah 7:14)

which, being interpreted is, *"God with us."* Then Joseph, awakened from sleep, did as the angel of the LORD had commanded him, and took his wife to him. He did not know her until after she had borne her firstborn son; and he called his name Jesus.

It came to pass in those days that there went out a decree from Caesar Augustus, that all the world should be registered. This first census was made when Cyrenius was governing Syria, and everyone went to be registered, everyone to his own city. Joseph also went up from Galilee, out of the city of Nazareth to Judea, to the city of David, which is called Bethlehem—because he was of the house and lineage of David—to be registered with Mary his betrothed wife; Mary being heavy with child.

So it was, that while they were there, the days were completed that she would deliver. She brought forth her firstborn son, wrapped him in swaddling clothes and laid him in a feeding trough, because there was no room for them at the inn.

There were in the same region shepherds staying in the fields, keeping watch over their flocks at night. The angel of the Lord appeared to them, and the glory of the Lord shone all about them; and they were very afraid.

The angel said to them, "Do not be afraid, for see I bring you good tidings of great joy, which will be to all people. For to you is born this day in the city of David, a Savior, who is Christ the Lord. This will be a sign to you: you will find the baby wrapped in swaddling clothes, lying in a feeding trough."

And suddenly there was with the angel a multitude of the angelic host praising God, and saying, "Glory to God in the highest, and on earth peace toward men of goodwill."

And so it happened, that when the angels had left them and gone back into heaven, the shepherds said to one another, "Let us now go to Bethlehem and see this thing that has come to pass, which the Lord has made known to us." They went quickly, and found Mary, and Joseph; the baby Jesus was lying in a feeding trough. When they had seen it, they told to everyone what had been told them concerning the child.

All those who heard it wondered about those things that were told to them by the shepherds, but Mary treasured everything in her heart, and pondered them. The shepherds returned, glorifying and praising God for all the things they had heard and seen—just as it was said to them.

When Jesus was born in Bethlehem of Judea in the days of Herod the king, wise men came to Jerusalem from the east, saying, "Where is he who has been born King of the Jews? For we have seen his star in the east and have come to worship him."

When Herod the king heard of these things, he was troubled, and all Jerusalem with him. When he had gathered all the chief priests and scribes of the people together, he inquired of them where the Christ would be born. They said to him, "In Bethlehem of Judea, for so it is written by the prophet:

And you Bethlehem, in the land of Judah, are not the least among the princes of Judah; for out of you will come a ruler who will govern my people Israel

(Micah 5:2).

Then Herod, when he had secretly called the wise men to him, carefully inquired of them at what time the star had appeared. He sent them to Bethlehem, and said, "Go and thoroughly search for the young child, and when you have found him bring word back to me that I might also come and worship him."

When they had heard the king, they left; and behold, the star, which they had seen in the east, went ahead of them until it came to rest over where the young child was. When they saw the star, they rejoiced with an exceptionally great amount of joy.

When they had entered into the house, they saw the young child with Mary his mother, and they fell down and worshiped him; and when they had opened their treasures, they presented him with gifts of gold, and frankincense, and myrrh.

When eight days were completed for the circumcising of the baby, his name was called Jesus, which was the name the angel had given him before he was conceived in the womb.

When the days of her purification according to the Law of Moses were completed, they brought Jesus to Jerusalem to present him to the LORD—as it is written in the Law of the LORD: "*Every male that opens the womb shall be called holy to the LORD*" (Exodus 13:2)—and to offer a sacrifice according to that which is written in the Law of the LORD: "*A pair of turtle-doves, or two young pigeons*" (Leviticus 15:14).

And, behold, there was a man in Jerusalem whose name was Simeon, and he was righteous and devout and waiting for the Consolation of Israel; and the Holy Spirit was upon him. It was revealed to him by the Holy Spirit that he would not see death before he had seen the LORD's Christ.

Simeon came by the Spirit into the temple, and when the parents brought in the child Jesus, to do for him according to the custom of the Law, he took him up in his arms and blessed God, and said, "LORD, now let your servant depart in peace according to your word; for my eyes have seen your *salvation* which you have prepared before the face of all peoples; a light of revelation to the Gentiles; and the glory of your people Israel."

Joseph and his mother marveled at those things that were spoken about Jesus. Simeon blessed them, and said to Mary his mother, "Behold, this child is set for the fall and rising again of many in Israel; and for a sign that will be spoken against. Yes, a sword will also pierce through your own soul, that the thoughts of many hearts may be revealed."

And there was one Anna, a prophetess, the daughter of Phanuel, of the tribe of Asher. She was of a great age and had lived with a husband seven years from her virginity; and she was a widow of about eighty-four years, who never departed from the temple, but served God with fasting and prayers night and day. Anna came in just at that moment and likewise gave thanks to the LORD, and spoke of Jesus to all those who looked for *redemption* in Jerusalem.

When they had completed everything according to the Law of the LORD, they returned to Galilee, to Nazareth their own city.

The genealogy[4] *of* Jesus Christ, the Son of David, the Son of Abraham: God created Adam, who fathered Seth, who fathered Enosh, who fathered Cainan, who fathered Mahalalel, who fathered Jared, who fathered Enoch, who fathered Methuselah, who fathered Lamech, who fathered Noah, who fathered Shem, who fathered Arphaxad, who fathered Cainan, who fathered Shelah, who fathered Eber, who fathered Peleg, who fathered Reu, who fathered Serug, who fathered Nahor, who fathered Terah, and Terah was the father of Abraham.

Abraham fathered Isaac, Isaac fathered Jacob, and Jacob fathered Judah and his brothers. Judah fathered Perez and Zerah by Tamar, Perez fathered Hezron, and Hezron fathered Ram. Ram fathered Amminadab, Amminadab fathered Nahshon, and Nahshon fathered Salmon. Salmon fathered Boaz by Rahab, Boaz fathered Obed by Ruth, Obed fathered Jesse, and Jesse was the father of David the king.

David the king was the father of Solomon and Nathan by her who had been the wife of Uriah the Hittite.

Solomon fathered Rehoboam, Rehoboam fathered Abijah, and Abijah fathered Asa, Asa fathered Jehoshaphat, Jehoshaphat fathered Joram, and Joram fathered Uzziah. Uzziah fathered Jotham, Jotham fathered Ahaz, and Ahaz fathered Hezekiah. Hezekiah fathered Manasseh, Manasseh fathered Amon, and Amon fathered Josiah. Josiah was the father of Jeconiah and his brothers about the time they were carried away to Babylon.

Nathan, the son of David, fathered Mattathah, who fathered Menan, who fathered Melea, who fathered Eliakim, who fathered Jonan, who fathered Joseph, who fathered Judah, who fathered Simeon, who fathered Levi, who fathered Matthat, who fathered Jorim, who fathered Eliezer, who fathered Jose, who fathered Er, who fathered Elmodam, who fathered Cosam, who fathered Addi, who fathered Melchi, who fathered Neri, who was the father of Shealtiel.

Shealtiel fathered Zerubbabel, and Zerubbabel was the father of Abiud and Rhesa. Abiud fathered Eliakim, and Eliakim fathered Azor. Azor fathered Zadok, Zadok fathered Achim, and Achim fathered Eliud. Eliud fathered Eleazar, Eleazar fathered Matthan, and Matthan fathered Jacob. And Jacob, through the widow of Heli, was the father of Joseph the husband of Mary, of whom was born Jesus who is called Christ.

Zerubbabel fathered Rhesa, who fathered Joannas, who fathered Judah, who fathered Joseph, who fathered Semei, who fathered Mattathiah, who fathered Maath, who fathered Naggai, who fathered Esli, who fathered Nahum, who fathered Amos, who fathered Mattathiah, who fathered Joseph, who fathered Janna, who fathered

Melchi, who fathered Levi, who fathered Matthat, who fathered Heli, and Heli, through his widow, was the father of Joseph.

So all the generations from Abraham to David [in Solomon's genealogical list] are fourteen generations, and from David until the carrying away into Babylon are fourteen generations, and from the carrying away into Babylon to the Christ are fourteen generations. Jesus himself began His ministry at about thirty years of age, being (as was supposed) the son of Joseph.

The wise men, being warned by God in a dream that they should not return to Herod, departed to their own country by another way. When they had left, behold, the angel of the LORD appeared to Joseph in a dream, saying, "Arise, and take the young child and his mother, and flee into Egypt, and stay there until I bring you word; for Herod will seek the young child to destroy him."

When he got up, he took the young child and his mother and left for Egypt at night, and remained there until the death of Herod; that it might be fulfilled which was spoken of the LORD by the prophet, saying: "*Out of Egypt I have called my son*" (Hosea 11:1).

Then Herod, when he saw that he had been outwitted by the wise men, became very angry and sent out and killed all the male children that were in Bethlehem and in all the coastlands, from two years old and under, according to the time that he had ascertained after inquiring of the wise men. Then was fulfilled that which was spoken by Jeremiah the prophet, saying:

In Rama there was a voice heard, lamentation, and weeping, and great mourning; Rachel weeping for her children and could not be comforted, because they were no more (Jeremiah 31:15).

When Herod was dead, behold, an angel of the LORD appeared in a dream to Joseph in Egypt, saying, "Arise, and take the young child and his mother and go into the land of Israel, for those who sought the young child's life are dead." Joseph arose, and took the young Jesus and his mother and came into the land of Israel, but when he heard that Archelaus reigned in Judea in place of his father Herod, he was afraid to go there. Being warned by God in a dream, he turned aside into the regions of Galilee. He came and lived in a city called Nazareth; that it might be fulfilled which was spoken by the prophets: "He shall be called a Nazarene."

Jesus grew, and increased in strength of spirit, filled with wisdom; and the grace of God was upon him. His parents went to Jerusalem every year at the feast of the Passover, and when he was twelve years old, they went up to Jerusalem after the custom of the feast. When they had fulfilled the days, as they returned, the boy Jesus remained behind in Jerusalem; and Joseph and his mother did not know it. But they, supposing Jesus to have been in the company, went a day's journey; and they looked for him among their relations and acquaintances. When they did not find him, they returned again to Jerusalem, continuing to look for him.

And so it was that after three days they found Jesus in the temple, sitting in the midst of the doctors of the Law, both listening to them and asking them questions. Everyone who heard him were astonished at his understanding and answers.

When his parents saw him, they were amazed, and his mother said to him, "Son, why have you done this to us? Look, your father and I have anxiously sought you!" He said to them, "How is it that you sought me? Did you not know that I would be about my Father's business?" They did not understand the word that he spoke to them.

Jesus went down with them, and they came to Nazareth. Jesus was obedient to them; but his mother kept all these sayings in her heart. And Jesus increased in wisdom and stature, and in favor with both God and man.

The beginning of the gospel of Jesus Christ, the Son of God: There was a man sent from God, whose name was John. He came to be a witness, to bear witness of the Light, that through him all men might believe. He was not that Light, but was sent to bear witness of the Light—the true Light, which lights every man who comes into the world.

In the fifteenth year of the reign of Tiberius Caesar, Pontius Pilate being governor of Judea, and Herod being tetrarch of Galilee, and his brother Philip tetrarch of Ituraea and of the region of Trachonitis, and Lysanias the tetrarch of Abilene, Annas and Caiaphas being the high priests, the word of God came to John the son of Zacharias in the wilderness.

He came into all the country around Jordan, preaching the baptism of repentance for the forgiveness of sins; as it

is written in the book of the words of Isaiah the prophet, saying:
> *Behold, I send my messenger before your face, who will prepare the way before you.*
>
> *The voice of one crying in the wilderness, prepare the way of the* Lord, *make his paths straight.*
>
> *Every valley will be filled and every mountain and hill will be brought low; and the crooked places will be made straight, and the rough ways will be made smooth; and all flesh will see the salvation of God* (Isaiah 40:3–5).

John had clothing of camel's hair, and wore a leather belt about his waist; and his food was locusts and wild honey. John baptized in the wilderness and preached a baptism of repentance for the forgiveness of sins saying, "Repent, for the kingdom of heaven is near at hand." All the people went out to him from all the land of Judea and Jerusalem, and everyone was baptized by him in the River Jordan, confessing their sins.

Then John said to the Pharisees and Sadducees who came to his baptism, "O generation of vipers, who has warned you to flee from the wrath to come?" And said to all the multitude that came out to be baptized by him: "Bring forth fruits worthy of repentance, and do not begin to say to yourselves, 'We have Abraham as our father'; for I say to you that God is able to raise up children to Abraham from these stones. The axe is laid to the root of the trees, therefore every tree that does not produce good fruit is cut down and thrown into the fire."

The people asked him, saying, "What shall we do then?" He answered and said to them, "He who has two coats, let him give one to him who does not have a coat; and he who has food, let him do likewise."

Then tax collectors came to be baptized also, and one said to him, "Master, what shall we do?" He said to them, "Take no more than that which is lawful for you." Soldiers likewise asked him, saying, "What shall we do?" He said to them, "Do no violence to anyone, nor falsely accuse anyone, and be content with your wages."

All the people were in expectation, and everyone wondered in their hearts about John, whether he was the Christ or not. John answered, saying to them all, "I indeed baptize you with water; but one mightier than I comes, and I am not fit to remove his sandals, nor loosen the strap of his sandals. He will baptize you with the Holy Spirit and with fire. His winnowing fork is in his hand and he will throughly clean his floor and will gather the wheat into his storehouse, but the chaff he will burn with unquenchable fire." And many other things he preached in his exhortation to the people.

When all the people were baptized, it happened that Jesus also came from Galilee to the Jordan to John, to be baptized by him. John restrained him, saying, "I have need to be baptized of you, and you come to me?" Jesus answering, said to him, "Allow it now to be so, for we must fulfill all righteousness." Then John consented. And Jesus, when he was baptized, came up out of the water, and as he prayed the heavens were opened immediately above him. John saw the Spirit of God descending in a bodily shape like a dove, and alighting upon Jesus; and a voice came from heaven, which said, "You are my beloved Son, in you I am well pleased."

Jesus, being full of the Holy Spirit, returned from the Jordan, and was led by the Spirit into the wilderness to be tempted for forty days by the devil. During those forty days he fasted and ate nothing. He was with the wild beasts; and the angels ministered to him; and when the days were ended, he was hungry.

The devil said to him, "If you are the Son of God, command this stone that it be made into bread." Jesus answered him, saying, "It is written, *'Man shall not live by bread alone, but by every word that proceeds out of the mouth of God'* " (Deuteronomy 8:3). And the devil, taking him up into a high mountain, showed to him all the kingdoms of the world in a moment of time. The devil then said to him, "All this power I will give you, and the glory of them, for it was given to me, and to whomever I want I will give it. If you will worship me, it shall all be yours."

Jesus answered and said to him, "Away with you! Get behind me, Satan, for it is written: *'You shall worship the* LORD *your God, and him only shall you serve'* " (Deuteronomy 6:13).

He brought him to Jerusalem, and set him on a pinnacle of the temple, and said to him, "If you are the Son of God, throw yourself down from here, for it is written, *'He shall give his angels charge over you, to keep you; and in their hands they shall bear you up, lest at any time you dash your foot against a stone'* " (Psalms 91:11-12). Jesus answering said to him, "It is said, *'You shall not tempt the* LORD *your God'* " (Deuteronomy 6:16).

When the devil had ended all the temptations, he left him alone for a while, and behold, angels came and ministered to Him.

This is the record of John, when the Jews[5] sent priests and Levites from Jerusalem to ask him, "Who are you?" He told the truth, and confessed, "I am not the Christ." They asked him, "Who then? Are you Elijah?" He said, "I am not." "Are you the Prophet?" He answered, "No." Then they said to him, "Who are you then? We need to give an answer to those who sent us. What do you say about yourself?" He said, "I am *the voice of one crying in the wilderness, 'Make straight the way of the* LORD*'* (Isaiah 40:3), as the prophet Isaiah said."

Those who were sent were Pharisees, and they asked John, and said to him, "Why do you baptize then, if you are not the Christ, neither Elijah, nor the Prophet?" John answered them, saying, "I baptize with water, but one stands among you whom you do not know. It is he who, coming after me, is preferred before me; whose sandal's strap I am not worthy to loosen."

These things were done in Bethany beyond Jordan, where John was baptizing. The next day John saw Jesus coming to him, and John cried out, saying, "See, the Lamb of God, who takes away the sin of the world. This is he of whom I said, 'After me comes a man who is preferred before me, for he was before me.' I did not know him, but I have come baptizing with water so that he would be revealed to Israel."

John bore witness, saying, "I saw the Spirit descending from heaven like a dove, and it alighted upon him. I did not know him, but he who sent me to baptize with water, said to me, 'Upon whom you will see the Spirit descending and remaining on him, this is he who baptizes with the Holy Spirit.' I saw, and testify that this is the Son of God."

The next day John stood with two of his disciples, and looking upon Jesus again as he walked, he said, "See!, the Lamb of God!" The two disciples heard him speak, and they followed Jesus.

Then Jesus turned, and saw them following, and he said to them, "What do you want?" They said to him, "Rabbi (which, being interpreted, means, "Teacher"), where are you staying?" He said to them, "Come and see." They came and saw where he lived, and stayed with him that day; for it was about the tenth hour.

One of the two who had heard John speak, and followed him, was Andrew, Simon Peter's brother. He first found his own brother Simon, and said to him, "We have found the Messiah" (which, being interpreted means, "the Christ"). And he brought him to Jesus.

The following day Jesus went into Galilee and found Philip, and said to him, "Follow me." Now Philip was of Bethsaida, the city of Andrew and Peter. Philip found Nathanael, and said to him, "We have found him of whom Moses in the Law and the Prophets wrote—Jesus of Nazareth, the son of Joseph." Nathanael said to him, "Can anything good come out of Nazareth?" Philip said to him, "Come and see."

Jesus saw Nathanael coming toward him and said of him, "Look, an Israelite indeed, in whom is no deceit!" Nathanael said to him, "From where do you know me?" Jesus answered him and said, "Before Philip even called you, when you were under the fig tree, I saw you." Nathanael answered and said to him, "Rabbi, you are the Son of God, you are the King of Israel!" Jesus answered and said to him, "Because I said to you, I saw you under the fig tree, you already believe? You will see greater things than this." He said to him, "Indeed, I say to you, henceforth you will see heaven open, and the angels of God ascending and descending upon the Son of Man[6]."

Two days later there was a wedding in Cana of Galilee, and the mother of Jesus was there, and both Jesus and his disciples were also invited to the wedding. When the wine ran low and they needed more, the mother of Jesus said to him, "They have no wine." Jesus said to her, "Woman, what have I got to do with your concern? My hour has not yet come." His mother said to the servants, "Whatever he says to you, do it."

There were six stone water pots sitting there according to the manner of the purifying of the Jews, each containing twenty gallons or more apiece. Jesus said to them, "Fill the water pots with water." They filled them to the brim, and then he said to them, "Now draw some out and take it to the master of the feast." They took it to him. When the master of the feast tasted the water that had been made into wine, and did not know where it came from (but the servants who drew the water knew), the master of the feast called the bridegroom and said to him, "Every man at the beginning sets out his good wine, and when guests have well drunk, then that which is inferior; but you have kept the good wine until now." This beginning of miracles

Jesus did in Cana of Galilee, publicly displaying his glory; and his disciples believed in him.

After that he went down to Capernaum, he, and his mother, and his brothers, and his disciples; and they remained there for a few days. The Passover feast was at hand, and Jesus went up to Jerusalem and found those who sold oxen and sheep and doves sitting in the temple, and the money changers. After he had made a scourge of small cords, he drove them all out of the temple, and the sheep, and the oxen; and poured out the changers' money, and overthrew the tables. And Jesus said to those who sold doves, "Take these things from here, do not turn my Father's house into a house of merchandise!" And his disciples remembered that it was written, "*The zeal for your house has consumed me*" (Psalms 69:9).

Then the Jews answered and said to him, "What sign do you show us, seeing that you do these things?" Jesus answered them and said, "Destroy this temple and in three days I will raise it up." Then the Jews said, "It took forty-six years to build this temple, and will you raise it up in three days?" However, Jesus spoke of the temple of his body.

Consequently, when Jesus was risen from the dead, his disciples remembered he had said this to them; and they believed the Scripture, and the word that he had spoken.

When Jesus was in Jerusalem, at the Passover during the feast days, many believed in his name when they saw the miracles that he did. But Jesus did not commit himself to them, because he knew all men, and did not need anyone to testify about man; for he knew what man was capable of.

There was a man of the Pharisees, named Nicodemus, a ruler of the Jews; he came to Jesus by night, and said to him, "Rabbi, we know that you are a teacher come from God; for no one can do the miracles that you do, except God is with him." Jesus answered and said to him, "Indeed, I say to you, unless a man is born again, he cannot see the kingdom of God." Nicodemus said to him, "How can a man be born when he is old? Can he enter the second time into his mother's womb, and be born?"

Jesus answered, "Indeed, I say to you, unless a man is born of water and of the Spirit, he cannot enter the kingdom of God. That which is born of the flesh is flesh, and that which is born of the Spirit is Spirit. Do not marvel that I said to you, you must be born again. The wind blows where it wants and you hear the sound of it, but you cannot tell from where it comes or where it goes; so is everyone who is born of the Spirit."

Nicodemus answered and said to him, "How can these things be?" Jesus answered and said to him, "Are you the teacher of Israel, and yet do not know these things? Indeed, I say to you, we speak what we do know and testify of what we have seen; and you do not receive our witness. If I have told you earthly things and you do not believe them, how can you believe if I tell you of heavenly things?

"No man has ascended up to heaven, except he who came down from heaven, even the Son of Man who is in heaven. As Moses lifted up the serpent in the wilderness, even so the Son of Man must be lifted up; that whoever believes in him would not perish, but have eternal life. For God so loved the world, that he gave his only begotten Son, that whoever believes in him would not perish, but have everlasting life.

"God did not send his Son into the world to condemn the world, but that through him the world might be saved. He who believes in him is not condemned, but he who does not believe is already condemned, because he has not believed in the name of the only begotten Son of God. This is the condemnation, that light has come into the world, and men loved the darkness rather than the light, because their deeds were evil. Everyone who commits evil hates the light, neither does he come to the light, lest his deeds should be rebuked. He that does good works comes to the light, so that his deeds may be clearly seen, that they are done in God."

After these things Jesus came with his disciples into the land of Judea; and there they baptized, and he delayed leaving. John was also baptizing in Aenon near Salim, because there was a lot of water there; and people came and were baptized. John had not yet been thrown into prison.

There arose a question between some of John's disciples and the Jews about purification. They came to John, and said to him, "Rabbi, he who was with you beyond the Jordan, to whom you bore witness, indeed, he baptizes and all are coming to him." John answered and said, "A man can receive nothing, unless it is given to him from above. You yourselves bear me witness that I said, 'I am not the Christ, but that I am sent before him.' He who has the bride is the bridegroom, but the friend of the bridegroom who stands and hears him, greatly rejoices because of the bridegroom's voice; therefore in this my joy is fulfilled. He must increase, but I must decrease.

"He who comes from above is above all; he who is of the earth is earthly, and speaks of the earth; he who comes from heaven is above all. What he has seen and heard, that he testifies to; and no man receives his testimony. He who has received his testimony certifies that God is true. For he whom God has sent speaks the words of God; for God does not give the Spirit to him by measure. The Father loves the Son, and has given all things into his hand. He who believes in the Son has everlasting life; he who does not believe in the Son will not see life, but the wrath of God abides upon him."

Therefore, when the Lord knew the Pharisees had heard that Jesus made and baptized more disciples than John, (though Jesus himself did not baptize, but his disciples), he left Judea. But Herod the tetrarch, being reproved by John for Herodias his brother Philip's wife, and for all the evils that Herod had done, added this to them all—he locked John up in prison.

When Jesus heard that John had been thrown into prison, he returned in the power of the Spirit to Galilee and he needed to go through Samaria. He came to a city of Samaria, which is called Sychar, near to the parcel of ground that Jacob gave to his son Joseph. Now Jacob's well was there. Jesus, being weary from his journey, sat down beside the well; and it was about the sixth hour.

There came a woman of Samaria to draw water. Jesus said to her, "Give me a drink" (for his disciples had gone away into the city to buy food). Then the Samaritan woman said to him, "How is it that you, being a Jew, ask for a drink from me, who is a woman of Samaria?" (For the Jews have no dealings with the Samaritans.) Jesus answered and said to her, "If you knew the gift of God, and who it is that said to you, 'Give me a drink'; you would have asked him and he would have given you living water." The woman said to him, "Sir, you have nothing to draw with, and the well is deep; from where then have you that living water? Are you greater than our father Jacob, who gave us the well, and drank from it himself, and his children, and his cattle?"

Jesus answered and said to her, "Whoever drinks of this water will thirst again, but whoever drinks of the water that I will give him will never thirst. The water that I will give him will be in him a well of water springing up into everlasting life." The woman said to him, "Sir, give me this water, so that I do not thirst, neither have to come here to draw it."

Jesus said to her, "Go, call your husband, and come here." The woman answered and said, "I have no husband." Jesus said to her, "You have said well, 'I have no husband,' for you have had five husbands, and he whom you have now is not your husband; in that you spoke truthfully." The woman said to him, "Sir, I perceive that you are a prophet. Our fathers worshiped on this mountain; and you say that in Jerusalem is the place where men ought to worship." Jesus said to her, "Woman, believe me, the hour comes, when you will neither on this mountain, nor even at Jerusalem, worship the Father. You do not know what you worship; we know what we worship, for salvation is from the Jews. The hour comes, and is already here, when true worshipers will worship the Father in Spirit and in truth; for the Father seeks those to worship him. God is a Spirit; and those who worship him must worship him in Spirit and in truth." The woman said to him, "I know that Messiah will come, who is called Christ; when he has come, he will tell us all things." Jesus said to her, "I who am speaking to you am he."

Just then his disciples came and they marveled that he talked with the woman, yet no one said, "What do you want?" or, "Why are you talking with her?" The woman then left her water pot and made her way into the city, and said to the men, "Come, see a man who told me all things that I ever did; is this not the Christ?" Then they went out of the city, and came to him.

In the meantime, his disciples implored him, saying, "Master, eat." He said to them, "I have food to eat that you know nothing about." Therefore the disciples said to one another, "Has anyone brought him anything to eat?" Jesus said to them, "My food is to do the will of him who sent me, and to finish his work. Do you not say, 'There are another four months and then comes the harvest?' Indeed, I say to you, lift up your eyes and look at the fields, for they are already ripe for harvesting. He who reaps receives wages and gathers fruit to eternal life; that he who sows and he who reaps may both rejoice together. In this the saying is true, 'One sows, and another reaps.' I sent you to reap where you did not labor; other men labored and you have entered into their labors."

Many of the Samaritans of that city believed in him because of the woman who testified, "He told me everything that I ever did." So when the Samaritans had come to him, they asked that he would stay with them; and he stayed there two days. Many more believed because of his own word, and they said to the woman, "Now we believe, not because of your witness, for we have heard him ourselves, and know that this is indeed the Christ, the Savior of the world."

After two days he left there and went to Galilee; for Jesus himself testified that a prophet has no honor in his own country. Then when he came into Galilee, the Galileans received him, having seen all the things that he did at Jerusalem at the feast; for they also went to the feast. The fame of him went throughout all the area round about. He taught in their synagogues, being glorified by all, preaching the gospel of the kingdom of God and saying, "The time is fulfilled and the kingdom of God is at hand; repent and believe the gospel."

Jesus came again into Cana of Galilee, where he had turned the water into wine, and there was a certain nobleman whose son was sick at Capernaum. When he heard that Jesus had come out of Judea into Galilee, he went to him and begged him that he would come down and heal his son; for he was at the point of death.

Then Jesus said to him, "Unless you see signs and wonders you will not believe." The nobleman said to him, "Sir, come down before my child dies." Jesus said to him, "Go your way, your son lives." The man believed the word that Jesus had spoken to him, and he went his way. As he was going down his servants met him and told him, saying, "Your son lives." Then he inquired of them the hour when he began to recover. They said to him, "Yesterday at the seventh hour the fever left him." So the father knew that it was at the same hour in which Jesus said to him, "Your son lives"; and he and his whole house believed. This was the second miracle that Jesus did, when he had come out of Judea into Galilee.

Jesus went out from there and came into his own country, and his disciples followed him. When the Sabbath day had come he began to teach in the synagogue, and many who heard him were astonished, saying, "From where has this man these things? What wisdom is this that has been given to him, that even such mighty miracles are wrought by his hands? Is this not the carpenter, the son of Mary, the brother of James, and Joses, and of Judah, and Simon? Are not his sisters here with us?" And they were offended at him.

He came to Nazareth where he had been brought up, and as was his custom he went into the synagogue on the Sabbath day, and stood up to read; and there was handed to him the scroll of the prophet Isaiah. When he had opened the scroll, he found the place where it was written:

> *The Spirit of the LORD is upon me, because he has anointed me to preach the gospel to the poor; he has sent me to heal the broken-hearted, to preach deliverance to the captives, and recovering of sight to the blind, to set at liberty those who are oppressed; to preach the acceptable year of the LORD* (Isaiah 61:1).

Jesus closed the scroll, gave it back to the attendant, and sat down. The eyes of all those who were in the synagogue were fixed steadily on him. He began to say to them, "Today this Scripture is fulfilled in your hearing." Everyone bore witness to him, and marveled at the gracious words that came out of his mouth. They said, "Is this not Joseph's son?"

He said to them, "You will surely say this proverb to me, 'Physician, heal yourself.' Whatever we have heard done in Capernaum, also do here in your hometown."

He said, "Truly I say to you, no prophet is accepted in his own hometown. And I tell you truthfully, many widows were in Israel in the days of Elijah when the heaven was shut up three years and six months, when there was great famine throughout all the land, but Elijah was sent to none of them, except to Zarephath, a widow in an area of Sidon. Many lepers were in Israel in the time of Elisha the prophet, and none of them was cleansed except Na'aman the Syrian."

When they heard these things, everyone in the synagogue was filled with rage, and got up and forcibly pushed him out of the city and led him to the brow of the hill on which the city was built, intending to throw him headlong over the cliff, but he passed through the midst of them and went his way.

Leaving Nazareth, he came and dwelt in Capernaum, a city of Galilee, which is by the sea in the regions of Zebulun and Naphtali, and taught them on the Sabbath days that it might be fulfilled that which was spoken by Isaiah the prophet:

> *The land of Zebulun and the land of Naphtali, by the way of the sea, beyond the Jordan, Galilee of the Gentiles.*
>
> *The people who sat in darkness have seen a*

great light, and upon those who sat in the region and shadow of death light has dawned (Isaiah 9:1).

From that time on Jesus began to preach and to say, "The time is fulfilled, repent, for the kingdom of heaven is at hand."

They went into Capernaum, and straight away on the Sabbath day he entered the synagogue and taught. They were astonished at his doctrine, for he taught them as one that had authority and not as the scribes; for his word was with power. In the synagogue there was a man who had a spirit of an unclean demon, and he cried out with a loud voice, saying, "Let us alone, what have we to do with you, Jesus of Nazareth? Have you come to destroy us? I know who you are—the Holy One of God." Jesus rebuked him, saying, "Hold your peace, and come out of him."

When the demon had thrown him down in their midst, he came out of him and did not hurt him, and they were all amazed and spoke among themselves, saying, "What is this word! For with authority and power he commands the unclean spirits, and they come out." And the fame of him spread throughout all the region, into every place of the country round about Galilee and throughout all of Syria.

Jesus got up and went out of the synagogue and entered the house of Simon and Andrew, with James and John. Simon's wife's mother lay sick with an intense fever, and they appealed to him for help. He came and stood over her, touched her and rebuked the fever and it left her. He took her by the hand and lifted her up, and immediately she ministered to them.

In the evening, when the sun was setting, they brought to him all who were diseased and those who were possessed with demons; and he laid his hands on every one of them and healed them, that it might be fulfilled what was spoken by Isaiah the prophet, saying: "*He took our sicknesses, and bore our sorrows*" (Isaiah 53:4). He cast out the demons with a word and they knew him and came out of many crying out, and saying, "You are Christ the Son of God." He rebuked them and would not allow them to speak; for they knew that he was the Christ. They brought those who were lunatics and those who were paralyzed; and he healed them. Great multitudes of people followed him from Galilee, and from Decapolis, and from Jerusalem, and from Judea, and from beyond the Jordan.

In the morning, rising up a long while before daylight, he departed and went into a solitary place and there prayed. Simon and the people who were with him sought him, and came to him and said to him, "Everyone looks for you," and they tried to detain him so that he would not go away from them. He said to them, "I must preach the kingdom of God to other cities also; for this reason I have been sent." And he continued to preach and cast out demons in the synagogues of Galilee.

It came about, as Jesus walked by the lake—the sea of Galilee—he saw Simon and Andrew his brother, casting a net into the sea, for they were fishermen. Jesus stood by the lake and the people pressed upon him to hear the word of God. He saw two boats standing by the lake, but the fishermen were gone out of them and were washing their nets. He got into one of the boats, which was Simon's, and asked him if he would push out a little from the land. Jesus sat down and taught the people from out of the boat.

When he had finished speaking, he said to Simon, "Launch out into the deep and let down your nets for a catch." Simon, answering, said to him, "Master, we have toiled all the night, and have caught nothing; nevertheless, at your bidding I will let down the net." When they had done this, they caught a great number of fish and their net almost broke. They beckoned to their partners who were in the other boat, that they should come and help them. They came and filled both the boats, so that they began to sink. When Simon Peter saw it, he fell down at the feet of Jesus, saying, "Go away from me, for I am a sinful man, O Lord." For he, and all who were with Simon, was astonished at the catch of fish which they had taken. So also was James and John, the sons of Zebedee, who were partners with Simon. Jesus said to Simon, "Do not be afraid, from now on you will catch men." When they had brought their boats to land, they left their nets, abandoned everything, and followed him.

Jesus saw the two other brothers, James the son of Zebedee, and John his brother, in a boat with Zebedee their father, mending their nets. Jesus called them and they left their father Zebedee in the boat with the hired men and followed him.

It came to pass, when Jesus was in a certain city, behold, a man full of leprosy saw him, and falling on his face, worshiped and implored him, saying, "Lord, if you want to, you can make me clean." Jesus put out his hand and touched him, saying, "I want to; be clean." Immediately the leprosy was cleansed and gone from him. Jesus told him not to tell anyone, but to go and show himself to the priest, and offer the gift for his cleansing just as Moses commanded as a testimony to them. However, the man went out and began to tell about it, and he spread the news so freely that Jesus could no longer openly enter the city. Jesus remained outside the city in deserted areas; and they came to Him from every direction. His reputation spread about all the more; and great crowds came together to hear him and to be healed of their sicknesses. He would often withdraw himself into the wilderness and prayed.

Jesus entered into a boat, crossed over to the other side of the lake, and came to his own city and entered Capernaum. After some days it became known that he was in the house and immediately many gathered together, so many came that there was no room to receive them, not even around the doorway; and he preached the word to them.

And so it was, on a certain day, as he was teaching, that there were Pharisees and doctors of the Law sitting there, who had come from every town of Galilee, and Judea, and Jerusalem; and the power of the LORD was present to heal.

And behold, four men brought a man on a bed who was paralyzed, and they attempted to bring him in and to lay him before Jesus. When they could not find a way to bring him in because of the crowd, they went up onto the roof and, when they had broken through the tiling, they let the man down on his bed into the midst in front of Jesus. When Jesus saw their faith, he said to him, "Man, your sins are forgiven you." The scribes and the Pharisees began to discuss among themselves, saying, "Who is this who speaks blasphemies? Who can forgive sins but God alone?"

When Jesus perceived their thoughts, he answered them and said, "Why do you question in your hearts? Why must you think evil? Which is easier to say to the paralytic, 'Your sins are forgiven you,' or to say, 'Rise up and walk?' However, that you may know that the Son of Man has power on earth to forgive sins," he said to the paralyzed man, "I say to you, arise, take up your bed, and go to your house." Immediately he got up from before them, and picked up what he had been laying on, and went to his own house glorifying God. They were all amazed, and they glorified God and were filled with fear, saying, "We have seen strange things today."

After these things Jesus went out and saw a tax collector, named Matthew Levi, the son of Alphaeus, sitting at the tax booth, and Jesus said to him, "Follow me." He got up, left everything, and followed him.

Matthew Levi made him a great feast in his own house, and there was a great company of tax collectors and others who sat down with him and his disciples. However, the scribes and Pharisees complained against him and his disciples, saying, "Why do you eat and drink with tax collectors and sinners?" Jesus answering, said to them, "You go and learn what this means, '*I will have mercy, and not sacrifice*' (Hosea 6:6). Those who are well do not need a physician, but those who are sick. I did not come to call the righteous, but sinners to repentance."

The disciples of John and of the Pharisees used to fast, and they came and said to him, "Why do the disciples of John fast often and make prayers, and also the disciples of the Pharisees, but yours eat and drink?" He said to them, "Can you make those of the bridal party fast while the bridegroom is with them? As long as they have the bridegroom with them they cannot fast. The days will come when the bridegroom will be taken away from them, and then they will fast."

He spoke also a parable to them: "No man sews a piece of a new garment onto an old garment, because the new will make a tear and the piece that was taken out of the new will not match with the old.

"No one puts new wine into old wineskins, because the new wine will burst the wineskins and be spilled, and the wineskins will perish. New wine must be put into new wineskins, and both are preserved. Also, no one having drunk old wine immediately desires new wine; for he says, 'The old is better.' "[7]

After this there was a feast of the Jews, and Jesus went up to Jerusalem. Now there is in Jerusalem, by the sheep market, a pool, which is called in Hebrew, Bethesda, having five porches. In these lay a great number of helpless people—blind, crippled, paralyzed—waiting for the moving of the water. For an angel went down at a certain time into the pool, and stirred up the water; whoever stepped in first after the stirring of the water was made whole of whatever disease he had.

A certain man was there who had an infirmity for thirty-eight years. When Jesus saw him lying there, and knew that he had been a long time in that condition, he said to him, "Do you want to be made well?" The powerless man answered him, "Sir, I have no one to put me into the pool when the water is stirred up, but as I am coming, someone else steps down before me. Jesus said to him, "Get up, pick up your bed, and walk." Immediately the man was made well, and took up his bed and walked; and it was the Sabbath day. The Jews said to him who was made well, "It is the Sabbath day; it is not lawful for you to carry your bed." He answered them, "He who made me well said to me, 'Take up your bed and walk.'" Then they asked him, "Who is the man who said to you, 'Take up your bed and walk'?" He who was healed did not know who it was, for Jesus had disappeared into the crowd that was there.

Afterward, Jesus found the healed man in the temple, and said to him, "See, you have been made well. Sin no more, lest something worse happens to you." The man went away and told the Jews that it was Jesus who had made him well. Therefore the Jews persecuted Jesus and sought to kill him, because he had done these things on the Sabbath day. Jesus answered them, "My Father still works, and I also work." Therefore the Jews sought all the more to kill him, because he had not only broken the Sabbath, but also said that God was his Father, making himself equal with God.

Then Jesus responded and said to them, "Indeed, I say to you, the Son can do nothing of himself, but only what he sees the Father do; for whatever things he does, these the Son also does. For the Father loves the Son, and shows him all things that he himself does, and he will show him greater works than these, that you may marvel. For just as the Father raises up the dead and gives them life; even so the Son gives life to whom he will. For the Father judges no man, but has entrusted all judgment to the Son so that all men should honor the Son, even as they honor the Father. He who does not honor the Son does not honor the Father who has sent him. Indeed, I say to you, he who hears my word and believes in him who sent me, has everlasting life and will not come into condemnation, but has passed from death to life.

"Indeed, I say to you, the hour is coming, and has now already come, when the dead will hear the voice of the Son of God; and those who hear will live.[8] For as the Father has life in himself, so he has given to the Son to have life in himself; and has given him authority to execute judgment also, because he is the Son of Man. Do not marvel at this, for the hour is coming in which all who are in the graves will hear his voice and will come out;[9] those who have done good, to the resurrection of life; and those who have done evil, to the resurrection of condemnation. I can of myself do nothing; as I hear, I judge. And my judgment is just, because I do not seek my own will, but the will of the Father who has sent me. If I bear witness of myself, my witness is not true. There is another who bears witness of me; and I know that the witness which he testifies of me is true.

"You sent to John, and he bore witness to the truth. I do not receive testimony from man; but I say these things that you might be saved. John was a burning and a shining light; and you were willing for a season to rejoice in his light. I have greater witness than that of John, for the works which the Father has given me to finish, the works that I do, bear witness of me that the Father has sent me.

The Father himself, who has sent me, has borne witness of me. You have never heard his voice, nor seen his form. You do not have his word abiding in you, for whom he has sent, him you do not believe. Search the Scriptures, for in them you think you have eternal life; and they are those which testify of me. You will not come to me that you might have life.

"I do not receive honor from men, but I know you, that you do not have the love of God in you. I have come in my Father's name, and you do not receive me; if another will come in his own name, him you will receive. How can you believe, you who receive honor one from another, and who do not seek the honor that comes from the only God? Do not think that I will accuse you to the Father; there is one who accuses you—Moses, in whom you trust. For had you believed Moses you would have believed me; for he wrote of me. If you do not believe his writings, how will you believe my words?"

At that time it came to pass, on the second Sabbath after the first,[10] that Jesus went through the grain fields and his disciples picked heads of grain as they went, and ate, rubbing them in their hands. Certain of the Pharisees said to them, "Why do you do what is not lawful on the Sabbath day?" Answering them Jesus said, "Have you not even read what David did when he was hungry, as were all those who were with him? How he went into the house of God in the days of Abiathar the high priest, and took and ate of the consecrated bread and also gave to those who were with him, which it is not lawful to eat, except for the priests alone?" He said to them, "The Sabbath was made for man, and not man for the Sabbath. The Son of Man is also Lord of the Sabbath day."

It also happened, on another Sabbath, that Jesus entered into the synagogue and taught, and there was a man whose right hand was withered. The scribes and Pharisees asked Jesus, "Is it lawful to heal on the Sabbath days?" They watched him, to see whether he would heal on the Sabbath day, that they might make an accusation against him. However, he knew their thoughts, and said to the man who had the withered hand, "Come and stand here in the midst." He arose and stood there.

Then Jesus said to them, "I will ask you one thing, is it lawful on the Sabbath day to do good, or to do evil? To save life, or to destroy it?" He said to them, "What man is there among you who will have one sheep, and if it falls into a pit on the Sabbath day, will not take hold of it and lift it out? How much more value is a man than a sheep? Therefore it is lawful to do well on the Sabbath days."

Looking around at them all with anger, he said to the man, "Stretch out your hand." He did so, and his hand was restored as whole as the other. The Pharisees were filled with rage; and counseled together with the Herodians, how they might destroy Jesus. When Jesus knew it, he withdrew himself from there with his disciples to the sea. A great multitude followed him from Galilee, and from Judea, and from Jerusalem, and from Idumea, and from beyond the Jordan, and many from around Tyre and Sidon—a great multitude came to him when they heard what wonderful things he did, and he healed them all.

He spoke to his disciples that a small boat should be made ready for him because of the huge number of people, in case they should crush him. For he had healed many to such an extent that all who had sicknesses pressed upon him, just to touch him. Unclean spirits, when they saw him, fell down before him and cried out, saying, "You are the Son of God." He strictly charged them that they should not make him known. That it might be fulfilled that which was spoken by Isaiah the prophet, saying:

> *Behold, my servant whom I have chosen; my beloved in whom my soul is well pleased. I will put my Spirit upon him and he will show justice to the Gentiles. He will not quarrel, nor cry out; neither will anyone hear his voice in the streets. A bruised reed he will not break, and a smoking flax he will not extinguish, until he sends out justice to victory; and in his name the Gentiles will trust* (Isaiah 42:1-3).

It came about in those days that Jesus went out to a mountain to pray, and continued all night in prayer to God. When it was day he called to himself those whom he wanted, and they came to him. Of those he chose and ordained twelve, whom he also named apostles, that they should be with him, and that he might send them out to preach, and to have power to heal sicknesses, and to cast out demons. Simon—whom he also named Peter—and Andrew his brother. James the son of Zebedee, and John the brother of James whom he surnamed Boanerges, which means, "The sons of thunder." Philip and Bartholomew, Matthew and Thomas, James the son of Alphaeus, and Simon the Canaanite—called the Zealot—and Judas the brother of James, and Judas Iscariot, who also was the traitor who betrayed Jesus. They went into a house and the multitude came together again, so that they could not so much as eat. When his friends heard about it they went out to get him, for they said, "He is beside himself!"

He came down with them and stood on a level plain with his group of disciples, and a great multitude of people out of all Judea and Jerusalem, and from the sea coast of Tyre and Sidon, came to hear him and be healed of their diseases. Also those who were troubled by unclean spirits were healed. The whole multitude sought to touch him, for power went out from him and healed them all. He focused his eyes on his disciples, opened his mouth and taught them, saying:

> Blessed are the poor in spirit, for theirs is the kingdom of God.
> Blessed are those who mourn, for they shall be comforted.
> Blessed are the meek, for they will inherit the earth.
> Blessed are those who hunger and thirst after righteousness, for they will be filled.
> Blessed are the merciful, for they will obtain mercy.
> Blessed are the pure in heart, for they will see God.
> Blessed are the peacemakers, for they will be called the children of God.
> Blessed are those who are persecuted for righteousness' sake, for theirs is the kingdom of heaven.
> Blessed are you when men will revile you, and persecute you, and will say all manner of evil against you falsely, for my sake. Rejoice, and be extremely glad, for great is your

reward in heaven, for so they also persecuted the prophets who were before you.

Woe to you who are rich, for you have received your consolation.

Woe to you who are full, for you will suffer hunger.

Woe to you who laugh now, for you will mourn and weep.

Woe to you when all men speak well of you, for so their fathers spoke of the false prophets.

"You are the salt of the earth,[11] but if the salt has lost its flavor, with what will it be salted? It is good for nothing, except to be thrown out and trodden under foot.

"You are the light of the world. A city that is set on a hill cannot be hidden. Neither do men light a candle and put it under a basket, but on a candlestick, and it gives light to all who are in the house. Let your light so shine before men that they may see your good works and glorify your Father who is in heaven.

"Do not think that I have come to destroy the Law, or the Prophets. I have not come to destroy, but to fulfill. For truly I say to you, until heaven and earth pass away, not one jot or one tittle will pass from the Law until everything is fulfilled.

"Therefore, whoever breaks one of the least of these commandments, and teaches others to do the same, he will be called the least in the kingdom of heaven; but whoever keeps and teaches them, he will be called great in the kingdom of heaven. For I say to you, that unless your righteousness exceeds the righteousness of the scribes and Pharisees, you will never enter the kingdom of heaven.

"*You have* heard that it was said to those of old, '*You shall not murder, and whoever commits murder will be in danger of judgment*' (Exodus 20:13). But I say to you that whoever is angry with his brother without cause will be in danger of judgment, and whoever will say to his brother, 'Raca!' will be in danger of the council, but whoever will say, 'You fool,' will be in danger of hell fire.

"Therefore, if you bring your gift to the altar and then remember that your brother has something against you, leave your gift there before the altar and go your way; first be reconciled to your brother, and then come and offer your gift.

"Agree with your adversary quickly, while you are on the way with him, lest at any time the adversary deliver you to the judge, and the judge deliver you to the officer, and you get thrown into prison. Truly I say to you, you will by no means come out of there until you have paid the last penny.

"You have heard that it was said to those of old, '*You shall not commit adultery*' (Exodus 20:14). but I say to you, that whoever looks upon a woman and lusts after her has already committed adultery with her in his heart.

"And if your right eye offends you, pluck it out and throw it away; for it is more profitable that one of your members should perish, and not that your whole body be sent into hell. If your right hand offends you, cut if off, and throw it away; for it is more profitable that one of your members should perish, and not that your whole body be sent into hell.

"It has been said, '*Whoever will put away his wife, let him give her a writing of divorce*' (Deuteronomy 24:1, 3); but

I say to you, that whoever will put away his wife, saving for the cause of sexual immorality, causes her to commit adultery; and whoever marries her who is divorced commits adultery.

"Again, you have heard that it has been said to those of old, '*You shall not swear falsely, but shall honor the* LORD *with your oaths*' (Leviticus 19:12). I say to you, do not swear oaths at all; neither by heaven, for it is God's throne, nor by the earth, for it is his footstool, neither by Jerusalem, for it is the city of the great King (Psalms 48:2). Neither shall you swear by your head, because you cannot make one hair white or black. Let your 'Yes' be 'Yes,' and "No" be 'No,' for whatever is more than this comes from evil.

"You have heard it said, '*An eye for an eye, and a tooth for a tooth*' (Exodus 21:24), but I say to you that you do not resist evil men; whoever slaps you on your right cheek, turn to him the other also. If any man sues you at law and takes away your coat, let him have your cloak also. And whoever compels you to go a mile, go with him two.

"Give to him who asks of you, and do not turn away him who would borrow from you.

"You have heard it said, 'You shall love your neighbor, and hate your enemy' (Leviticus 19:18). I say to those who hear, love your enemies, bless those who curse you, do good to those who hate you, and pray for those who despitefully use and persecute you, that you may be the children of your Father who is in heaven. For he makes the sun to rise both on evil men and also on the good, and sends rain on the righteous and also on the unrighteous.

"Give to everyone who asks of you, and of him who takes away your goods, do not ask for them back again. As you would have men do to you, do that to them.

"If you love only those who love you, what reward do you have? Do not even the sinners and tax collectors do the same? If you greet only your brothers, what more do you do than others? Do not even the tax collectors do that? Therefore be merciful, as your Father is merciful, be perfect, just as your Father, who is in heaven, is perfect.

"If you lend to those from whom you hope to receive back, what thanks do you have? For sinners also lend to sinners, to receive as much back again. Love your enemies, and do good and lend, hoping for nothing in return; and your reward will be great, and you will be children of the Highest, for he is kind both to the unthankful and to the evil men.

"Judge not, and you will not be judged; condemn not, and you will not be condemned; forgive, and you will be forgiven.

"Give, and it will be given to you, good measure, pressed down, shaken together, and running over, will men pour into your lap. For with the same measure that you use it will be measured back to you again."

He spoke a parable to them: "Can the blind lead the blind? Will they not both fall into the ditch? The disciple is not above his master, but everyone who is perfect will be as his master. Why look at the splinter that is in your brother's eye, but do not see the plank that is in your own eye? How can you say to your brother, 'Brother, let me pull out the splinter that is in your eye,' when you yourself do not see the plank that is in your own eye? You hypocrite, first take the plank out of your own eye, and then you will see clearly to pull out the splinter that is in your brother's eye."

"*A good* tree does not bear corrupt fruit, neither does a corrupt tree bear good fruit. For every tree is known by his own fruit, for men do not gather figs from thorns, nor from a bramble bush do they gather grapes. A good man out of the good treasure of his heart brings out that which is good, and an evil man out of the evil treasure of his heart brings out that which is evil, for out of the abundance of the heart the mouth speaks.

"Do not give that which is holy to the dogs, neither cast your pearls before swine, lest they trample them under their feet and turn around and attack you. Ask, and it will be given to you, seek, and you will find, knock, and it will be opened to you; for everyone who asks receives, and he who seeks finds, and to him who knocks it will be opened."

"*Why call* me, 'Lord, Lord,' and do not do the things that I say? Whoever comes to me and hears my sayings, and does them, I will show you to whom he is like. He is like a man who built a house, and dug deep and laid the foundation on a rock; and when a flood came, the water beat strongly against that house and could not shake it, because it was built upon a rock. He who hears my words and does not do them, is like a man who built a house upon the earth without a foundation, against which the water beat strongly, and immediately it collapsed; and the ruin of that house was great."

When he had ended all his sayings in the hearing of the people, he entered Capernaum. A certain centurion's servant, who was dear to him, was sick with a paralysis, grievously tormented and ready to die. When he heard of Jesus, he sent to him the elders of the Jews who pleaded with him to come and heal his servant.

When they came to Jesus they appealed to him instantly, saying, "He is worthy for whom you should do this, for he loves our nation and has built us a synagogue." Jesus said to them, "I will come and heal him."

Then Jesus went with them. When he was not far from the house the centurion sent friends to him, saying to him, "Lord, do not trouble yourself for I am not worthy that you should come under my roof. Neither did I think myself worthy to come to you, but say a word and my servant will be healed. For I also am a man placed under authority, having soldiers under me, and I say to one, 'Go,' and he goes, and to another, 'Come,' and he comes, and to my servant, 'Do this,' and he does it."

When Jesus heard these things, he marveled at him, and turned around and said to the people who followed him, "I say to you, I have not found such great faith, no, not in Israel. I say to you, that many will come from the east and the west and will sit down with Abraham, and Isaac, and Jacob, in the kingdom of heaven. However, the children of the kingdom will be cast out into outer darkness; there will be weeping and gnashing of teeth."

Jesus said to the centurion, "Go your way, and as you have believed so it is also done to you." And his servant was healed in that same hour. Returning to the house, the centurion found the servant who had been sick, fully healed.

It came about the next day that he went into a city called Nain, and many of his disciples went with him, and many other people also. When he came near the gate of the city, behold, there was a dead man being carried out, the only son of his mother, and she was a widow; and many people from the city were with her. When the Lord saw her, he had compassion on her, and said to her, "Do not weep." He came and touched the bier, and those who carried him stood still. He said, "Young man, I say to you, arise." He who was dead sat up, and began to speak. And Jesus presented him to his mother.

Fear came upon everyone, and they glorified God, saying, "A great prophet has risen up among us" and, "God has visited his people." This report of Jesus went about throughout all Judea, and throughout all the surrounding region.

The disciples of John told him about all these things. When John had heard in the prison about the works of Christ, he sent two of his disciples to Jesus, saying, "Are you the One that should come? Or do we look for another?" When the men came to him they said, "John the Baptist has sent us to you, saying, 'Are you he that should come? Or do we look for another?' " In that same hour Jesus cured many people of their infirmities and diseases, and evil spirits, and to many who were blind he gave sight.

Then Jesus, answering John's disciples, said to them, "Go your way and tell John again what things you have seen and heard: how the blind see, the lame walk, the lepers are cleansed, the deaf hear, the dead are raised, the gospel is preached to the poor. Blessed are those who will not be offended by me."

When the messengers of John had departed, he began to speak to the people concerning him: "What did you go out into the wilderness to see? A reed shaken in the wind? What did you go out to see? A man clothed in soft clothing? Indeed, those who wear gorgeous apparel and live in luxury are in kings' courts. What did you go out to see? A prophet? Yes, I say to you, and much more than a prophet. This is he of whom it is written: '*Behold, I send my messenger before your face, who will prepare the way before you*' (Malachi 3:1). For I say to you, among those who are born of women there is no greater prophet than John the Baptist, but he that is least in the kingdom of God is greater than John. From the days of John the Baptist until now the kingdom of heaven suffers violence, and the violent take it by force. For all the Prophets and the Law prophesied until John, and if you will hear it, this is Elijah who was to come. He who has ears to hear, let him hear."

All the people who heard Jesus, even the tax collectors, justified God, being baptized with the baptism of John. However, the Pharisees and lawyers rejected the purpose of God for themselves, and were not being baptized by him.

The Lord said, "How will I liken the men of this generation? What are they like? They are like children sitting in the marketplace, and calling to one another saying, 'We have played the pipe for you, and you have not danced; we have mourned for you, and you have not wept or lamented.' For John the Baptist came neither eating bread nor drinking wine, and you say, 'He has a demon.' The Son of Man came eating and drinking and you say, 'See, a gluttonous man and a drunkard, a friend of tax collectors and sinners'! But wisdom is justified by all her children."

One of the Pharisees requested that he should eat with him. He went into the Pharisee's house and sat down to eat. And behold, a woman in the city, who was a sinner, when she knew that Jesus sat at the table in the Pharisee's house, brought an alabaster box of ointment and knelt at his feet behind him weeping, and began to wash his feet with her tears and wipe them with the hair of her head; and kissed his feet and anointed them with the ointment.

When the Pharisee, who had invited him, saw it, he spoke within himself, saying, "This man, if he were a prophet, would have known who and what manner of woman this is that touches him, for she is a sinner." Responding to the Pharisee's thoughts, Jesus said to him, "Simon, I have something to say to you." He said, "Rabbi, say it."

"There was a certain creditor who had two debtors, one owed five hundred *denarii*, and the other fifty. When they had nothing with which to pay, he freely forgave them both. Tell me therefore, which of them will love him the most?" Simon answered and said, "I suppose that he to whom he forgave most." He said to him, "You have judged rightly."

He turned to the woman, and said to Simon, "You see this woman? I entered into your house, you gave me no water for my feet, but she has washed my feet with her tears and wiped them with the hair of her head. You gave me no kiss, but this woman since the time I came in has not ceased to kiss my feet. You did not anoint my head with oil, but this woman has anointed my feet with ointment. Therefore I say to you, her sins, which are many, are forgiven, for she loved much; but to whom little is forgiven, the same loves little."

He said to her, "Your sins are forgiven." Those that sat at the table with him began to say within themselves, "Who is this that also forgives sins?" He said to the woman, "Your faith has saved you, go in peace."

And so it was, that afterward Jesus went throughout every city and village, preaching and sharing the glad tidings of the kingdom of God, and the twelve were with him. Certain women also, who had been healed of evil spirits and infirmities—Mary called Magdalene, out of whom went seven demons, and Joanna the wife of Chuza, Herod's steward, and Susanna, and many others who provided for him from their private resources.

Jesus began again to teach by the sea's edge, and there was a great multitude gathered to him that had come to him from out of every city. He entered into a boat and sat in the boat on the sea, and the whole multitude was on the land, on the shore. He taught them many things by parables, and said to them in his teaching, "Listen, a sower went out to sow his seed, and as he sowed some seed fell by the wayside, and it was trodden down and the birds of the air ate it. Some fell upon a rock, and as soon as it sprang up it was scorched when the sun was up, and withered away because it lacked moisture and had no depth of soil.

Some fell among thorns, and the thorns sprang up with it and choked it and it yielded no fruit. Other seed fell on good ground and sprang up, and bore fruit and increased, and brought forth some thirty, and some sixty, and some a hundredfold." When he had said these things he cried loudly, "He who has ears to hear, let him hear!"

The disciples of Jesus asked him, saying, "Why do you speak to them in parables? What might this parable be?" He said, "To you it has been given to know the mysteries of the kingdom of God, but to them it is not given. For whoever has, to him more will be given and he will have an abundance, but whoever does not have, from him will be taken away even what little he does have.

"Therefore I speak to them in parables, that seeing they might not see, and hearing they might not understand. And in them is fulfilled the prophecy of Isaiah, which says:

> *Hearing you will hear, and will not understand, and seeing you will see and will not perceive, for this people's heart has grown fat, and their ears are dull of hearing, and their eyes they have closed, lest they should turn again, and their sins be forgiven them*
> (Isaiah 6:9-10).

But blessed are your eyes, for they see, and your ears, for they hear. For truly I say to you that many prophets and righteous men have desired to see the things which you see, and have not seen them; and to hear the things that you hear, and have not heard them. He said to them, "Do you not understand this parable? How then will you understand all the parables? Therefore hear the parable of the sower: The seed is the word of God. Those by the wayside are those who hear; then Satan comes and takes away the word out of their hearts, lest they should believe and be saved. Those on the rock are those who, when they hear, receive the word with joy; and these have no root, who for a while believe, and in time of temptation fall away. Those that fell among thorns are those who, when they have heard, go out and are choked with the cares and riches and pleasures of this life, and bring no fruit to maturity. Those on the good ground are those who, with an honest and good heart, having heard the word, keep it, and with patience bring forth fruit, some thirtyfold, some sixty, and some a hundred.

"No one, when he has lit a candle, covers it with a vessel, or puts it under a bed, but sets it on a candlestick, that those who enter may see the light. For nothing is secret that will not be revealed, nor anything hidden that will not be made known and shed abroad. If any man has ears to hear, let him hear.

"Therefore take heed how you hear, for whoever has, to him more will be given. Whoever does not have, from him will be taken even that which he seems to have. With whatever measure you use, it shall be measured back to you."

Jesus said, "the kingdom of God is as if a man should sow seed into the ground and then sleeps and rises night and day, and the seed springs up and grows, and he does not know how. For the earth brings forth fruit of herself, first the blade, then the ear, after that the full grain in the ear. But when the fruit is ripe and ready, he immediately puts in the sickle because the harvest is ready."

Then he said, "To what shall we liken the kingdom of God? Or with what shall we compare it? The kingdom of heaven is like a grain of mustard seed, which, when it is sown in the earth, is less than all the seeds that are on the earth. When it is sown, it grows up and becomes greater than all herbs and becomes a tree, and shoots out great branches; so that the birds of the air might lodge in the branches and rest under the shadow of it."

Again he said, "To what shall I liken the kingdom of God? It is like leaven, which a woman took and mixed into three measures of meal, until the whole lump was leavened."

Another parable he put forth to them, saying, "The kingdom of heaven is likened to a man who sowed good seed in his field. But, while his men slept, his enemy came and sowed tares among the wheat, and went his way. When the blades had sprung up and brought forth fruit, then the tares appeared also.

"So the servants of the owner came and said to him, 'Sir, did you not sow good seed in your field? From where then has it got tares?' He said to them, 'An enemy has done this.' The servants said to him, 'Do you want us to go and gather them up?' He said, 'No, lest while you are gathering up the tares you also root up the wheat along with them. Let both grow together until the harvest, and in the time of harvest I will say to the reapers: 'Gather together the tares first, and bind them in bundles to burn them, but gather the wheat into my barn.' "

Then Jesus sent the multitude away, and went into the house, and his disciples came to him, saying, "Explain to us the parable of the tares of the field. He answered and said to them, "He that sows the good seed is the Son of Man; the field is the world; the good seed are the children of the kingdom; but the tares are the children of the evil one; the enemy that sowed them is the devil; the harvest is the end of the world; and the reapers are the angels.

"Therefore, just as the tares are gathered and burned in the fire, so it will be at the end of this age. The Son of Man will send forth his angels and they will gather out of his kingdom everything that offends, and all those who practice wickedness. They will be cast into a furnace of fire; there will be wailing and gnashing of teeth. Then the righteous will shine forth like the sun in the kingdom of their Father. He who has ears to hear, let him hear.

"Again, the kingdom of heaven is like treasure hidden in a field, which, when a man has found it, he hides it, and for joy goes and sells everything he has, and buys the field. Again, the kingdom of heaven is like a merchant seeking excellent pearls and who, when he had found one pearl of great price, went and sold all that he had and bought it.

"Again, the kingdom of heaven is like a net which was cast into the sea, and gathered every kind of fish. When it was full, they drew to shore and sat down, gathering the good fish into containers, but throwing the bad away. So will it be at the end of the age; the angels will come out and separate the wicked from among the righteous, and will throw them into the furnace of fire; there will be wailing and gnashing of teeth."

Jesus said to the disciples, "Have you understood all these things?" They say to him, "Yes, Lord." Then he said to them, "Every scribe therefore, who is instructed in the kingdom of heaven, is like a householder who brings out of his treasure new things and old. With many such parables he spoke the word to them, as they were able to hear it. Without a parable he did not speak to them, that it might be fulfilled which was spoken by the prophet, saying:

> *I will open my mouth in parables; I will utter things which have been kept secret from the foundation of the world* (Psalms 78:2-3).

All these things Jesus spoke to the multitude in parables, and when they were alone he expounded everything to his disciples. When Jesus had finished these parables, he departed from that place.

Then his mother came to him and his brothers, and they could not come near him because of the crowd of people. It was told him that, "Your mother and your brothers are standing outside wanting to see you." He answered and said to them, "Who is my mother and who are my brothers?" He stretched out his hand toward his disciples and said, "Here are my mother and my brothers; my mother and my brothers are those who hear the word of God and do it."

It happened on a certain day, when Jesus saw great crowds around him, that he got into a boat with his disciples and said to them, "Let us go over to the other side of the lake." When they had sent the crowd away they launched out, and there were also other little ships with them. But as they sailed Jesus fell asleep and there came a windstorm on the lake, a great tempest, and the waves beat into the boat so that it filled with water and they were in danger.

They went to Jesus and awoke him, saying, "Master, master, we perish!" Then he stood up and rebuked the wind and the raging of the water, and said to the sea, "Peace, be still," and it ceased and there was a great calm. He said to them, "Why are you so fearful? Where is your faith?" They were afraid and wondered, saying one to another, "What manner of man is this! For he even commands the winds and water, and they obey him."

They arrived at the country of the Gadarenes, which is over the lake, opposite Galilee. When he set foot on land, there immediately met him out of the city a certain man possessed with demons for a long time. He neither wore clothes, nor lived in a house, but in the tombs. Always, night and day, he was in the mountains, and in the tombs, crying, and cutting himself with stones; neither could anyone subdue him. When he saw Jesus afar off, he ran and worshiped him, cried out, and fell down before him. And with a loud voice said, "What have I to do with you, Jesus, you Son of God Most High? Have you come here to torment us before the time? I beseech you—adjure you by God—torment me not!" For he had commanded the unclean spirit to come out of the man, for it had often seized him and he was kept bound in chains and shackles; and he broke the bonds and was driven by the demons into the wilderness.

Jesus asked him, saying, "What is your name?" He said, "Legion," because many demons had entered him. The demons begged him that he would not command them to go into the abyss. Now there was a herd of many swine feeding there on the mountain, and they pleaded with him that he would allow them to enter into the swine. He permitted them and said to them, "Go!" Then the demons went out of the man and entered the pigs, and the whole herd ran violently down a steep hill into the lake, and drowned in the water.

When those who fed them saw what was done, they fled and went and told it in the city and in the country. Then the whole city came out to meet Jesus, to see what was done. They came to Jesus and found the man out of whom the demons had gone, sitting at the feet of Jesus, clothed, and in his right mind, and they were afraid. Also, those who saw it told them how it happened to him who was possessed with the demons, and also concerning the pigs, by what means he who was possessed of the demons was healed.

Then the whole multitude round about the region of the Gadarenes begged him to go away from them, for they were taken with great fear. He got into the boat again and went back.

The man out of whom the demons had gone, begged him that he might go with him, but Jesus sent him away, saying, "Return to your own house, to your friends, and show what great things God has done for you and has had compassion on you. He went his way and made known throughout the whole Decapolis region what great things Jesus had done to him, and everyone marveled.

It came about, that when Jesus returned again by boat to the other side, many people gladly received him, for they were all waiting for him. And behold, there came a man named Jairus, and he was a ruler of the synagogue and he fell down at Jesus' feet and worshiped him. He begged

Jesus that he would come to his house, for he had only one daughter of about twelve years of age, and she lay dying. "Come I beg you, and lay your hands on her that she may be healed; and she will live. Jesus arose, and followed him, and so did his disciples. And as Jesus went the people thronged around him.

A certain woman who was sick with having an issue of blood twelve years, who had spent all of her living upon physicians, and had suffered many things of many physicians and could not be healed by them, but rather grew worse. She came behind Jesus, and touched the fringe of his garment, for she said within herself, "If I may just touch his garment I will be healed," and immediately her issue of blood was stanched and she felt in her body that she was healed of the affliction. Jesus, immediately knowing in himself that power had gone out of him, turned around in the crowd and said, "Who touched me?"

When all denied it, Peter and those who were with him said, "Master, the crowd throngs and presses against you, and you say, "Who touched me?" Jesus said, "Somebody touched me, for I felt power go out of me."

When the woman saw that she was not hidden, she came fearing and trembling, knowing what had been done in her, and falling down before him she declared to him before all the people why she had touched him and how she was immediately healed. He said to her, "Daughter, be of good cheer, your faith has made you whole; go in peace." And the woman was healed from that moment.

While he was still speaking there came one from the synagogue ruler's house, saying to him, "Your daughter is dead, do not trouble the Master." However, when Jesus heard it, he answered him, saying, "Do not fear, only believe, and she will be made well."

When he came into the house of the ruler of the synagogue, he allowed no one to go in except Peter, and James, and John, and the father and the mother of the young girl. All wept and lamented for her, but he said, "Why do you make such a tumult? Do not weep, she is not dead, but sleeping." And they laughed him to scorn, knowing that she was dead. He put them all out and entered in where the young girl was lying. He took the young girl by the hand, and said to her, *"Talitha cumi,"* which is, being interpreted, "Little girl, arise." Her spirit returned, and she got up straight away and walked, for she was twelve years of age. He commanded that something should be given her to eat. Her parents were greatly astonished, but he charged them that they should not tell anyone what was done. And his fame spread throughout all the land.

When Jesus departed from there, two blind men followed him, crying out, and saying, "You Son of David, have mercy on us." When he had come into the house, the blind men came to him. Jesus said to them, "Do you believe that I am able to do this?" They said to him, "Yes, Lord." Then he touched their eyes, saying, "According to your faith let it be to you." Their eyes were opened, and Jesus strictly charged them, saying, "See that no man knows about it." However, they, when they had left, spread their news in all the region.

As they went out they brought to him a mute man possessed by a demon. When the demon was cast out, the mute spoke, and the multitudes marveled, saying, "It has never been seen before in Israel." However, the Pharisees said, "He casts out demons through the ruler of the demons."

When Jesus and his disciples came into his own country, and the Sabbath day had come, he taught them in their synagogue and many were astonished, and said, "Where did this man get this wisdom, and these miracles that are done through his hands? Is this not the carpenter's son? Is his mother not called Mary? And his brothers, James, and Joses, and Simon, and Judas? And his sisters, are they not all with us? Where then did this man get all these things?" And they were offended at him. Jesus said to them, "A prophet is not without honor, except in his own hometown, and in his own house, among his own family." And he could do no mighty miracle there, except that he laid his hands upon a few sick people and healed them. He marveled because of their unbelief.

Jesus went round all the cities and villages, teaching in their synagogues, and preaching the gospel of the kingdom, and healing every sickness and every disease among the people. When he saw the multitudes, he was moved with compassion for them, because they fainted, and were scattered about like sheep without a shepherd.

Then he called his twelve disciples together and gave them power and authority over all unclean spirits, to cast them out and to cure all manner of sickness and all manner of diseases. He sent them to preach the kingdom of God, and to heal the sick, and he said to them: "Take nothing for your journey, only a staff. Neither gold, nor silver, nor money, nor brass in your purses, neither bag, nor have two coats apiece, nor shoes, neither bread, for the workman is worthy of his food. Into whatever city or town you will enter, inquire in it who is worthy, and live there until you leave.

"When you come into a house, greet it. If the house is worthy, let your peace come upon it, but if it is not worthy let your peace return to you. Whoever will not receive you, when you go out of that city, shake off the very dust from your feet for a testimony against them. Truly I say to you, it will be more bearable for Sodom and Gomorrah in the day of judgment, than for that city."

Jesus sent the twelve out by two and two, and commanded them, saying, "Do not go into the areas of the Gentiles, and do not enter any city of the Samaritans, but go only to the lost sheep of the house of Israel. As you go, preach, saying, 'The kingdom of heaven is at hand.' Heal the sick, cleanse the lepers, raise the dead, cast out demons—freely you have received, freely give.

"Surely, I send you out as sheep in the midst of wolves, therefore be as wise as serpents and as harmless as doves. Beware of men, for they will deliver you up to the councils, and they will scourge you in their synagogues; and you will be brought before governors and kings for my sake, for a testimony against them and the Gentiles. When they deliver you up, take no thought how or what you will speak, for it will be given you that same hour what you will speak. For it is not you who will speak, but the Spirit of your Father that will speak in you.

"Brother will deliver up his brother to death, and the father his child, and the children will rise up against their parents and cause them to be put to death. You will be hated by everyone for my name's sake, but he who endures to the end will be saved. When they persecute you in this city, flee to another, for truly I say to you, you will not have gone through all the cities of Israel before the Son of Man will come.

"The disciple is not above his master, nor the servant above his lord. It is enough for the disciple that he be as his master, and the servant as his lord. If they have called the master of the house 'Beelzebub,' how much more will they call those of his household? Do not fear them, for there is nothing covered that will not be revealed, or hidden, that will not be known. What I tell you in darkness, speak it in the light, and what you hear in your ear, preach it from the housetops.

"Do not fear those who kill the body, but are unable to kill the soul, but rather fear him who is able to destroy both soul and body in hell. Are not two sparrows sold for a quarter of a penny? Not one of them will fall on the ground without your Father's permission. The very hairs of your head are all numbered, therefore do not fear, for you are of more value than many sparrows."

"Whoever confesses me before men, I will also confess him before my Father who is in heaven. Whoever denies me before men, I will also deny him before my Father who is in heaven.

"Do not think that I have come to bring peace on earth, I did not come to bring peace, but a sword. I have come to set a man at variance against his father, and the daughter at variance against her mother, and the daughter-in-law at variance against her mother-in-law. And a man's foes will be those of his own household.

"He who loves father or mother more than me is not worthy of me, and he who loves son or daughter more than me is not worthy of me. He who does not take up his cross and follow after me, is not worthy of me. He who finds his life will lose it; he who loses his life for my sake will find it.

"He who receives you receives me, and he who receives me receives him who sent me. He who receives a prophet in the name of a prophet will receive a prophet's reward, and he who receives a righteous man in the name of a righteous man will receive a righteous man's reward. And whoever will give one of these little ones just a cup of cold water to drink in the name of a disciple, truly I say to you, he will in no way lose his reward."

The disciples departed from there and went throughout the towns, preaching the gospel and that all men should repent, and they cast out many demons, and anointed with oil those who were sick, and healed them.

*K*ing Herod the tetrarch heard of all that was done by Jesus—for his name was being spread around—and he was puzzled, for it was said by some that John the Baptist had risen from the dead and therefore mighty works were being done through him. Some said that Elijah had appeared, and others that one of the old prophets had risen again. Herod said, "John I had beheaded, so who is this of whom I hear such things?" He desired to see him.

Herod himself had sent men and they laid hold upon John, and bound him, and put him in prison for Herodias' sake, his brother Philip's wife, for he had married her. John had said to him, "It is not lawful for you to have your brother's wife."

Therefore Herodias had a quarrel against John and would have killed him, but she could not, for Herod feared him, knowing that he was a righteous and holy man. He protected him and happily listened to him, enjoying what he did. He would have put him to death, but he feared the multitude because they looked upon John as a prophet.

Then an opportune day came when Herod's birthday was observed, and Herod made a supper for his lords, high military captains, and chief leaders of Galilee. When the daughter of Herodias came in and danced, it pleased Herod and those who sat with him. The king said to the young girl, "Ask of me whatever you will, and I will give it to you." He swore to her with an oath, "Whatever you shall ask of me, I will give it to you—up to half of my kingdom!"

She went and said to her mother, "What shall I ask?" Then the girl, being instructed by her mother, said, "Give me John the Baptist's head on a platter." The king was exceptionally sorry, nevertheless, for the oath's sake and those who sat with him at the table, he could not deny her; he commanded it to be given her. Immediately the king sent an executioner and commanded his head to be brought, and he went and beheaded John in the prison. His head was brought on a platter and given to the young girl, and she took it to her mother.

His disciples came and took up the body, and laid it in a tomb, and went and told Jesus.

The apostles, when they had returned, told him all things, both what they had done, and what they had taught. He said to them, "Come apart by yourselves and rest a while in a quiet place," for there were many people coming and going and they had no time even to eat. He took them and went away privately by boat over the lake—sea of Galilee, which is the sea of Tiberias—into a deserted place belonging to the city of Bethsaida.

The people, when they knew of it, followed him on foot out of the cities because they saw his miracles which he did on those who were diseased. He received them, a great multitude, and was moved with compassion toward them because they were like sheep without a shepherd; and he began to teach them many things and spoke to them of the kingdom of God, and healed those that had need of healing. Jesus then went up onto a mountain, and there he sat with his disciples. The Passover, a feast of the Jews, drew near.

When the day began to draw to a close, the twelve came and said to him, "Send the multitude away, so that they may go into the towns and area round about and find lodging, and buy themselves food, for they have nothing to eat and we are in a deserted place." He said to them, "They need not go away, you give them something to eat."

Jesus raised his head and looked, and he saw a great company coming to him; he said to Philip, "Where will we buy bread that these may eat?" He said this to test him, because he knew what he was going to do. Philip answered him, "Two hundred *denarii* worth of bread is not sufficient for them, that everyone might have a little."

One of his disciples, Andrew, Simon Peter's brother, said to him, "There is a lad here who has five barley loaves and two small fish, but what are they among so many?" For there were about five thousand men besides women and children. Now there was a lot of grass in that place; and he said to his disciples, "Make them sit down in companies of fifties on the green grass." And they did so; they sat down in ranks, by hundreds, and by fifties.

Then He said, "Bring the loaves, and fish here to me," and when he had taken the five loaves and the two fish, and looking up to heaven he blessed them, and broke the loaves, and gave them to the disciples to set before the multitude, and the two fish he divided among them all and they ate as much as they wanted.

When they were full, he said to his disciples, "Gather up the fragments that remain, that nothing is lost." Therefore they gathered them all together and filled twelve baskets with the remaining fragments of the five barley loaves and the two fish—twelve full baskets. Immediately Jesus made his disciples get into a boat and go ahead of him to the other side of the lake, while he sent the multitudes away.

Then those who had seen the miracle that Jesus did, said, "Of a truth this is the Prophet that was to come into the world. Therefore, when Jesus understood that they would come and take him by force to make him a king, he went up on a mountain alone to pray; and when evening had come, he was there alone.

*W*hen *evening had* come his disciples went down to the sea of Galilee and got into a boat, and they went over the lake toward Capernaum. It was now dark, and Jesus had not come to them.

The sea arose because of a great wind that was blowing. The boat was now in the middle of the sea, tossed about by the waves, for the wind was contrary, and he was alone on the land and he saw them straining at rowing. About the fourth watch of the night, when they had rowed about three or four miles, they saw Jesus walking on the sea, and was drawing near to the boat and would have passed them by. They were afraid; they cried out in fear, saying, "It is a spirit." At once Jesus spoke to them and said to them, "Be of good cheer, it is I, do not be afraid." Peter answered him and said, "Lord, if it is you, tell me to come to you on the water." He said, "Come!" When Peter got down out of the boat, he walked on the water to go to Jesus, but when he saw the boisterous wind he was afraid and, beginning to sink, he cried out, saying, "Lord, save me!" Immediately Jesus stretched out his hand and caught him, and said to him, "O you of little faith, why did you doubt?"

Then they gladly received Jesus into the boat, and when they had gotten into the boat the wind ceased. Then those who were in the boat worshiped him, saying, "Of a truth you are the Son of God." Immediately the boat was at the land where they were going, and they were really amazed beyond measure, and wondered. For they did not consider the miracle of the loaves, for their hearts were hardened.

When they had crossed over the lake, which is the sea of Galilee, they came to the land of Gennesaret and anchored near the shore. When they had got out of the boat, straight away the men of that place recognized him. They ran out into all the area, through the whole region, and began to carry about on beds those who were sick to where they heard he was. They brought to him all that were suffering from disease. Whenever he entered into villages, or cities, or regions, they laid the sick in the streets and implored him that they may just touch the fringe of his garment, and as many as touched him were made perfectly well.

The following day, when the people who stood on the other side of the lake saw that there was no other boat there except the one into which his disciples had entered, and saw that Jesus did not go with his disciples into the boat—his disciples had gone away alone. Other boats came from Tiberias near to the place where they ate the bread after the Lord had given thanks and therefore, when the people realized that Jesus was not there, nor his disciples, they also took boats and went to Capernaum, looking for him.

When they had found him on the other side of the lake, they said to him, "Rabbi, when did you come here?" Jesus answered them and said, "Indeed, I say to you, you look for me, not because you saw the miracles, but because you ate of the loaves and were satisfied. Do not toil for the food that perishes, but for the food that endures to everlasting life, which the Son of Man will give to you; for upon him God the Father has set his seal."

Then they said to him, "What shall we do, that we might work the works of God?" Jesus answered and said to them, "This is the work of God, that you believe in him whom he has sent." Therefore they said to him, "What sign do you show then, that we might see and believe you? What miracle will you do? Our fathers all ate manna in the wilderness, as it is written: '*He gave them bread from heaven to eat*' " (Nehemiah 9:15).

Then Jesus said to them, "Indeed, I say to you, Moses did not give you that bread from heaven, but my Father gives you the true bread from heaven. For the bread of God is he who comes down from heaven and gives life to the world." Then they said to him, "Lord, give us this bread forever." Jesus said to them, "I am the bread of life, he who comes to me will never hunger, and he who believes in me will never thirst.

"I said to you, that you have also seen me, but do not believe. All whom the Father gives me will come to me; and those who come to me I will never cast out. For I came down from heaven, not to do my own will, but the will of him who sent me. And this is the Father's will who has sent me, that of all those whom he has given me I would lose none, but would raise them up again at the last day. This is the will of him who sent me, that everyone who sees the Son and believes in him may have everlasting life, and I will raise him up at the last day."

The Jews then found fault with him, because he said, "I am the bread which came down from heaven." They said, "Is this not Jesus, the son of Joseph, whose father and mother we know? How is it then that he says, I came down from heaven?" Jesus therefore answered and said to them, "Do not complain among yourselves. No one can come to me, unless the Father who has sent me draws him, and I will raise him up at the last day. It is written in the prophets, '*And they shall all be taught by God*' (Isaiah 54:13). Therefore, everyone who has heard, and has learned from the Father, comes to me. Not that anyone has seen the Father, except he who is of God, he has seen the Father. Indeed, I say to you, he that believes in me has everlasting life.

"I am that bread of life. Your fathers ate manna in the wilderness and are dead. This is the bread that comes down from heaven, which a man may eat and not die. I am the living bread that came down from heaven. If any man eats of this bread he will live forever; and the bread that I will give is my flesh, which I will give for the life of the world."

Therefore the Jews argued among themselves, saying, "How can this man give us his flesh to eat?" Then Jesus said to them, "Indeed, I say to you, unless you eat the flesh of the Son of Man, and drink his blood,[12] you have no life in you. Whoever eats my flesh, and drinks my blood, has eternal life, and I will raise him up at the last day. For my flesh is food indeed, and my blood is drink indeed. He that eats my flesh and drinks my blood lives in me, and I in him. As the living Father has sent me, and I live by the Father, so he that feeds on me, he will even live by me.

"This is that bread that came down from heaven, not as your fathers ate manna, and are dead; he who eats of this bread will live forever." These things Jesus said in Capernaum, as he taught in the synagogue.

Therefore, many of his disciples, when they had heard this word, said, "This is a hard saying, who can accept it?" When Jesus knew in himself that his disciples complained, he said to them, "Does this offend you? What if you should see the Son of Man ascend up to where he was before? It is the Spirit that quickens, the flesh profits nothing. The words that I speak to you, they are Spirit, and they are life, but there are some of you who do not believe." For from the beginning Jesus knew who they were who did not believe, and who would betray him.

He then said, "Therefore I said to you, that no man can come to me, unless it is given to him of my Father." From that time many of his disciples turned back, and followed him no more. Then Jesus said to the twelve, "Will you go away also?" Then Simon Peter answered him, "Lord, to whom will we go? You have the words of eternal life. We believe and know that you are the Christ, the Son of the living God." Jesus answered them, "Have I not chosen you, the twelve, and one of you is a devil?" He spoke of Judas Iscariot the son of Simon, for he it was who would betray him, he being one of the twelve.

After these things Jesus walked in Galilee, for he would not walk in Jerusalem, because the Jews sought to kill him. There came to Jesus certain of the scribes and Pharisees who had come from Jerusalem. They saw some of his disciples eat bread with *defiled,* that is to say, with unwashed hands, and they found fault. For the Pharisees, and all the Jews, unless they wash their hands often, will not eat,[13] holding to the tradition of the elders. When they come from the market, unless they wash, they do not eat. Many other things there are, which they traditionally hold to, such as the washing of cups, and pots, brass vessels, and of tables.

Then the Pharisees and scribes asked him, "Why do your disciples not live according to the tradition of the elders? For they do not wash their hands before eating." He answered and said to them, "Why do you transgress the commandment of God by your tradition? You totally reject the commandment of God, so that you may keep your own tradition. For God commanded, saying, 'Honor your father and mother,' and 'He that curses father or mother, let him be put to death.' Now you say, 'Whoever says to his father or his mother, "Whatever you might have profited from me is Corban" (that is to say, a gift to God), he will be free and need not honor his father or his mother.' You allow him to do nothing for his father or his mother, thus you negate the commandment of God by your tradition. And many other such things you do. You hypocrites, well did Isaiah prophesy about you, when he said:

This people draw near to me with their mouths, and honor me with their lips, but their hearts are far from me. In vain they worship me, teaching for doctrines the commandments of men (Isaiah 29:13).

Jesus called the crowd to him, and said to them, "Hear, and understand every one of you, there is nothing from outside of a man that entering into him can *defile* him, but the things that come out of him, those are what *defile* a man. If anyone has ears to hear, let him hear."

When he had entered into the house away from the people, his disciples came and said to him, "Do you know that the Pharisees were offended after they heard that saying?" He answered and said, "Every plant that my heavenly Father has not planted will be uprooted. Let them alone, they are blind leaders of the blind and if the blind lead the blind, both will fall into the ditch."

Then Peter answered and said to him, "Explain this parable to us." Jesus said, "Are you also without understanding? Do you not understand that whatever enters in through the mouth goes into the stomach and is eliminated from the body, purging all foods, it cannot *defile* him. Those things that proceed out of the mouth come from the heart, and they *defile* the man. For out of the heart proceed evil thoughts, murders, adulteries, sexual sins, thefts, false witness, wickedness, deceit, lasciviousness, an evil eye, pride, foolishness, blasphemies; these are the things that *defile* a man, but to eat with unwashed hands does not *defile* a man."

Jesus departed from there and went into the borders of Tyre and Sidon, and entered into a house. He wanted no one to know of it, but he could not be hidden. And, behold, a certain woman of Canaan, a Gentile, a Syro-Phoenician by birth, heard of him and came out of the same coastlands, and came and fell down at his feet. She cried out to him, saying, "Have mercy on me, O Lord, you Son of David, my daughter is grievously troubled by a demon." He answered her not a word. His disciples came and entreated him, saying, "Send her away, because she cries out after us!"

He answered and said, "I have been sent only to the lost sheep of the house of Israel." Then the woman came and worshiped him, saying, "Lord, help me!" He answered and said, "Let the children be filled first: for it is not right to take the children's bread and to throw it to dogs." She said, "True, Lord, yet even the dogs eat the children's crumbs that fall from their masters' table." Then Jesus answered and said to her, "O woman, great is your faith; be it unto you even as you would have it." And her daughter was made well that very same hour. When she came to her house, she found the demon had gone, and her daughter laying on the bed.

Jesus departed again from the coasts of Tyre and Sidon and came near to the sea of Galilee through the region of Decapolis, and went up onto a mountain and sat down. They brought to him one who was deaf and who also had an impediment in his speech. They implored him to put his hand upon him. He took him aside from the multitude, and put his fingers into his ears, and he spat, and touched his tongue. Looking up to heaven, he sighed, and said, "*Ephphatha*," that is, "Be opened." Straight away his ears were opened, and the impediment of his tongue was gone, and he spoke plainly.

Great multitudes came to him, having with them those who were lame, blind, mute, maimed, and many other things, and put them down at Jesus' feet, and he healed them. Insomuch that the multitude wondered when they saw the mute speak, the maimed made whole, the lame walking, and sight restored to the blind; and they glorified the God of Israel.

He charged them that they should tell no one, but the more he instructed them, so much the more freely they spread it about. They were astounded beyond belief, saying, "He has done all things well."

In those days the multitude was very great, and they had nothing to eat. Jesus called his disciples to him and said, "I have compassion on the multitude, because they continue with me now for three days and have had nothing to eat. I will not send them away fasting, they will faint by the way for many of them have come a long way."

His disciples say to him, "Where could we get so much bread in the wilderness so as to satisfy so great a multitude of people? Jesus said to them, "How many loaves do you have?" They said, "Seven, and a few little fish." He commanded the multitude to sit down on the ground. He took the seven loaves and the fish, and he blessed and gave thanks, and broke them up and gave to his disciples, and commanded the disciples to set them before the multitude.

They all ate and were filled, and they took up the spare food that was left—seven full baskets. Those that ate were about four thousand men, beside women and children. Then he sent them away.

After he sent the multitude away, he got into a boat with his disciples and came into the coastal area of Magdala, into the region of Dalmanutha. The Pharisees along with the Sadducees came out, and began to argue with him, seeking from him a sign from heaven, testing him.

He sighed deeply in his spirit and answered them saying, "When it is evening, you say, 'It will be fair weather, for the sky is red.' In the morning, 'It will be foul weather today because the sky is red and threatening.' O you hypocrites, you can discern the face of the sky, but you cannot discern the signs of the times? A wicked and adulterous generation seeks after a sign, and there will be no sign given to it except the sign of the prophet Jonah."

Jesus left them, and getting into the boat again departed with his disciples to the other side. Now the disciples had forgotten to take bread, neither did they have with them in the boat more than one loaf. Then Jesus instructed them, saying, "Take heed, beware of the leaven of the Pharisees and of the Sadducees, and of the leaven of Herod." They reasoned among themselves, saying, "It is because we have forgotten to take bread." Which, when Jesus became aware of it, he said to them, "O you of little faith, why do you discuss among yourselves that you have brought no bread? Do you not realize, nor understand? Is your heart still hardened? Having eyes, can you not see? Having ears, do you not hear? Do you not remember the five loaves of the five thousand, and how many baskets you picked up?" They say to him, "Twelve."

"Neither the seven loaves of the four thousand, and how many baskets full of pieces you collected?" They said, "Seven." How is it that you do not understand that I did not speak to you concerning bread, but that you should beware of the leaven of the Pharisees and of the Sadducees?" Then they understood that he did not tell them to beware of the leaven of bread, but of the doctrine of the Pharisees and of the Sadducees.

He came to Bethsaida; and they brought a blind man to him, and begged him to touch him. He took the blind man by the hand and led him out of the town, and when he had spat on his eyes and had put his hands upon him, he asked him if he saw anything. He looked up and said, "I see men as trees, walking."

After that he put his hands on his eyes again, and made him look up; and his sight was restored and he saw everything clearly. He sent him away to his house, saying, "Neither go into the town, nor tell it to anyone in the town."

Jesus and his disciples came into the towns of Caesarea Philippi; and it came to pass, as he was alone praying, he asked his disciples who were with him, saying, "Whom do the people say that I am?" They, answering, said, "Some say that you are John the Baptist, but some say Elijah; and others say Jeremiah, or that one of the old prophets has risen again." He said to them, "But whom do you say that I am?" Simon Peter answering said, "You are the Christ, the Son of the living God." Jesus answered and said to him, "Blessed are you, Simon Bar-Jonah, for flesh and blood has not revealed this to you, but my Father who is in heaven.

Jesus looked at him and said, "You shall be called Cephas"[14] (which is, by interpretation, "a stone"). I also say to you that upon this rock I will build my church and the gates of hell will not prevail against it. I will give to you the keys of the kingdom of heaven, and whatever you will bind on earth will be bound in heaven, and whatever you will loose on earth will be loosed in heaven." He strictly charged his disciples, and commanded them to tell no one that he was Jesus the Christ.

Jesus began to teach them saying, "The Son of Man must go to Jerusalem and suffer many things, and be rejected by the elders and chief priests and scribes, and be killed, and after three days be raised on the third day." He spoke this word openly.

Then Peter took him aside and began to rebuke him, saying, "Far be it from you, Lord; this shall not happen to you." When he had turned around and looked on his disciples, he rebuked Peter, saying, "Get behind me, Satan, you are an offense to me, you do not care for the things that are of God, but those that are of men."

He said to all his disciples, "If any man wants to come after me, let him deny himself and take up his cross daily, and follow me. For whoever will save his life will lose it, but whoever will lose his life for my sake, the same will find and save it. For what will it profit a man if he gain the whole world, and lose his own soul? Or be cast away? Or what will a man give in exchange for his soul?

"Whoever is ashamed of me and my words in this adulterous and sinful generation, of him will the Son of Man be ashamed when he will come in his own glory, and in his Father's, and that of the holy angels. For the Son of Man will come in the glory of his Father with his angels; and then he will reward every man according to his works. And I tell you truthfully, there are some standing here who will not taste death until they see the kingdom of God come with power."

It came to pass about six or eight days after those sayings, that Jesus took Peter and John, and his brother James, and went up onto a high mountain apart by themselves to pray. As he prayed, the appearance of his face was altered, and his clothing became white, and glistering, and shining, exceptionally white as snow, such as no launderer on earth can bleach them; and he was transfigured before them. His face shone like the sun, and behold, there appeared to them two men, who were talking with him. Moses and Elijah, who appeared in glory, spoke of his departure which he would accomplish at Jerusalem. Now Peter and those who were with him were heavy with sleep, and when they were awake they saw the glory of Jesus, and the two men who stood with him. And it came about that, as Moses and Elijah parted from Jesus, Peter said to him, "Master, it is good for us to be here, and if you will, let us make three tabernacles; one for you, and one for Moses, and one for Elijah—not knowing what he said for they were very much afraid.

While he was speaking there came a bright cloud, that overshadowed them; and they were fearful as they entered the cloud. There came a voice out of the cloud, saying, "This is my beloved Son in whom I am well pleased; hear him!" When the disciples heard it, they fell on their faces, and were even more afraid. Jesus came and touched them, and said, "Get up, and do not be afraid." Suddenly, when they had looked around, they saw no one any more, only Jesus along with themselves.

As they came down from the mountain, Jesus charged them, saying that they should tell no one what things they had seen until the Son of Man had risen again from the dead. They kept that saying among themselves, questioning one with another what the rising from the dead could mean. They kept it a secret and told no one in those days any of the things which they had seen.

*H*is *disciples asked* Jesus, saying, "Why then do the scribes say that Elijah must come first?" He answered and said to them, "Elijah truly will first come, and restore all things. However, I say to you that Elijah has come already, and restores all things, and they knew him not, but have done to him whatever they pleased. Likewise it is written that the Son of Man must also suffer from them and be treated as nothing. Then the disciples understood that he spoke to them of John the Baptist.

It happened, that, on the next day, when they had come down from the mountain, he came to his disciples and saw about them a great multitude, and the scribes questioning them. Straight away, when all the people saw him, they were awestruck, and running to him greeted him. He asked the scribes," What are you questioning them about?"

Then, behold, a certain man of the company came to him, knelt down and cried out, saying, "Master, I implore you, look upon my son for he is my only child; for he is a lunatic, and sorely troubled; for often he falls into the fire, and often into the water. And, lo, a spirit takes him, and he suddenly cries out; and it tears him so that he foams at the mouth, and it bruises him badly before departing from him. I begged your disciples to cast him out, and they could not."

Jesus answering said, "O faithless and perverse generation, how long shall I be with you, and how long shall I put up with you? Bring your son here to me." Straight away, as he was still coming, the demon threw him down and convulsed him, and he fell on the ground and rolled about, foaming at the mouth. Jesus asked his father, "How long is it since this came to him?" He said, "Since he was a child. Often it has thrown him into the fire, and into the waters, to destroy him, but if you can do anything, have compassion on us, and help us. Jesus said to him, "If you can? All things are possible to him who believes." Immediately the father cried out, and said with tears, "Lord, I believe, please help my unbelief!"

When Jesus saw that the people came running together, he rebuked the foul spirit saying to him, "You dumb and deaf spirit, I charge you, come out of him and enter into him no more." The spirit cried out, and greatly convulsed him, and came out of him; and he was so much like one who is dead that many said, "He is dead." Jesus took the healed child by the hand and lifted him up; and he stood up. And they were all amazed at the mighty power of God.

When he had come into the house, his disciples asked him privately, "Why could we not cast him out?" Jesus said to them, "Because of your unbelief; for truly I say to you, if you have faith as a grain of mustard seed, you will say to this mountain, remove from here to a place yonder, and it will go; and nothing will be impossible to you. He said to them, "However, this kind can come out by nothing other than prayer and fasting."

While everyone wondered at all the things that Jesus did, they departed from there and passed through Galilee; and he did not want anyone to know about it. Jesus said to his disciples, "Let these sayings settle down into your ears; the Son of Man will be delivered into the hands of men. They will kill him, and after he is killed, the third day he will be raised up again." But they did not understand this saying, and it was hidden from them, that they may not grasp it; and they were afraid to ask him about that saying.

When they had come to Capernaum, those who received the temple tax money came to Peter and said, "Does your master not pay the temple tax?" He said, "Yes." When he had come into the house, Jesus preempted him, saying, "What do you think, Simon? Of whom do the kings of the earth take custom or tax? Of their own children, or of strangers?" Peter said to him, "Of strangers." Jesus said to him, "Then the children are free. Nevertheless, in case we should offend them, go to the sea, throw in a hook and take the first fish that comes up, and when you open its mouth you will find a piece of money; take that and give it to them for me and for you."

Jesus came to Capernaum; and being in the house he asked them, "What was it that you were disputing among yourselves along the way?" But they said nothing, for along the way there had arose a dispute among themselves as to who would be the greatest. He sat down, and called the twelve, and said to them, "If anyone desires to be first, the same shall be last of all, and servant of all."

He took a child and set him in the midst of them, and when he had taken the child in his arms, he said to them, "Truly I say to you, unless you turn and become like little children, you will not enter the kingdom of heaven. Whoever will humble himself like this little child, the same is greatest in the kingdom of heaven. Whoever will receive one such child in my name, receives me, and whoever will receive me, receives not only me, but also him that sent me; for he that is least among you all, that one will be great."

John answered and said "Master, we saw someone casting out demons in your name, and we forbade him because he does not follow with us." Jesus said to him, "Do not forbid him for there is no one who will do a miracle in my name, that afterward will easily speak evil of me, for he that is not against us is for us. For whoever will give you a cup of water to drink in my name because you belong to Christ, truly I say to you, he will not lose his reward.

"Whoever offends one of these little ones who believe in me, it would be better for him if a millstone were hung around his neck and he is thrown into the depth of the sea and drowned. Take care that you do not despise one of these little ones, for I say to you, that in heaven their angels always see the face of my Father who is in heaven. Woe to the world because of offenses! Offenses must come, but woe to that man by whom the offense comes!

"*The Son* of Man has come to save that which was lost. What do you think? If a man has a hundred sheep and one of them goes astray, does he not leave the ninety-nine and go into the hills and look for the one that has gone astray? If it happens that he finds it, truly I say to you, he rejoices more over that one sheep than over the ninety-nine that did not go astray. Even so it is not the will of your Father who is in heaven, that one of these little ones should perish."

"*If your* hand offends you, cut it off. It is better for you to enter into life crippled than having two hands to be cast into hell, the fire that will never be quenched, where the worm does not die. If your foot offends you, cut it off. It is better for you to enter into life lame than having two feet to be cast into hell, where the worm does not die, and the fire is never quenched.

"If your eye offends you, pluck it out. It is better for you to enter into the kingdom of God with one eye, than having two eyes to be cast into hell fire, where the worm does not die and the fire is never quenched. For everyone will be seasoned with fire, and every sacrifice will be seasoned with salt. Salt is good, but if the salt has lost its flavor, with what will you season it? Have salt in yourselves, and have peace one with another. Moreover if your brother sins against you, go and tell him his fault between you and him alone. If he will hear you, you have gained your brother. However, if he will not hear you, then take with you one or two others, that in the mouth of two or three witnesses every word may be established. If he refuses to hear them, tell it to the church, but if he refuses to hear the church, let him be to you as a heathen and a tax collector.

"Truly I say to you, whatever you will bind on earth will be bound in heaven, and whatever you will loose on earth will be loosed in heaven. Again I say to you, that if two of you will agree on earth as touching anything that they will ask, it will be done for them by my Father who is in heaven. For where two or three are gathered together in my name, there am I in the midst of them."

Then Peter came to Jesus and said, "Lord, how often shall my brother sin against me, and I forgive him? Up to seven times?" Jesus said to him, "I will not say to you, up to seven times, but, until seventy times seven. Pay attention to yourselves, if your brother sins against you, rebuke him, and if he repents, forgive him. If he sins against you seven times in a day, and seven times in a day returns to you, saying, 'I repent,' you shall forgive him.[15]

"Therefore the kingdom of heaven is like a certain king who would settle accounts with his servants. When he had begun his reckoning, one was brought to him who owed him ten thousand talents. Because he had nothing to pay with, his lord commanded him to be sold, along with his wife and children and all that he owned, and payment be

made. Therefore the servant dropped to his knees and begged him, saying, 'Master, have patience with me, and I will pay you all.' Then the master of that servant was moved with compassion, and let him go and forgave him the debt. However, the servant went out, and found one of his fellow servants who owed him a hundred *denarii*, and he grabbed him and took him by the throat, saying, 'Pay me what you owe.' His fellow servant fell down at his feet, and implored him, saying, 'Have patience with me, and I will pay you everything.' He would not listen, but went and threw him into prison until he should pay the debt. So when his fellow servants saw what he had done, they were very upset, and came and told their master all that was done.

Then his master, after he had called the servant, said to him, 'O you wicked servant, I forgave you all that debt because you pleaded with me. Should you not also have had compassion on your fellow servant, even as I had pity on you?' His master was very angry, and delivered him to the tormentors, until he should pay everything that was due to him. So also will my heavenly Father do likewise to you if you do not from your hearts forgive every brother his sins."

The Jew's feast of tabernacles was at hand. Therefore his brothers said to him, "Leave here, and go into Judea, where your disciples may also see the works that you do. For no one does anything in secret, because he himself wants to be known openly. If you do these things, show yourself to the world." For his brothers did not believe in him. Then Jesus said to them, "My time has not come yet, but your time is always here. The world cannot hate you, but it hates me because I testify that its works are evil. You go up to this feast; I will not go up to this feast yet for my time has not fully come." When he had said these words to them, he still remained in Galilee, but when his brothers had gone up, then he also went up to the feast, not openly, but in secret as it were.

And so it was, when the time had come that he should be received up, he steadfastly set his face to go to Jerusalem. Messengers were sent ahead of him and they went and entered into a village of the Samaritans to make preparations for him, but they did not receive him because his face was set to go to Jerusalem. When his disciples James and John saw this, they said, "Lord, will you allow that we command fire to come down from heaven, and consume them, even as Elijah did?" He turned and rebuked them, saying, "You do not know what manner of Spirit you are of. For the Son of Man has not come to destroy men's lives, but to save them." And they went to another village.

It came about, that, as they were going along the way, a certain scribe said to him, "Lord, I will follow you wherever you go." Jesus said to him, "Foxes have holes, and birds of the air have nests, but the Son of Man has nowhere to lay his head." He said to another, "Follow me." He said, "Lord, allow me to first go and bury my father." Jesus said to him, "Let the dead bury their dead, but you go and preach the kingdom of God."

Also another disciple said, "Lord, I will follow you, but first let me go and say farewell to those who are at home at my house." Jesus said to him, "No one who puts his hand to the plow and looks back is fit for the kingdom of God."

The Jews looked for Jesus at the feast, and said, "Where is he?" There was much murmuring among the people concerning him, for some said, "He is a good man," others said, "No, he deceives the people." However, no one spoke openly about him for fear of the Jews.

About the middle of the feast Jesus went up into the temple, and taught. The Jews marveled, saying, "How does this man know letters, having never learned?" Jesus answered them, and said, "My doctrine is not mine, but his who sent me. If any man will do his will, he will know of the doctrine, whether it is of God, or whether I speak from myself. He who speaks from himself seeks his own glory, but he who seeks the glory of him who sent him, the same is true, and no unrighteousness is in him.

"Did not Moses give you the Law, and yet none of you keep the Law? Why do you go around seeking to kill me?" The people answered and said, "You have a demon; who goes around seeking to kill you?" Jesus answered and said to them, "I have done one work, and you all marvel. Moses gave you circumcision—not because it is of Moses, but of the fathers—and you will circumcise a man on the Sabbath day. If a man receives circumcision on the Sabbath day, that the Law of Moses should not be broken, are you angry at me because I have made a man completely whole on the Sabbath day? Do not judge according to the appearance, but judge with righteous judgment."

Then some of them from Jerusalem said, "Is not this he whom they seek to kill? But listen, he speaks boldly, and they say nothing to him. Do the rulers know that this is indeed the real Christ? However, we know this man from where he comes, but when Christ comes, no man knows where he is from."

Then Jesus cried out in the temple as he taught, saying, "You both know me, and you know from where I came; and I have not come of myself, but he who sent me is true, whom you do not know. But I know him; for I am from him, and he has sent me." Then they tried to take him, but no one laid hands on him because his hour had not come yet.

Many of the people believed in him, and said, "When Christ comes, will he do more miracles than those which this man has done?" The Pharisees heard the people murmuring such things about Jesus, and the Pharisees and the chief priests sent officers to take him. Then Jesus said to them, "Only a little while longer will I be with you, and then I go to him who sent me. You will seek me and will not find me; and where I am, there you cannot come."

Then the Jews said among themselves, "Where will he go that we will not find him? Will he go to the dispersed among the Gentiles, and teach the Gentiles? What sort of saying is this that he says, you will seek me and will not find me; and where I am, there you cannot come?"

On the last day, the great day of the feast, Jesus stood and cried out, saying, "If any man thirst, let him come to me, and drink. He that believes in me, as the Scripture has said, out of his innermost being will flow rivers of living water. (Now this he spoke concerning the Spirit, which those who believe in him would receive; for the Holy Spirit had not yet been given because Jesus was not yet glorified.) Therefore, many of the people, when they heard this, said,

"Of a truth this is the Prophet." Others said, "This is the Christ." But some said, "Will Christ come out of Galilee? Does not the Scripture say that Christ comes of the seed of David, and out of the town of Bethlehem, where David was?" So there was a division among the people because of him. Some of them would have taken him, but no one laid hands on him.

Then came the officers to the chief priests and Pharisees, and they said to them, "Why have you not brought him?" The officers answered, "Never did a man speak like this man." Then the Pharisees answered them, "Are you also deceived? Have any of the rulers or of the Pharisees believed in him? This people who do not know the Law are cursed."

Nicodemus said to them (he who came to Jesus by night, being one of them), "Does our law judge anyone before it hears him, and knows what he does?" They answered and said to him, "Are you also from Galilee? Search, and see, for no prophet arises out of Galilee."

Then Jesus spoke to them again, saying, "I am the light of the world; he who follows me will not walk in darkness, but will have the light of life." Therefore the Pharisees said to him, "You bear record of yourself, your record is not true." Jesus answered and said to them, "Even though I bear witness of myself, yet my witness is true, for I know from where I came and where I will go, but you cannot tell where I came from, and where I go. You judge after the flesh; I judge no man. And even if I do judge, my judgment is true for I am not alone, because the Father who sent me is with me. It is also written in your law, that the testimony of two men is true. I am one that bears witness of myself, and the Father who sent me also bears witness of me. Then they said to him, "Where is your Father?" Jesus answered, "You neither know me, nor my Father; if you had known me, you would have known my Father also." These words Jesus spoke in the treasury, as he taught in the temple, and no one laid hands on him because his hour had not come.

Then Jesus said to them again, "I go my way, and you will seek me, and will die in your sins; where I go, you cannot come." Then the Jews said, "Will he kill himself? Because he said, where I go, you cannot come." Jesus said to them, "You are from beneath, I am from above; you are of this world, I am not of this world. I therefore said to you, that you will die in your sins; for if you do not believe that I am he, you will die in your sins."

Then they said to him, "Who are you?" Jesus said to them, "I am still the same that I said to you from the beginning. I have many things to say and to judge concerning you; he that sent me is true and I speak to the world those things which I have heard from him." They did not understand that he spoke to them of the Father. Then Jesus said to them, "When you have lifted up the Son of Man, then you will know that I am he, and that I do nothing of myself; but as my Father has taught me, so I speak these things. He who sent me is with me, the Father has not left me alone for I always do those things that please him." As he spoke these words, many believed in him.

Then Jesus said to those Jews who believed in him, "If you continue in my word, then you are indeed my disciples; and you will know the truth, and the truth will make you free." They answered him, "We are Abraham's seed, and were never in bondage to anyone; how is it that you say, "You will be made free?" Jesus answered them, "Indeed, I say to you, whoever commits sin is the servant of sin. The servant abides not in the house forever, but the Son abides forever. If the Son will make you free, you will be free indeed. I know that you are Abraham's seed, but you seek to kill me, because my word has no place in you. I speak that which I have seen with my Father, and you do that which you have seen with your father." They answered and said to him, "Abraham is our father." Jesus said to them, "If you were Abraham's children, you would do the works of Abraham. But now you seek to kill me, a man who has told you the truth, which I heard from God; Abraham did not do this. You do the deeds of your father."

Then they said to him, "We were not born out of fornication; we have one Father—God." Jesus said to them, "If God were your Father, you would love me, for I began with God and came from him; nor did I come by myself, but he sent me. Why do you not understand my speech? Because you are unable to bear hearing my word. You are of your father the devil, and the works of your father you will also do. He was a murderer from the beginning, and stood not in the truth, because there is no truth in him. When he speaks a lie, he speaks of his own; for he is a liar, and the father of lies. And because I tell you the truth, you will not believe me. Which of you convinces me of sin? If

I say the truth, why do you not believe me? He that is of God hears God's words, you do not hear them because you are not of God."

Then the Jews answered, and said to him, "Do we not rightly say that you are a Samaritan, and that you have a demon?" Jesus answered, "I do not have a demon; I honor my Father, and you dishonor me. I do not seek my own glory; there is one who seeks and judges. Indeed, I say to you, if a man keeps my word, he will never see death." Then the Jews said to him, "Now we know that you have a demon. Abraham is dead, and the prophets; and you say, 'If a man keeps my word, he will never taste death.' Are you greater than our father Abraham, who is dead? And the prophets are dead; whom do you make yourself out to be?"

Jesus answered, "If I honor myself, my honor is nothing. It is my Father who honors me; of whom you say that he is your God. Yet you have not known him, but I know him, and if I should say 'I do not know him' I would be a liar like to you; but I know him and keep his word. "Your father Abraham rejoiced to see my day,[16] and he saw it and was glad." Then the Jews said to him, "You are not yet fifty years old, and have you seen Abraham?" Jesus said to them, "Indeed, I say to you, before Abraham was, *I AM*. Then they took up stones to throw at him, but Jesus hid himself and went out of the temple, passing through the midst of them.

After this the Lord also appointed seventy others, and sent them out two and two before him into every city and place where he himself would come. He said to them, "The harvest is truly great, but the laborers are few, therefore pray that the Lord of the harvest would send out laborers into his harvest. Go on your way; surely, I send you forth as lambs among wolves. Carry neither purse, nor bag, nor sandals, and greet no one along the way.

Into whatever house you enter, first say, 'Peace be to this house.' If a son of peace is there, your peace will rest upon it, if not, it will return to you again. Remain in the same house, eating and drinking such things as they give you, for the laborer is worthy of his hire. Do not go from house to house. Into whatever city you enter, and they receive you, eat such things as are set before you; and heal the sick that are there and say to them, 'The kingdom of God has come near to you.' Whatever city you enter into, and they do not receive you, go out into the streets of the city, and say, 'Even the dust of your city, which clings to us, we wipe off against you. Nevertheless, you can be sure of this, the kingdom of God has come near to you.'

"I say to you, that it will be more tolerable in that day for Sodom, than for that city. He who hears you hears me, and he that despises you despises me; and he who despises me despises him who sent me."

Then he began to upbraid the cities where many of his mighty miracles were done, because they did not repent: "Woe to you, Chorazin! Woe to you, Bethsaida! For if the mighty works done in you had been done in Tyre and Sidon, they would have repented long ago and sat in sackcloth and ashes. I say to you, it will be more tolerable for Tyre and Sidon in the day of judgment than for you. And you, Capernaum, who are exalted to heaven, will be brought down to hell; for if the mighty works done in you had been done in Sodom, it would have remained until to-day. I say to you, that it will be more tolerable for the land of Sodom in the day of judgment than for you."

"Come to me, all you who labor and are heavily laden, and I will give you rest. Take my yoke upon you, and learn from me for I am gentle and humble in heart, and you will find rest for your souls. For my yoke is easy, and my burden is light."

The seventy returned with joy, saying, "Lord, even the demons are subject to us in your name." He said to them, "I saw Satan fall like lightning from heaven. Indeed, I give to you power to tread on serpents and scorpions, and over all the power of the enemy, and nothing will by any means hurt you. Nevertheless, do not rejoice in this, that the spirits are subject to you, but rather rejoice because your names are written in heaven."

At that time Jesus rejoiced in Spirit and said, "I thank you, O Father, LORD of heaven and earth, that you have hidden these things from the wise and prudent, and have revealed them to children. Just so, Father, for so it seemed good in your eyes. All things have been delivered to me by my Father, and no one knows who the Son is, except the Father, and who the Father is except the Son, and he to whom the Son wills to reveal him."

He turned to his disciples and said, privately, "Blessed are the eyes which see the things that you see; for I tell you that many prophets and kings have desired to see the things which you see, and have not seen them, and to hear the things which you hear, and have not heard them."

And, behold, a certain lawyer stood up and tested him, saying, "Master, what shall I do to inherit eternal life?" He said to him, "What is written in the Law? how do you read it?" Answering him he said:

> *"You shall love the* Lord *your God with all your heart, and with all your soul, and with all your strength, and with all your mind; and your neighbor as yourself"* (Deuteronomy 6:5/ Leviticus 19:18).

He said to him, "You have answered correctly, do this and you will live."

However, wanting to justify himself, the lawyer said to Jesus, "Who is my neighbor?" Answering him, Jesus said, "A certain man went down from Jerusalem to Jericho, and fell among thieves who wounded him and stripped him of his clothing and then departed, leaving him half dead. By chance there came down a certain priest that way, and when he saw him he passed by on the other side. So likewise did a Levite when he came to the place; he looked at him and passed by on the other side. But a certain Samaritan, as he journeyed, came to where he was, and when he saw him he had compassion on him. He went to him and bound up his wounds, pouring on oil and wine, and sat him on his own animal and brought him to an inn, and took care of him. The next morning, when he departed, he took out two *denarii* and gave them to the host and said to him, 'Take care of him, and whatever more you spend, when I come again I will repay you.' Now, which of those three do you think was a neighbor to him who fell among the thieves?" He said, "He who showed mercy to him." Then Jesus said to him, "Go, and do likewise."

And so it was, that, as they went on their way, he entered into a certain village, and a woman named Martha received him into her house. She had a sister called Mary, who also sat at Jesus' feet, and listened to his word.

Martha was distracted about a lot of serving, and came to him and said, "Master, do you not care that my sister has left me alone to serve? Tell her that she should help me." Jesus answered and said to her, "Martha, Martha, you are mindful and troubled about many things, but only one thing is necessary, and Mary has chosen the good part, which will not be taken away from her. Take care that you do not do your works of charity before men, to be seen of them, else you will have no reward from your Father who is in heaven. Therefore, when you do good works, do not sound a trumpet before you as the hypocrites do in the synagogues and in the streets, that they may have glory from men. Truly I say to you, they have their reward.

"When you do charitable acts, do not let your left hand know what your right hand does, that your acts may be in secret; and your Father, who sees in secret, will himself reward you openly."

It came to pass, as Jesus was praying in a certain place, that when he ceased one of his disciples said to him, "Lord, teach us to pray as John taught his disciples. He said to them, "When you pray, you must not be as the hypocrites, for they love to pray standing in the synagogues and on the street corners that they may be seen by men. Truly I say to you, they have their reward. You, when you pray, enter into your closet, and when you have shut the door pray to your Father who is in secret, and your Father, who sees in secret, will reward you openly. When you pray, do not use vain repetitions as the heathen do, for they think that they will be heard because of their many words. Therefore, do not be like them, for your Father knows what things you have need of before you ask him. Therefore pray after this manner:

"Our Father who is in heaven,
Hallowed be your name.
Your kingdom come.
Your will be done on earth, as it is in heaven.
Give us this day our necessary daily bread.
And forgive us our debts, as we forgive our debtors.
Lead us not into temptation, but deliver us from evil.
For yours is the kingdom, and the power, and the
    glory, forever. Amen.

"For if you forgive men their sins, your heavenly Father will also forgive you, but if you do not forgive others their sins, neither will your Father forgive your sins. Moreover, when you fast, do not be like the hypocrites and wear a sad expression, for they disfigure their faces so that they may appear to others to be fasting. Truly I say to you, they have their reward. But you, when you fast, anoint your head and wash your face so that you do not appear to others to be fasting, but only to your Father who is in heaven, and your Father, who sees in secret, will reward you openly."

He said to them, "Which of you will have a friend, and will go to him at midnight, and say to him, 'Friend, lend me three loaves, for a friend of mine on a journey has come to me, and I have nothing to set before him?' He from within will answer and say, 'Do not trouble me, the door is now shut, and my children are with me in bed; I cannot rise and give you.' I say to you, though he will not arise and give to him because he is his friend, but because of his persistence he will arise and give him as many as he needs.

"I say to you, ask, and it will be given to you, seek, and you will find, knock, and it will be opened to you. For everyone who asks receives, and he who seeks finds, and to him who knocks it will be opened.

"If a son will ask for bread from any of you who is a father, will he give him a stone? Or if he asks for a fish, will he for a fish give him a serpent? Or if he will ask for an egg, will he offer him a scorpion? If you then, being evil, know how to give good gifts to your children, how much more will your heavenly Father give the Holy Spirit to them that ask him?"

"The light of the body is the eye, if your eye is good, your whole body will be full of light. But if your eye is bad, your whole body will be full of darkness. If, therefore, the light that is in you is darkness, how great is that darkness!"

"Whatever things you would have men do to you, that do even to them, for this is the Law and the Prophets.

Enter in at the narrow gate; for wide is the gate and broad is the way that leads to destruction, and many there are who go that way. Narrow is the gate and narrow is the way that leads to life, and there are few who find it.

"Beware of false prophets who come to you in sheep's clothing, but who inwardly are ravening wolves. You will know them by their fruits. Do men gather grapes from thorn bushes, or figs from thistles? Even so, every good tree bears good fruit, but a corrupt tree bears bad fruit. A good tree cannot produce bad fruit, neither can a bad tree produce good fruit. Every tree that does not bear good fruit is cut down and thrown into the fire. Therefore, by their fruits you will know them.

"Not everyone who says to me, 'Lord, Lord,' will enter the kingdom of heaven, only he who does the will of my Father who is in heaven. Many will say to me in that day, 'Lord, Lord, have we not prophesied in your name? And in your name have cast out demons? And in your name done many wonderful works?' Then will I announce to them, 'I never knew you. Depart from me, you who work wickedness.'"

And so it was, that when Jesus had ended these sayings, that the people were astonished at his doctrine, for he taught them as one having authority and not as the scribes.

He was casting out a demon, and it was blind, and mute. When the demon had gone out, the blind and mute man both spoke and saw; and the people wondered and were amazed, and said, "Is this not the Son of David?" But some of the Pharisees said, "He casts out demons through Beelzebub the chief ruler of the demons."

Others, testing him, wanted him to show a sign from heaven. But Jesus, knowing their thoughts, said to them, "Every kingdom divided against itself is brought to desolation; and a house divided against a house cannot stand. How can Satan cast out Satan? If Satan is divided against himself, how can his kingdom stand? — it has an end. You say that I cast out demons through Beelzebub. If I cast out demons by Beelzebub, by whom do your sons cast them out? Therefore, they will be your judges. However, if

I cast out demons with the finger of God, then no doubt the kingdom of God has come upon you.

"When a strong, armed man keeps his palace, his goods are secure, but when someone stronger than he comes upon him and overcomes him, he takes from him all his armor in which he trusted and divides his spoil. How can one enter into a strong man's house, and take his goods except that he first binds the strong man? Then he plunders his house. He that is not with me is against me, and he that does not gather with me scatters. "Therefore I say to you, all manner of sin and blasphemy will be forgiven men, but blasphemy against the Holy Spirit will not be forgiven men. Whoever speaks a word against the Son of Man, it will be forgiven him, but whoever speaks against the Holy Spirit, it will not be forgiven him, neither in this world, nor in the world to come—he never has forgiveness." He is in danger of eternal damnation, because they said He has an unclean spirit.

"Either make the tree good, and its fruit good, or else make the tree bad, and its fruit bad, for a tree is known by its fruit. O generation of vipers, how can you, being wicked, speak good things? For out of the abundance of the heart the mouth speaks. A good man out of the good treasure of his heart brings forth good things, and a wicked man out of his evil treasure brings forth wicked things. I say to you, that every idle word that men will speak, they will give account for in the day of judgment. For by your words you will be justified, and by your words you will be condemned."

"When an unclean spirit goes out of a man, he walks through dry places seeking rest, and finding none he says, 'I will return to my house from where I came out.' When he comes, he finds it swept and ordered. Then he goes and takes with him seven other spirits more wicked than himself, and they enter in and live there; and the last state of that man is worse than the first. Even so will it be also with this wicked generation."

It came to pass, as he spoke these things, that a certain woman in the crowd raised her voice and said to him, "Blessed is the womb that bore you, and the breasts at which you nursed." He said, "Blessed rather are those that hear the word of God, and keep it."

Then certain of the scribes and Pharisees answered, saying, "Master, we would see a sign from you." When the people were thickly gathered together, he began to say, "This is an evil generation; they seek a sign, and there shall be no sign given, but the sign of Jonah the prophet. For as Jonah was three days and three nights in the whale's belly, so will the Son of Man be three days and three nights in the heart of the earth. For as Jonah was a sign to the Ninevites, so also will the Son of Man be to this generation.

"The Queen of the South will rise up in the judgment with the men of this generation, and condemn them; for she came from the utmost parts of the earth to hear the wisdom of Solomon, and, indeed, a greater than Solomon is here. The men of Nineveh will rise up in the judgment with this generation, and will condemn it; for they repented at the preaching of Jonah, and, indeed, a greater than Jonah is here."

"No man, when he has lit a candle, puts it in a secret place, or under a basket, but on a candlestick so that those who come in may see the light. The light of the body is the eye; therefore, when your eye is single, your whole body is full of light, but when your eye is wicked, your body is full of darkness. Take care therefore that the light which is in you is not darkness. If your whole body is full of light, having no dark part, the whole will be full of light, like when the bright shining of a lamp gives you light."

As he spoke, a certain Pharisee invited him to dine with him, and he went in, and sat down to eat. When the Pharisee saw it, he marveled that he had not first washed before eating. The Lord said to him, "Now you Pharisees clean the outside of the cups and the platters, but your inward part is full of lust, wickedness, and self-indulgence. You foolish people, did not he who made the outside make the inside also? Rather, give the poor charitable gifts from such things as you have, and look, all things will be clean to you.

"Woe to you, scribes and Pharisees, hypocrites! For you are like whitewashed tombs, which outwardly appear beautiful, but inside are full of dead men's bones and all uncleanness. You are like unseen graves that men walk over and are not aware of them. You outwardly appear righteous to men, but inside you are full of hypocrisy and lawlessness.

"Woe to you, scribes and Pharisees, hypocrites! For you tithe mint and rue, and cummin, and all manner of garden herbs, but pass over judgment, mercy, and the love of God; these you ought to have done and not to leave the other undone. Woe to you, Pharisees, for you love the best seats in the synagogues, and greetings in the market places.

"Then answered one of the Lawyers, who said to him, "Master, speaking thus you reproach us also." He said, "Woe to you also, you lawyers! For you load men with grievous burdens that need to be borne, and you yourselves touch not one of the burdens with your fingers. Woe to you! For you build the tombs of the prophets and adorn the tombs of the righteous, and say, 'If we had been living in the days of our fathers, we would not have been partners with them in shedding the blood of the prophets.' Truly you bear witness against yourselves in that you condone the deeds of your fathers; for indeed they killed them and you build their tombs. Fill up then the measure of your fathers' guilt. You serpents, you offspring of vipers, how can you escape the damnation of hell?

"Therefore also the wisdom of God said, 'I will send them prophets and apostles, and some of them they will slay and persecute, that the righteous blood of all the prophets, which was shed from the foundation of the world, may be required of this generation—from the blood of Abel to the blood of Zacharias, who perished between the altar and the temple; truly I say to you, it will be required of this generation.

"Woe to you, lawyers! For you have taken away the key of knowledge; you did not enter in yourselves and you hindered those who were entering in." As he said these things to them, the scribes and Pharisees began to be intensely hostile to him and trying to provoke him into speaking of many things. They were laying in wait for him, seeking to catch him saying something that they might accuse him.

In the mean time, when there had gathered together an innumerable multitude of people, so many that they trod one upon another, he began to say to his disciples first of all, "Beware of the leaven of the Pharisees, which is hypocrisy. For there is nothing covered, that will not be revealed, neither hidden, that will not be known. Therefore, whatever you have spoken in the darkness will be heard in the light, and that which you have spoken in the ear in secret will be proclaimed from the housetops.

"I say to you my friends, do not be afraid of those that kill the body and after that they can do no more. I will forewarn you whom you shall fear; fear him, who after he has killed has power to cast into hell; yes, I say to you, fear him.

"Are not five sparrows sold for half a penny, and not one of them is forgotten before God? Even the very hairs of your head are all numbered, fear not therefore, you are of more value than many sparrows.

"Also I say to you, whoever will confess me before men, him will the Son of Man confess before the angels of God; but he who denies me before men will be denied before the angels of God. Whoever will speak a word against the Son of Man, it will be forgiven him, but to him that blasphemes against the Holy Spirit it will not be forgiven. When they bring you to the synagogues, and before the magistrates and powers, take no thought of how or what thing you will answer, or what you will say, for the Holy Spirit will teach you in that hour what you should say."

No Other NAME

One of the crowd said to him, "Master, speak to my brother that he might divide the inheritance with me." He said to him, "Man, who made me a judge or a divider over you?" He said to them, "Take care, and beware of covetousness; for a man's life does not consist in the abundance of the things he possesses."

He spoke a parable to them, saying, "The ground of a certain rich man brought forth plentifully; and he thought within himself, saying, 'What shall I do, because I have no room where to store my produce?' He said, 'This is what I will do: I will pull down my barns, and build greater; and there I will store all my crops and my goods. I will say to my soul, 'Soul, you have much goods laid up for many years, take your ease, eat, drink, and be merry.' But God said to him, 'You fool, this night your soul will be required of you; then whose things will they be, those things that you have collected together?' So is it with him that lays up treasure for himself and is not rich toward God."

Jesus said to his disciples, "Therefore I say to you, take no thought for your life, what you will eat, nor for the body, what you will put on. The life is more than food, and the body is more than clothing. Consider the ravens, for they neither sow nor reap, they have neither storehouse nor barn; and God feeds them. How much more value are you than the birds of the air?

"Which of you by taking thought can add one foot to his stature? If then, you are not able to do that which is least, why do you take thought for the rest? Consider how the lilies grow; they do not work, they do not spin, and yet I say to you that Solomon in all his glory was not arrayed like one of these. If then, God so clothes the grass, which today is in the field and tomorrow is thrown into the furnace, how much more will he clothe you, O you of little faith?

"Do not be concerned about what you will eat, or what you will drink, neither be of an anxious mind. For all these things the nations of the world seek after, and your Father knows that you have need of these things. But rather seek after the kingdom of God and his righteousness, and all these things will be given to you. Therefore, take no thought for tomorrow, for tomorrow will take care of itself. Sufficient for each day is its own trouble.

"Fear not, little flock, for it is your Father's good pleasure to give you the kingdom. Sell what you have and give gifts to the poor and needy, provide yourselves with bags that do not grow old, a treasure in the heavens that never fails, where no thief breaks through and steals, neither does moth or rust consume. For where your treasure is, there your heart will be also."

"***Gird yourself and*** be ready with your lamps burning bright. Be like those who wait for their master's return from the wedding, that they may open to him immediately when he comes and knocks. Blessed are those servants whom the master will find watching for his return; truly I say to you that he will gird himself, and make them sit down to eat while he comes and serves them. If he will come in the second watch, or come in the third watch and find them watching for him, blessed are those servants.

"Know this, that if the master of the house had known what hour the thief would come, he would have been watching and would not have allowed his house to be broken into. Therefore, you also be ready, for the Son of Man will come at an hour when you do not expect him."

Then Peter said to him, "Lord, are you speaking this parable to us, or to everyone?" The Lord said, "Who then is the faithful and wise steward whom his master will make ruler over his household, to give them their portion of food at the correct times? Blessed is that servant, whom, when his master comes, finds him so doing. Of a truth I say to you, that he will make him ruler over all that he has. But if that servant says in his heart, 'My master delays his coming'; and then begins to beat the male and female servants; and eats and drinks and becomes drunk. The master of that servant will come on a day when he is not expecting him, and at an hour of which he is unaware, and will cut him in pieces and will make him share the lot of the unbelievers.

"And that servant, who knew his master's will, and who neither prepared himself, nor did according to his will, will be given many lashes. And he who did not know, and did commit things worthy of punishment, will be given only a few lashes. For to whomever much is given, of him much will be required; and to whom men have committed much, of him they will ask more."

"I came to cast fire on the earth, and how I wish that it were already kindled. I have a baptism to be baptized with, and how disquieted I am until it be accomplished! Do you suppose that I came to bring peace on earth? I tell you, no, but rather division; for from now on there will be five in one house divided three against two, and two against

three. The father will be divided against the son, and the son against the father, the mother against the daughter, and the daughter against the mother, the mother-in-law against her daughter-in-law, and the daughter-in-law against her mother-in-law."

He also said to the people, "When you see a cloud rise out of the west, straight away you say, 'There comes a shower,' and so it is. When you see the south wind blow, you say, 'There will be heat,' and it comes to pass. You hypocrites! You can discern the face of the sky and of the earth, but how is it that you do not discern this time?

"Yes, and why, even of yourselves, do you not judge what is right? When you go with your accuser to the magistrate, as you are on the way make diligent effort to come to an agreement, lest he haul you before the judge and the judge delivers you to the officer, and the officer throws you in prison. I tell you, you will not get out of there until you have paid the very last penny."

There were some present at that time who told him of the Galileans, whose blood Pilate had mingled with their sacrifices. Jesus answering, said to them, "Do you suppose that those Galileans were worse sinners than all the other Galileans because they suffered such things? I tell you, no; but unless you repent you will all likewise perish. Or those eighteen, upon whom the tower in Siloam fell and killed them, do you think they were worse sinners that all those that dwelt in Jerusalem? I tell you, no; but unless you repent, you will all likewise perish."

He also spoke this parable: "A certain man had a fig tree planted in his vineyard, and he came looking for fruit on it, and found none. Then he said to his vinedresser, 'Look, these past three years I came looking for fruit on this fig tree, and found nothing. Cut it down; why should it use the ground?' Answering, he said to him, 'Master, leave it alone this year also, wait until I have dug around and fertilized it. If it bears fruit, good, but if not, then after that you can cut it down.' "

He was teaching in one of the synagogues on the Sabbath. And behold, there was a woman who had a spirit of infirmity eighteen years, and was bowed over, and could in no way straighten herself up. When Jesus saw her he called her to him, and said to her, "Woman, you are loosed from your infirmity." He laid his hands on her, and immediately she was made straight and glorified God. But because Jesus had healed on the Sabbath day, the ruler of the synagogue answered with indignation, and said to the people, "There are six days on which men ought to work; therefore come and be healed on them, and not on the Sabbath day." Then the Lord answered and said to him, "You hypocrite! Does not each one of you on the Sabbath day free his ox or his ass from the stall, and lead him to water? Ought not this woman, being a daughter of Abraham, whom Satan has bound for these past eighteen years, be loosed from this bond on the Sabbath day?" When he had said these things, all his adversaries were ashamed; and the people rejoiced because of all the glorious things that were done by him.

On a certain day, as Jesus passed by, he saw a man who was blind from birth. His disciples asked him, saying, "Master, who sinned, this man, or his parents, that he was born blind?" Jesus answered, "Neither this man, nor his parents sinned, but that the works of God should be displayed in him.

"I must work the works of him who sent me while it is still day; the night comes when no man can work. As long as I am in the world, I am the light of the world." After he had spoken that, he spat on the ground and made clay from the saliva, and he anointed the eyes of the blind man with the clay, and said to him, "Go, wash in the pool of Siloam," which, being interpreted, means "Sent." Therefore he went his way, and washed, and came back seeing. Therefore the neighbors and those who had seen before that he was blind, said, "Is this not he who sat and begged?" Some said, "This is he," others said, "He is like him," but he said, "I am he." Therefore they said to him, "How were your eyes opened?" He answered and said, "A man who is called Jesus made clay, and anointed my eyes, and said to me, 'Go to the pool of Siloam and wash'; and I went and washed, and I received sight." Then they said to him, "Where is he?" He said, "I do not know." They brought him who was previously blind to the Pharisees. It was the Sabbath day when Jesus made the clay, and opened his eyes.

Then the Pharisees asked him again how he had received his sight. He said to them, "He put clay upon my eyes, and I washed, and now see." Therefore some of the Pharisees said, "This man is not of God because he does not keep the Sabbath day." Others said, "How can a man who is a sinner do such miracles?" And there was a division among them.

They said to the blind man again, "What do you say about him who has opened your eyes?" He said, "He is a prophet." The Jews did not believe him, that he had been blind, and received his sight until they called the parents of him who had received his sight. They asked them, saying, "Is this your son, whom you say was born blind? How then does he now see?" His parents answered them and said, "We know that this is our son, and that he was born blind. By what means he now sees we do not know, or know who has opened his eyes; he is of age, ask him; he can speak for himself." His parents spoke these words because they feared the Jews; for the Jews had already agreed that if anyone confessed that he was Christ, he would be put out of the synagogue. Therefore his parents said, "He is of age, ask him."

Then they again called the man who was blind, and said to him, "Give God the glory, we know that this man is a sinner." He answered and said, "Whether he is a sinner or not I do not know; one thing I do know, that whereas I was blind, now I see." Then they said to him again, "What did he do to you? How did he open your eyes?" He answered them, "I have already told you, and you did not listen; why would you hear it again? Will you also become his disciples?" Then they railed at him and said, "You are his disciple, but we are disciples of Moses. We know that God spoke to Moses; as for this man, we do not know where he comes from."

The man answered and said to them, "Why, here is a marvelous thing, you do not know where he is from, and yet he has opened my eyes. We know that God does not hear sinners, but if anyone is a worshiper of God and does his will, him he hears. Since the world began it was never heard that anyone opened the eyes of one who was born blind. If this man were not of God, he could do nothing." They answered and said to him, "You were altogether born in sin, and do you teach us?" And they put him out.

Jesus heard that they had expelled him, and when he had found him, he said to him, "Do you believe in the Son of God?" He answered and said, "Who is he, Lord, that I might believe in him?" Jesus said to him, "You have both seen him, and it is he who talks with you." He said, "Lord, I believe!" And he worshiped him.

Jesus said, "For judgment I have come into this world, that those who do not see might see, and that those who see might become blind." Some of the Pharisees who were with him heard these words and said to him, "Are we blind also?" Jesus said to them, "If you were blind, you would have no sin, but in saying, 'We see,' your sin therefore remains.

"Indeed, I say to you, he who does not enter by the door into the sheepfold, but climbs up some other way, the same is a thief and a robber. He who enters in by the door is the shepherd of the sheep. To him the gatekeeper opens, and the sheep hear his voice; and he calls his own sheep by name and leads them out. And when he brings out his own sheep, he goes before them; and the sheep follow him, for they know his voice. A stranger they will not follow, but will flee from him, because they do not know the voice of strangers." Jesus spoke this parable to them, but they did not understand the figurative language in which he spoke to them.

Then Jesus said to them again, "Indeed, I say to you, I am the door of the sheep. All who came before me were thieves and robbers, but the sheep did not listen to them. I am the door, if anyone enters in through me he will be saved, and will go in and out and find pasture. The thief comes only to steal, and to kill, and to destroy; I have come that they may have life, and that they may have it more abundantly.

"I am the good shepherd; the good shepherd gives his life for the sheep. He who is a hired man and not the shepherd, who does not own the sheep, sees the wolf coming and flees, leaving the sheep; and the wolf catches the sheep and scatters them. The hired man flees because he is a hired man and does not care for the sheep. I am the good shepherd and know my sheep, and I am known by my sheep. As the Father knows me, even so I know the Father, and I lay down my life for the sheep. I have other sheep that are not of this fold; those I must also bring, and they will hear my voice; and there will be one flock and one shepherd.

"Therefore my Father loves me, because I lay down my life that I may take it again. No one takes it from me, but I lay it down myself. I have power to lay it down, and I have power to take it up again. This commandment I have received from my Father."

Therefore there was again a division among the Jews because of these sayings. Many of them said, "He has a demon and is mad, why listen to him?" Others said, "These are not the words of one who has a demon. Can a demon open the eyes of the blind?"

It was in Jerusalem, at the feast of the dedication, and it was winter. Jesus walked in the temple, in Solomon's porch. Then the Jews came all around him and said to him, "How long will you leave us in doubt? If you are the Christ, tell us plainly." Jesus answered them, "I told you, and you did not believe me; the works that I do in my Father's name, they bear witness of me. You do not believe because, as I said to you, you are not my sheep. My sheep hear my voice and I know them, and they follow me. I give to them eternal life and they will never perish, neither will any man snatch them out of my hand. My Father, who gave them to me, is greater than all, and no man is able to snatch them out of my Father's hand. I and my Father are one."

Then the Jews took up stones again to stone him. Jesus said to them, "I have showed you many good works from my Father; for which of those works do you stone me?" The Jews answered him, saying, "For a good work we do not stone you, but for blasphemy, and because you being a man make yourself God." Jesus answered them, "Is it not written in your law, 'I said, you are gods'? If he called them gods, to whom the word of God came, and the Scripture cannot be broken, are you saying of him whom the Father has sanctified and sent into the world, 'You blaspheme,' because I said, I am the Son of God? If I do not do the works of my Father, do not believe me, but if I do, even though you do not believe me, believe the works that I do, that you may know and believe that the Father is in me, and I am in him." Therefore they again tried to take him, but he escaped out of their hand. He went away again, beyond the Jordan, into the place where John baptized at first, and there he stayed. Many came to him and said, "John performed no miracle, but all things that John spoke about this man were true." And many believed in him there.

He went through the cities and villages, teaching, as he journeyed toward Jerusalem. Then someone said to him, "Lord, are there but few who can be saved?" He said to them, "Strive earnestly to enter in at the narrow gate, for I say to you that many will seek to enter in and will not be able. When once the master of the house has arisen and has shut the door, and you begin to stand outside and knock at the door, saying, 'Lord, Lord, open to us,' and he will answer and say to you, 'I do not know you, or where you come from.' Then you will begin to say, 'We ate and drank in your presence, and you have taught in our streets.' But he will say, 'I tell you, I do not know you, or where you come from. Depart from me, all you workers of iniquity.'

There shall be weeping and gnashing of teeth when you will see Abraham, and Isaac, and Jacob, and all the prophets in the kingdom of God, and you yourselves shut out. They will come from the east and from the west, and from the north and from the south, and will sit down in the kingdom of God. Indeed, some who are last will be first, and some who are first will be last."

The same day there came certain of the Pharisees, saying to him, "Get out, go away from here, because Herod wants to kill you." He said to them, "Go and tell that fox, 'Observe, I cast out demons and do cures today and tomorrow, and the third day I will complete my course.' Nevertheless, I must continue on today, tomorrow, and the following day; for it cannot be that a prophet perishes outside of Jerusalem.

"O Jerusalem, Jerusalem, the city that kills the prophets and stones those sent to her. How often I have wanted to gather your children together as a hen gathers her chicks under her wings, and you would not have it! See, your house is left to you desolate; and truly I say to you, you will not see me, until the time comes when you will say, 'Blessed is he who comes in the name of the LORD.' "

It came to pass, as Jesus went into the house of one of the chief Pharisees to eat on the Sabbath day, that they watched him. And behold, there was a certain man before him who had dropsy. Jesus spoke to the lawyers and Pharisees, saying, "Is it lawful to heal on the Sabbath day?" They kept silent. He took him, and healed him, and let him go. And answered them, saying, "Which of you shall have an ass or an ox fallen into a pit, and will not immediately pull him out on the Sabbath day?" They could not answer him regarding these things.

He presented a parable to those who were invited, when he watched how they chose the places of honor, saying to them, "When you are invited by anyone to a wedding, do not sit down in the best place lest a more honorable man than yourself be invited by him. And he who invited you both come and say to you, 'Give your place to this man,' and you shamefully begin to take the lowest seat. Rather, when you are invited, go and sit down in the lowest place so that when he who invited you comes, he may say to you, 'Friend, go up higher'; then you will have honor in the presence of those who sit at the table with you. For whoever exalts himself will be humbled, and he who humbles himself will be exalted.

Then he said to him who invited him, "When you make a dinner or a supper, do not call your friends, nor your brothers, neither your relatives, nor your rich neighbors, lest they invite you back again and repay you. When you make a feast, call the poor, the maimed, the crippled, the blind. You will be blessed because they cannot repay you; for you will be repaid at the resurrection of the righteous." When one of those who sat at the table with him heard these things, he said to him, "Blessed are those who will eat bread in the kingdom of God."

Then Jesus said to him, "A certain man made a great feast and invited many. He sent his servant at supper time to say to those who were invited, 'Come, for all things are now ready.' They all, without exception, began to make excuses. The first said to him, 'I have bought a piece of land and I must go and see it; I ask that you excuse me.' Another said, 'I have bought five yoke of oxen and I must go and work them; I ask that you excuse me.' Another said, 'I have just married a wife; therefore I cannot come.' So that servant came and told his master these things.

Then the master of the house, being angry, said to his servant, 'Go out quickly into the streets and lanes of the city and bring in here the poor, and the maimed, and the lame, and the blind.' The servant said, 'Master, it is done as you have commanded, and still there is room.' The master said to the servant, 'Go out into the highways and hedges and compel them to come in, that my house may be filled. For I say to you that none of those men who were invited shall taste of my feast.' "

Great multitudes went with Jesus. He turned and said to them, "If anyone comes to me and does not think less of his father, and mother, and wife, and children, and brothers, and sisters, and yes, even his own life, than he does me, he cannot be my disciple. Whoever does not bear his cross and follow after me, cannot be my disciple. For which of you intending to build a tower, does not first sit down and count the cost, whether he has sufficient to complete it? Otherwise, after he has laid the foundation and is not able to finish it, all who see it begin to mock him, saying, 'This man began to build, and was not able to complete what he began.'

"Or what king going to make war against another king, does not first sit down and consult whether he is able with ten thousand men to overcome him that comes against him with twenty thousand? Or else, while the other is still a long way off, he sends an emissary and asks for terms of peace. So likewise, whoever of you who does not forsake all that he has, he cannot be my disciple. Salt is good, but if the salt has lost its flavor, with what will it be seasoned? It is neither fit for the land, nor even for the dunghill, but men throw it out. He who has ears to hear, let him hear."

Then all the tax collectors and sinners drew near to Jesus to hear him. The Pharisees and scribes complained, saying, "This man receives sinners and eats with them." Jesus spoke this parable to them, saying, "What man among you, having a hundred sheep, if he loses one of them, does not leave the ninety-nine in the wilderness and go after that which is lost, until he finds it? When he has found it, he puts it on his shoulders, rejoicing. When he comes home, he calls together his friends and neighbors, saying to them, 'Rejoice with me, for I have found my sheep that was lost.' I say to you, that likewise there will be joy in heaven over one sinner who repents, more than over ninety-nine righteous persons who need no repentance.

"Or what woman having ten pieces of silver, if she loses one piece, does not light a candle and sweep the house, and seek diligently until she finds it? When she has found it, she calls her friends and her neighbors together, saying, 'Rejoice with me, for I have found the piece that I had lost.' Likewise, I say to you, there is joy in the presence of the angels of God over one sinner who repents."

Jesus said, "A certain man had two sons. The younger of them said to his father, 'Father, give me the portion of goods that will come to me.' And the father divided his property between them. Not many days later the younger son gathered everything together and left on his journey into a far country, and there wasted his money with riotous living.

"When he had spent everything, there came a severe famine in that land, and he began to be in need. He went and joined himself to a citizen of that country who sent him into his fields to feed pigs. He would happily have filled his stomach with the carob pods that the pigs ate, but no one gave any to him. When he came to himself, he said, 'How many hired servants of my father's have food enough to spare, and I perish with hunger! I will arise and go to my father and will say to him, "Father, I have sinned against heaven[17] and before you; I am no longer worthy to be called your son; make me as one of your hired servants."

"He arose and came to his father. But when he was still a long way off, his father saw him and had compassion, and ran and fell on his neck and kissed him. The son said to him, 'Father, I have sinned against heaven, and in your sight; I am no longer worthy to be called your son.' The father said to his servants, 'Bring out the best robe and put it on him, and put a ring on his hand and sandals on his feet. Bring here the fatted calf and kill it, and let us eat and be merry; for my son was dead, and is alive again; he was lost, and is now found.' And they began to be merry.

"Now his eldest son was in the field, and as he came and drew near to the house, he heard music and dancing. He called one of the servants and asked what these things meant. He said to him, 'Your brother has come and your father has killed the fatted calf, because he has received him back safe and sound.' He was angry, and would not go in. Therefore his father came out and implored him.

"Answering he said to his father, 'Look, all these many years I have served you, never at any time have I transgressed your commandment, and yet you never gave me so much as a young goat that I might make merry with my friends, but as soon as this son of yours came, who has devoured your wealth with harlots, you killed the fatted calf for him.' The father said to him, 'Son, you are always with me and all that I have is yours. It was fitting that we should make merry and be happy; for your brother was dead, and is alive again; was lost, and is found.' "

Jesus said to his disciples, "There was a certain rich man, who had a steward. The steward was accused of having wasted his goods. He called him and said to him, 'How is it that I hear this of you? Give an account of your stewardship, for you can no longer be steward.' Then the steward said within himself, 'What shall I do? For my master takes away the stewardship from me. I cannot dig; I am too ashamed to beg. I have resolved what to do, so that when I am put out of the stewardship they might receive me into their houses.'

"So he called each one of his master's debtors to him, and said to the first, 'How much do you owe to my master?' He said, 'A hundred measures of oil.' He said to him, 'Take your bill, and sit down quickly and write fifty.' Then he said to another, 'how much do you owe?' He said, 'A hundred measures of wheat.' He said to him, 'Take your bill, and write eighty.' The master commended the unjust steward because he had done wisely; for the children of this world are in their generation wiser than the children of light. I say to you, make for yourselves friends with unrighteous mammon, so that when you fail, they may receive you into everlasting dwelling places.

"He who is faithful in what is a little is faithful also in what is much; and he that is dishonest in the least is also dishonest in much. Therefore, If you have not been faithful in unrighteous mammon, who will commit true riches to your trust? If you have not been faithful with what is another man's, who will give you that which is your own? No servant can serve two masters. Either he will hate the one and love the other, or else he will be devoted to the one and despise the other. You cannot serve both God and mammon."

The Pharisees, who were lovers of money, heard all these things, and they derided Jesus. He said to them, "You are those who justify yourselves before men, but God knows your hearts; for that which is highly esteemed among men is an abomination in the sight of God. The Law and the Prophets were until John. Since that time the kingdom of God is preached and everyone presses into it. It is easier for heaven and earth to pass, than one tittle of the Law to fail.

"*There was a* certain rich man, who was clothed in purple and fine linen, and fared sumptuously every day. And there was a certain beggar named Lazarus, who was laid at his gate, full of sores, who desired to be fed with the crumbs which fell from the rich man's table; moreover, the dogs came and licked his sores.

"It came to pass that the beggar died, and was carried by the angels into Abraham's bosom. The rich man also died, and was buried. Being in torment in hell, he raised his eyes and sees Abraham afar off, and Lazarus in his bosom. He cried out and said, 'Father Abraham, have mercy on me and send Lazarus, that he may dip the tip of his finger in water and cool my tongue, for I am tormented in this flame.' Abraham said, 'Son, remember that in your lifetime you received your good things, and Lazarus received bad things, but now he is comforted and you are tormented. Besides all this there is a great chasm fixed between us and you, so that those who would pass from here to you cannot, neither can those who want to come to us pass from there.'

"Then he said, 'I ask you therefore, father, that you would send him to my father's house, for I have five brothers,[18] that he may testify to them lest they also come to this place of torment.' Abraham said to him, 'They have Moses and the Prophets, let them hear them.' He said, 'No, father Abraham, but if someone goes to them from the dead, they will repent.' He said to him, 'If they do not hear Moses and the Prophets, neither will they be persuaded even though one rose from the dead.' "

The apostles said to the Lord, "Increase our faith." The Lord said, "If you have faith as a grain of mustard seed, you may say to this mulberry tree, 'Be uprooted and planted in the sea,' and it would obey you. Which of you, having a servant plowing or feeding sheep, will say to him when he has come in from the field, 'Go and sit down to eat'? Will he not rather say to him, 'Prepare my supper, and ready yourself to serve me until I have finished eating and drinking; and afterward you will eat and drink'? Does he thank that servant because he did the things that he was commanded to do? I think not. So likewise you, when you have done all the things you were commanded to do, say, 'We are unprofitable servants, we have done only that which was our duty to do.' "

A certain man was sick, named Lazarus, of Bethany, the town of Mary and her sister Martha (it was Mary who had anointed the Lord with ointment, and wiped his feet with her hair, whose brother Lazarus was sick). Therefore his sisters sent to him, saying, "Lord, behold, he whom you love is sick." When Jesus heard that, he said, "This sickness is not unto death, but for the glory of God, that the Son of God might be glorified through it."

Now Jesus loved Martha, and her sister, and Lazarus. When he had heard that Lazarus was sick, he remained another two days in the same place where he was. Then after that he said to his disciples, "Let us go into Judea again." His disciples say to him, "Teacher, of late the Jews sought to stone you; and you go there again?"

Jesus answered, "Are there not twelve hours in the day? If a man walks in the day he will not stumble, because he sees the light of this world, but if a man walks in the night, he stumbles, because the light is not in him." These things he said, and afterwards said to them, "Our friend Lazarus sleeps, but I go that I may awaken him out of sleep."[19] Then his disciples said, "Lord, if he sleeps, he will be safe." However, Jesus spoke of his death, but they thought he had spoken of Lazarus taking a rest in sleep.

Then Jesus said to them plainly, "Lazarus is dead. I am glad for your sakes that I was not there, so that you may believe; nevertheless let us go to him. Then said Thomas—who was also called Didymus—to his fellow disciples, "Let us go also, that we may die with him." When Jesus came, he found that Lazarus had already lain in the grave four days.

Now Bethany was near Jerusalem, about two miles away. Many of the Jews came to Martha and Mary, to comfort them concerning their brother. Then Martha, as soon as she heard that Jesus was coming, went and met him, but Mary remained sitting in the house.

Then Martha said to Jesus, "Lord, if you had been here, my brother would not have died. But I know that even now, whatever you will ask of God, God will give you." Jesus said to her, "Your brother will rise again." Martha said to him, "I know that he will rise again in the resurrection at the last day." Jesus said to her, "I am the resurrection and the life; he that believes in me, even though he dies he will yet live. Whoever lives and believes in me will never die. Do you believe this?" She said to him, "Yes, Lord, I believe that you are the Christ, the Son of God, who was to come into the world."

When she had said this she went her way and secretly called Mary her sister, saying, "The Teacher has come and is asking for you." As soon as she heard that she got up quickly, and came to him.

Now Jesus had not yet come into the town, but was in that place where Martha had met him. Then the Jews who were with her in the house comforting her, when they saw that Mary hastily got up and went out, they followed her, saying, "She is going to the grave to weep there." Then when Mary had come to where Jesus was, and saw him, she fell down at his feet, saying to him, "Lord, if you had been here, my brother would not have died."

When Jesus saw her weeping, and the Jews who came with her also weeping, he groaned in the spirit and was troubled. He said, "Where have you laid him?" They said to him, "Lord, come and see."

Jesus wept.

Then the Jews said, "Look how he loved him!" Some of them said, "Could not this man, who opens the eyes of the blind, have prevented this man from dying?" Therefore Jesus, groaning again in himself, came to the grave; it was a cave, and a stone lay across the opening. Jesus said, "Take away the stone." Martha, the sister of him who was dead, said to Jesus, "Lord, by this time he will stink, for he has been dead four days." He said to her, "Did I not say to you, that if you would believe you will see the glory of God?"

Then they took away the stone from the cave where Lazarus was lying. Jesus raised up his eyes toward heaven and said, "Father, I thank you that you have heard me. I know that you always hear me, but because of the people who stand watching I said it, that they may believe that you have sent me." When he had spoken this, he cried with a loud voice, "Lazarus, come out!" And he who was dead came out, bound hand and foot with grave linens, and his face was wrapped in a cloth. Jesus said to them, "Loose him, and let him go." Then many of the Jews who came with Mary and had seen the things which Jesus did, believed in him. But some of them went to the Pharisees and told them what things Jesus had done.

The chief priests and the Pharisees gathered a council together and said, "What do we do? This man does many miracles. If we leave him alone everyone will believe in him, and the Romans will come and take away both our place and our nation." One of them, named Caiaphas, being the high priest that year, said to them, "You know nothing at all, nor consider that it is expedient that one man should die for the people rather than the whole nation should perish." He did not speak this on his own accord, but being high priest that year he prophesied that Jesus would die for the nation. Not for the nation only, but also that he would gather together into one the children of God who were scattered abroad.

So from that day onward they counseled together to put him to death. Therefore Jesus no longer walked openly among the Jews, but went from there to an area near to the wilderness, into a city called Ephraim, and stayed there with his disciples.

It came to pass, as he went to Jerusalem, that he passed through the midst of Samaria and Galilee. As he entered into a certain village, there met him ten men who were lepers, who stood at a distance. They raised their voices and said, "Jesus, master, have mercy on us." When he saw them, he said to them, "Go show yourselves to the priests." It happened that as they went, they were cleansed. One of them, when he saw that he was healed, turned back, and with a loud voice glorified God and fell down on his face at his feet, giving him thanks; and he was a Samaritan.

Jesus responding said, "Were there not ten cleansed? Where are the other nine?[20] Have none returned to give glory to God save this foreigner?" He said to him, "Stand up and go on your way, your faith has made you whole."

When Jesus was asked by the Pharisees when the kingdom of God would come, he answered them and said, "The kingdom of God does not come with observation, neither shall they say, 'Here!' or, 'See there!' Because the kingdom of God is within you."[21]

He said to the disciples, "The days will come when you will desire to see one of the days of the Son of Man, and you will not see it. They will say to you, 'See here!' or, 'See there!' Do not go after them, nor follow them, for as the lightning that flashes out of one part of the sky shines to the other part of the sky, so also will the Son of Man be in his day. But first he must suffer many things, and be rejected by this generation.

"As it was in the days of Noah, so also will it be in the days of the Son of Man. They ate, they drank, they married wives, they were given in marriage, until the day that Noah entered into the ark and the flood came and destroyed them all.

"Likewise, just as it also was in the days of Lot, they ate, they drank, they bought, they sold, they planted, they built; but the same day that Lot went out of Sodom it rained fire and brimstone from heaven, and destroyed them all.

"Even so will it be in the day when the Son of Man is revealed. In that day, he who will be on the housetop, and his goods in the house, do not let him come down to take them away. He who is in the field, let him likewise not return back. Remember Lot's wife. Whoever will try to save his life will lose it; and whoever will lose his life will save it.

"I tell you, on that night there will be two men in one bed; one will be taken, and the other will be left. Two women will be grinding together; one will be taken, and the other left. Two men will be in the field; one will be taken, and the other left." They answered and said to him, "Where, Lord?" He said to them, "Wherever the body is, there the vultures will be gathered together."

He spoke a parable to them to the end that men should always pray, and not be discouraged. Saying, "In a city there was a judge who neither feared God, nor respected man. And there was a widow in that city, and she came to him, saying, 'Avenge me of my adversary.' For a while he would not, but afterward he said to himself, 'Though I do not fear God, nor regard man, but because this widow troubles me, I will avenge her, lest by her continual coming she wear me out.' "

The Lord said, "Hear what the unjust judge said. And will not God avenge his own elect who cry to him day and night, though he bears long with them? I tell you he will avenge them speedily. Nevertheless, when the Son of Man comes, will he find faith on the earth?"

He spoke this parable to those who trusted that they themselves were righteous, and despised others: "Two men went up into the temple to pray, one was a Pharisee, the other a tax collector. The Pharisee stood and prayed thus with himself: 'God, I thank you that I am not like other men are, extortioners, unrighteous, adulterers, or even like this tax collector; I fast twice in the week and I give tithes of all that I possess.' The tax collector, standing afar off, would not so much as raise his eyes to heaven, but beat his breast, saying, 'God, be merciful to me, a sinner!' I tell you, this man went down to his house justified rather than the other; for everyone who exalts himself will be humbled, and he who humbles himself will be exalted."

And so it was, that when Jesus had finished these sayings, he departed from Galilee and came into the coastal regions of Judea, beyond the Jordan, and great multitudes followed him. As was his custom, he taught them and healed them there.

The Pharisees also came to him, testing him, and saying, "Is it lawful for a man to put away his wife for any reason?" He answered and said to them, "Have you not read that he who made them at the beginning of the creation made them male and female, and said, 'For this reason a man shall leave his father and mother and be united with his wife; and the two will become one flesh'? Therefore, they are no longer two, but one flesh. So then, what God has joined together, let not man separate."

They said to him, "Why then did Moses command us to give a bill of divorce, and put her away?" Jesus said to them, "Moses, because of the hardness of your hearts, wrote you this precept and allowed you to divorce your wives, but from the beginning it was not so. I say to you, whoever divorces his wife, except for sexual immorality, and marries another, commits adultery against her; and whoever marries her who is divorced from her husband commits adultery."

His disciples said to him, "If this is the case with the man and his wife, it is better not to marry." He said to them, "Not all men can accept this saying, only those to whom it is given. For there are some eunuchs who were born eunuchs from their mother's womb, and there are some eunuchs who were made eunuchs by men; and there are eunuchs who have made themselves eunuchs for the sake of the kingdom of heaven. He who is able to receive this, let him receive it."

They also brought little children to Jesus, that he should put his hands on them and pray, but when his disciples saw it, they rebuked those who brought them. When Jesus saw it he was very displeased and called them to him, and said, "Allow the little children to come to me, and do not hinder them, for to such the kingdom of God belongs. Truly I say to you, whoever does not receive the kingdom of God as a little child will in no way enter in at all." He took them up in his arms, put his hands upon them, blessed them, and departed from there.

A *certain ruler* came running, and knelt before Jesus, and asked him, saying, "Good master, what good thing shall I do to inherit eternal life?" Jesus said to him, "Why do you call me good? No one is good, except one, that is, God. If you will enter into life, keep the commandments." He said to him, "Which ones?" Jesus said, "You know the commandments: *You shall not murder, you shall not commit adultery, you shall not steal, you shall not bear false witness, honor your father and your mother, and, you shall love your neighbor as yourself"* (Exodus 20:12-16 / Leviticus 19:18). He said, "All these I have kept from my youth up, what else do I lack?" Then Jesus, looking at him, loved him, and said to him, "You still lack one thing: if you want to be perfect, go and sell all that you have and distribute it to the poor, and you will have treasure in heaven; and come, take up your cross and follow me." When he heard this he was very sorrowful, for he was very rich and had great possessions.

When Jesus saw that he was very sorrowful, he said to his disciples, "Children, how hard it is for those who trust in riches to enter into the kingdom of God! Truly I say to you, it is easier for a camel to go through a needle's eye,[22] than it is for a rich man to enter into the kingdom of God."

The disciples were astonished at his words. Jesus said to them again, "Children, how hard it is for those who trust in riches to enter the kingdom of God." Those who heard it were extremely astonished, beyond measure, at his words, saying, "Who then can be saved?" He said, "With men it is impossible, but not with God, for all things are possible with God."

Then Peter said, "Look, we have left everything and followed you, therefore what will we have?" He said to them, "Truly I say to you, there is no one who has left house, or parents, or brothers, or wife, or children, for my sake, for the gospel's sake, and for the kingdom of God, who will not receive many times more in this present time, houses, and brothers, and sisters, and mothers, and children, and lands, with persecutions; and in the world to come everlasting life. However, many who are first will be last, and the last first. Truly I say to you, in the regeneration when the Son of Man sits on the throne of his glory, those of you who have followed me will also sit upon twelve thrones, judging the twelve tribes of Israel."

"The kingdom of heaven is like a master of a house who went out early in the morning to hire laborers to work in his vineyard. When he had agreed with the laborers for a *denarius* a day, he sent them into his vineyard.

"He went out about the third hour and saw others standing idle in the marketplace. He said to them, 'You also go into the vineyard, and whatever is right I will give you.' And they went their way.

"Again he went out about the sixth and ninth hours, and did the same. About the eleventh hour he went out and found others standing idle, and said to them, 'Why do you stand here idle all day?' They said to him, 'Because no one has hired us.' He said to them, 'You also go into the vineyard, and whatever is right, that you will receive.'

"When evening had come, the master of the vineyard said to his steward, 'Call the laborers and give them their wages, beginning from the last to the first.'

"When they came, those who were hired about the eleventh hour received each man a *denarius*. When the first came, they supposed that they would receive more, but they likewise received each man a *denarius*. When they had received it, they complained against the master of the house, saying, 'These last men have worked only one hour, and you have made them equal to us who have borne the burden and heat of the day.'

"He answered one of them, and said, 'Friend, I have done you no wrong, did you not agree with me for a *denarius*? Take what is yours and go your way; I will give to the last, even as to you. Is it not lawful for me to do what I want with my own money? Is your eye evil because I am good?' The last will be first, and the first last, for many are called, but few are chosen."

They were going on their way up to Jerusalem, and Jesus went before them. As they followed, they were astonished, and also afraid. Then he took the twelve disciples aside on the way, and said to them, "Look, we are going up to Jerusalem, and all things which are written by the prophets concerning the Son of Man will be accomplished. He will be betrayed to the chief priests and to the scribes, and then be delivered to the Gentiles, and will be mocked, and shamefully insulted, and spat upon. They will scourge him and crucify him, and put him to death; and the third day he will rise again." However, they understood none of these things, and this saying was hidden from them, neither had they come to know the things that were spoken.

Then the mother of Zebedee's children came to him with her sons, James and John, worshiping him, and saying, "We want you to do for us whatever we will ask." He said to her, "What do you want?" She said to him, "Grant that my two sons may sit one at your right hand, and the other at the left in your kingdom." Jesus answered and said, "You do not know what you ask. Are you able to drink from the cup that I will drink from, and be baptized with the baptism that I am to be baptized with?" They said to him, "We are able."

He said to them, "You will indeed drink from the cup that I will drink from, and with the baptism that I am to be baptized with you will be baptized, but to sit at my right hand, and at my left, is not mine to give, but it will be given to those for whom it is prepared by my Father." When the ten heard it, they were moved with indignation against the two brothers and they began to be very displeased with James and John.

Jesus called them over to him, and said, "You know that the rulers of the Gentiles lord it over them, and those who are great exercise authority over them; but it shall not be like that among you, whoever will be great among you let him be your servant, and whoever will be chief among you, let him be your slave. For even as the Son of Man did not come to be served, but to serve and to give his life a ransom for many."

They came to Jericho and as he went out of Jericho with his disciples and a great number of people, blind

Bartimaeus, the son of Timaeus, sat by the wayside begging. Hearing the crowd pass by, he asked what it meant. They told him, that Jesus of Nazareth was passing by. He cried out, saying, "Jesus, Son of David, have mercy on me." Those who were up ahead rebuked him, that he should keep quiet, but he cried out all the more, "Son of David, have mercy on me." Jesus stopped, and commanded him to be brought to him. They called the blind man, saying to him, "Be of good courage, get up, he calls for you." Throwing away his garment, he arose and came to Jesus. When he had come near, Jesus asked him, saying, "What do you want me to do for you?" He said, "Lord, that I may receive my sight." Jesus said to him, "Receive your sight, your faith has saved you." Immediately he received his sight and followed Jesus, glorifying God; and all the people, when they saw it, gave praise to God.

Departing from Jericho, a great multitude followed Jesus. And behold, two blind men were sitting by the wayside, and when they heard that Jesus was going by, cried out, saying, "Have mercy on us, O Lord, you Son of David." The multitude rebuked them, saying they should be quiet, but they cried all the more, saying, "Have mercy on us, O Lord, you Son of David." Jesus stood still, and called them, and said, "What do you wish that I will do for you?" They say to him, "Lord, that our eyes may be opened." So Jesus had compassion on them, and touched their eyes, and immediately their eyes received sight, and they followed him.

Jesus entered and passed through Jericho. And behold, there was a man named Zacchaeus, who was the chief among the tax collectors, and he was rich. He tried to see who Jesus was, and could not because of the crowd, since he was short in stature. He ran ahead and climbed up into a sycamore-fig tree to see him, because he was to pass that way. When Jesus came to the place, he looked up and saw him, and said to him, "Zacchaeus, make haste and come down, today I must stay at your house." He quickly came down, and received him joyfully.

When the people of the Jews saw it, they all complained, saying, "He has gone to be a guest of a man who is a sinner." Zacchaeus stood, and said to the Lord, "Look, Lord, half of my goods I give to the poor, and if I have taken anything from anyone by false accusation, I will restore it fourfold." Jesus said to him, "Today salvation has come to this house, for he also is a son of Abraham; for the Son of Man has come to seek and to save that which was lost."

As they listened to these things, Jesus added and spoke a parable, because he was near to Jerusalem, and because they thought that the kingdom of God would immediately appear.

Therefore, he said, "A certain nobleman went into a far country to receive for himself a kingdom, and then return. He called his ten servants and gave them ten *minas*, saying to them, 'Trade with this until I return.' But his citizens hated him, and sent a message after him, saying, 'We will not have this man to reign over us.'

"And it came to pass, that, when he had returned after having received the kingdom, he commanded his servants to be called to him, those to whom he had given the money, that he might know how much each man had gained by trading.

Then came the first, saying, 'Master, your *mina* has gained ten *minas*.' He said to him, 'Well done you good servant, because you have been faithful in a very little, you will have authority over ten cities.'

"The second came, saying, 'Master, your *mina* has gained five *minas*.' He said likewise to him, 'You will also be over five cities.' Another came, saying, 'Master, look, here is your *mina* which I have kept safe in a handkerchief. For I feared you, because you are an austere man, you gather up that which you did not deposit, and reap what you did not sow.'

"He said to him, 'Out of your own mouth I will judge you, you wicked servant. You knew that I was an austere man, taking up what I did not lay down, and reaping what I did not sow. Why then did you not give my money to the bank, that at my coming I might have gotten my own with interest?' He said to them that stood by, 'Take his *mina* and give it to him who has ten *minas*.' They said to him, 'But master, he has ten *minas*!' Therefore I say to you, that to everyone who has, more will be given, and from him that does not have, even what he has will be taken away from him. But those enemies of mine who would not have me reign over them, bring them here, and kill them in front of me." When he had spoken this, he went ahead, ascending up to Jerusalem.

The Passover of the Jews was close at hand, and many went up to Jerusalem from out of their regions before the Passover, to purify themselves. Then they looked for Jesus and spoke among themselves as they stood in the temple, "What do you think, that he will not come to the feast?" Both the chief priests and the Pharisees had given an order that, if any man knew where he was, he should make it known, that they might arrest him.

Six days before the Passover Jesus came to Bethany, where Lazarus was who had been dead, whom he had raised from the dead. There, in the house of Simon the leper, they made him a meal; Martha served and Lazarus was one of those who sat at the table with him.

Then Mary took an alabaster box holding a pound of ointment of spikenard, very precious, very costly, and she broke the box and poured it on his head, and anointed the feet of Jesus and wiped his feet with her hair; and the house was filled with the fragrance of the ointment.

Then said one of his disciples, Judas Iscariot, Simon's son, who would betray him, "To what purpose was this waste of the ointment made? Why was it not sold for three hundred *denarii* and given to the poor?" This he said, not that he cared for the poor, but because he was a thief, and had the bag, and carried what was put into it.

Then Jesus said, "Why do you trouble the woman? Let her alone, for she has done a good work on me, against the day of my burial she has done this, to anoint my body for the burial. For the poor you will always have with you, but me you will not always have. Truly I say to you, wherever this gospel will be preached throughout the whole world, this what she has done will also be spoken of as a memorial of her."

Many people of the Jews knew that Jesus was there, and they came not only for his sake, but that they might also see Lazarus, whom he had raised from the dead. But the chief priests also consulted how they might put Lazarus to death, because he was the reason many of the Jews went away believing in Jesus.

It came to pass on the next day, when he had come near to Bethphage and Bethany, at the mount called the Mount of Olives, he sent two of his disciples, saying, "You go into the village opposite you and when you enter you will find a colt tied, upon which no man ever sat. Untie him and bring him here. If anyone asks you, 'Why are you untying him?' You will say to him, 'Because the Lord has need of him.'"

Those who were sent went on their way and found it just as he had said to them. And as they were untying the colt the owners of it said to them, "Why do you untie the colt?" They said, "The Lord has need of him," and they let them go. They brought him to Jesus, and they threw their clothing upon the colt, and they sat Jesus on it. All this was done that it might be fulfilled which was spoken by the prophet, saying, "*Fear not, daughter of Zion: behold, your King comes to you, gentle, and sitting upon an ass, a colt, the foal of an ass*" (Zechariah 9:9).

Many people that had come to the feast and when they heard that Jesus was coming to Jerusalem, they took branches of palm trees, and went out to meet him. As Jesus went, they spread their clothes on the road, others cut down branches from the trees, and spread them on the road. When he was near, at the descent of the Mount of Olives, the whole multitude of the disciples began to rejoice and praise God with a loud voice for all the mighty works that they had seen.

The multitudes that went ahead, and those that followed, shouted, saying, "Hosanna to the Son of David!" "Blessed be the kingdom of our father David!" "***Blessed be the King of Israel who comes in the name of the L<small>ORD</small>!***"; "*Hosanna in the highest!*"; "*Peace in heaven, and glory in the highest!*" (Psalms 118:26f). These things his disciples did not understand at first, but when Jesus was glorified then they remembered that these things were written of him, and that they had done these things to him.

Some of the Pharisees from among the multitude said to him, "Master, rebuke your disciples." He answered and said to them, "I tell you that if these would hold their peace, the stones would immediately cry out. Yes, have you never read, '*Out of the mouth of babies and infants you have perfected praise*'?" (Psalms 8:2).

When Jesus had come near Jerusalem, he saw the city and wept over it, saying, "If you had known, even you, at least in this your day, the things which make for your peace! But now they are hidden from your eyes. For the days will come upon you that your enemies will build a siegework around you and surround you all about, and hedge you in on every side. They will level you and all your children within you to the ground; and they will not leave you one stone upon another because you did not know the time of your visitation."

When he had come into Jerusalem, all the city was moved, saying, "Who is this?" The multitude said, "This is Jesus, the prophet of Nazareth of Galilee." Therefore the people who were with him when he called Lazarus out of his grave and raised him from the dead, bore witness.

For this reason the people also met him, because they had heard that he had done this miracle. Therefore the Pharisees said among themselves, "Do you see how you accomplish nothing? Look, the world has gone after him."

Jesus entered Jerusalem, and went into the temple. When he had looked around at everything, and because the evening had come, he went out to Bethany with the twelve, and he lodged there.

In the morning, as he returned to the city, he was hungry. Seeing a fig tree a short distance away having leaves, he went to see if perhaps he might find something on it, but when he came to it he found nothing but leaves, for it was not yet the season for figs. Jesus said to it in response, "Let no fruit ever grow on you from now and forever." And his disciples heard it.

They came to Jerusalem and Jesus went into the temple of God, and began to throw out those who sold and bought in the temple, and overthrew the tables of the moneychangers, and the seats of those who sold doves. And he would not permit any man to carry any vessel through the temple, saying to them, "It is written, '*My house shall be called the house of prayer for all nations,*' but *you have made it 'a den of thieves'*" (Jeremiah 7:11).

The scribes and chief priests heard it, and they were very angry and sought a way how they might destroy Jesus, but they feared him, because all the people were amazed at his doctrine. Then everyone went to his own house. Jesus went to the Mount of Olives.

Early in the morning Jesus came into the temple again, and all the people came to him, and he sat down and taught them.

The scribes and Pharisees brought to him a woman taken in adultery; and when they had placed her in the midst, they said to him, "Master, this woman was taken in adultery, in the very act. In the law Moses commanded us that such should be stoned, but what do you say?" They said this to test him, that they might have something to accuse him of. Jesus stooped down and wrote on the ground with his finger, as though he had not heard them.

So when they continued asking him, he raised himself up and said to them, "He that is without sin among you, let him throw the first stone at her."

He stooped down again and wrote on the ground. Those who heard it, being convicted by their own conscience, went out one by one, beginning at the eldest, down to the youngest; and Jesus was left alone, and the woman standing in the midst.

When Jesus had raised himself up and saw no one except the woman, he said to her, "Woman, where are your accusers? Has no one condemned you?" She said, "No one, Lord." Jesus said to her, "Neither do I condemn you; go and sin no more."

Jesus taught daily in the temple, but the chief priests and the scribes and the chiefs of the people sought to destroy him. They could not, because all the people were very attentive to hear him.

There were certain Greeks among those who came up to worship at the feast. They came to Philip who was from

Bethsaida in Galilee, and asked him, saying, "Sir, we want to see Jesus." Philip came and told Andrew and then Andrew and Philip told Jesus.

Jesus responded to them, saying, "The hour has come that the Son of Man should be glorified. Indeed, I say to you, except a grain of wheat fall into the ground and die, it abides alone; but if it dies, it brings forth much grain. He who loves his life will lose it, and he who hates his life in this world will keep it to eternal life.

"If any man will serve me, let him follow me, and where I am, there my servant will be also; if any man serve me, him my Father will honor.

"Now is my soul troubled, and what shall I say? 'Father, save me from this hour'? But for this reason I came to this hour. 'Father, glorify your name.' " Then there came a voice from heaven, saying, "I have both glorified it, and will glorify it again." Therefore, the people who stood by heard it, and said that it had thundered; others said, "An angel spoke to him." Jesus answered and said, "This voice did not come because of me, but for your sakes. Now is the judgment of this world; now will the ruler of this world be cast out. And I, if I be lifted up from the earth, will draw all men to me." This he said, signifying what death he would die.

The people answered him, "We have heard from the law that Christ abides for ever, why do you say, 'The Son of Man must be lifted up?' Who is this Son of Man?"

Then Jesus said to them, "Only a little while longer the light is with you. Walk while you have the light, lest darkness comes upon you; for he who walks in darkness does not know where he goes. While you have light, believe in the light, that you may be the children of light."

Jesus spoke these things, then he departed and hid himself from them. Even though he had worked so many miracles before them, they still did not believe in him, so that the words of Isaiah the prophet might be fulfilled:

> LORD, who has believed our report? And to whom has the arm of the LORD been revealed? (Isaiah 53:1)

They could not believe, because again Isaiah said:

> He has blinded their eyes and hardened their heart, lest they should see with their eyes and understand with their heart, lest they turn again and I should heal them (Isaiah 6:10).

These things Isaiah said when he saw his glory and spoke of him. Nevertheless, many among the rulers believed in him, but because of the Pharisees they did not confess it, for fear they would be put out of the synagogue; for they loved the praise of men more than the praise of God.

Jesus cried out, saying "He who believes in me, does not believe in me, but in him who sent me. He who sees me sees him who sent me. I have come as a light into the world, that whoever believes in me would not remain in darkness.

"If anyone hears my words and does not believe, I do not judge him; for I did not come to judge the world, but to save the world. He who rejects me and does not receive my words has one who judges him; the words that I have spoken, those will judge him in the last day. For I have not spoken of myself, but the Father who sent me gave me a commandment, what I should say and what I should speak. I know that his commandment is everlasting life; therefore, whatever I speak, I speak just as the Father commanded me."

When evening had come, he went out of the city. In the morning, as they passed by, the disciples saw the fig tree withered from its roots. When they saw it, they marveled, saying, "How quickly has the fig tree withered away!" Peter, calling it to remembrance, said to Jesus, "Master, look, the fig tree that you cursed has withered away."

Jesus answered them and said, "Have faith in God. For truly I say to you, if you have faith, and doubt not, you will not only do what is done to the fig tree, but also that whoever will say to this mountain, 'Be removed and thrown into the sea,' and does not doubt in his heart, but will believe that the things that he says will come to pass; he will have whatever he says. All things, whatever you will ask in prayer, believing, you will receive.

"Therefore I say to you, whatever things you desire, when you pray, believe that you receive them, and you will have them. And whenever you stand praying, forgive, if you have something against anyone, so that your Father in heaven may forgive you your trespasses. If you do not forgive, neither will your Father in heaven forgive your trespasses."

They came again to Jerusalem, and it happened that one day, as Jesus taught the people in the temple and preached the gospel, that the chief priests and the scribes, with the elders, came to confront him. They spoke to him, saying, "Tell us, by what authority do you do these things?

Who is he who gave you this authority?" Jesus answered and said to them, "I will also ask you one question, which if you tell me, I will likewise tell you by what authority I do these things. 'John's baptism: was it from heaven, or from men'? Answer me." They reasoned among themselves, saying, "If we say, 'From heaven,' he will say, 'Why did you not believe him then?' If we say, 'Of men,' we fear the people because the people will stone us; for they are all persuaded and believe that John was indeed a prophet.'" They answered that they could not tell where it was from. So Jesus said to them, "Neither will I tell you by what authority I do these things.

What do you think? A certain man had two sons, and he came to the first, and said, 'Son, go work today in the vineyard.' He answered and said, 'I will not' but afterward he changed his mind and went. He came to the second son and said the same. He answered and said, 'I go, sir,' but he did not go. Which of the two did the will of his father?" They said to him, "The first."

Jesus said to them, "Truly I say to you, that the tax collectors and the prostitutes go into the kingdom of God before you. For John came to you in the way of righteousness, and you did not believe him, but the tax collectors and the prostitutes believed him; but you, when you saw it, you did not regret it afterward that you might believe him."

Then he began to speak to the people in parables: "A certain man planted a vineyard, and fenced it around and dug a winepress in it, and built a tower, and leased it to tenant-farmers, and then went away to a far country for a long time. At harvest time he sent servants to the tenant-farmers, that they should give him some of the fruit of the vineyard, but the tenant-farmers beat him and sent them away empty-handed.

"He sent another servant, and they beat him also and treated him shamefully, and sent him away empty-handed. Again he sent a third servant, and they stoned him, wounding him in the head, and threw him out. He sent other servants, more than at first; and they did the same to them.

"Then the master of the vineyard said, 'What shall I do? I will send my beloved son; it may be that they will respect him when they see him.' But when the tenant-farmers saw him, they talked among themselves, saying, 'This is the heir, come, let us kill him, then the inheritance will be ours.' So they threw him out of the vineyard and killed him.

"Therefore what will the master of the vineyard do to them? He will come and destroy those tenant-farmers and will give the vineyard to other tenant-farmers. Therefore I say to you, the kingdom of God will be taken from you, and given to a nation who will give him the fruits in their seasons." When they heard it, they said, "God forbid!" He looked at them and said, "Have you not read this Scripture that is written: *'The stone which the builders rejected has become the chief cornerstone; this is the Lord's doing, and it is marvelous in our eyes'* (Psalms 118:22–23)? Whoever falls upon that stone will be broken, but on whomever it will fall, it will grind him to powder." Right then the chief priests and the scribes wanted to lay hands on him, but they feared the people, for they understood that he had spoken the parable against them; and they left him, and went their way.

Jesus again spoke to them by way of a parable, and said, "The kingdom of heaven is like a certain king who arranged a marriage for his son, and sent out his servants to call those who were invited to the wedding; and they would not come.

"He sent out other servants, saying, "Tell those who are invited, 'Look, I have prepared my feast; my oxen and fattened cattle are killed, and all things are ready; come to the wedding.' " However, they made light of it and went their different ways, one to his farm, another to his business; and the others took his servants and treated them spitefully, and killed them.

"And when the king heard of it he was very angry; and he sent his armies, and destroyed the murderers and burned their city. Then he said to his servants, 'The wedding is ready, but those who were invited were not worthy. Therefore, go into the streets and as many as you can find, invite to the wedding.' So those servants went out into the streets and gathered together all those whom they found, both bad and good; and the wedding was filled with guests.

"When the king came in to see the guests, he saw a man who did not have on a wedding garment. He said to him, 'Friend, how did you come in here without having a wedding garment?' He was speechless. Then the king said to the servants, 'Bind him hand and foot, take him away and throw him into outer darkness; there will be weeping and gnashing of teeth.' For many are called, but few are chosen."

The Jews watched Jesus, and sent out disciples, spies of the Pharisees and the Herodians who would pretend to be righteous men, that they might seize upon his words and entangle him, so that they might deliver him to the power and authority of the governor. They asked him, saying, "Master, we know that you say and teach rightly, nor do you regard the outward appearance of a person, but teach the way of God in truth. Therefore is it lawful for us to give tax-tribute to Caesar, or not? Should we give, or should we not give?"

However, Jesus perceived their craftiness, and said to them, "Why do you test me you hypocrites? Show me the tax-tribute money." They brought to him a *denarius*. He asked, "Whose image and superscription is this?" They answered and said, "Caesar's." He said to them, "Therefore render to Caesar the things that are Caesar's, and to God the things that are God's." They could not catch him in his words before the people; and they marveled at his answer, and held their peace and went their way.

The same day certain of the Sadducees, who deny that there is any resurrection, came to him and asked him, saying, "Master, Moses wrote to us that if any man's brother die, having a wife, and he dies without children, that his brother should take his wife and raise up offspring to his brother.

"Now there were with us seven brothers, and the first took a wife and died without children. The second took her as his wife, and he died childless. The third took her, and in the same manner the seven also took her; and they died leaving no children. Last of all the woman died also. Therefore, in the resurrection, whose wife will she be? For all seven had her as wife."

Jesus answering, said to them, "You are mistaken, because you neither know the Scriptures, nor the power of God. The children of this world marry and are given in marriage, but those who will be counted worthy to obtain that world, and the resurrection from the dead, neither marry, nor are given in marriage. Neither can they die anymore; for they are equal to the angels of God in heaven and are the children of God, being the children of the resurrection.

"Now touching that the dead are raised, have you not read in the Book of Moses that which was spoken to you by God, saying, '*I am the God of Abraham, and the God of Isaac, and the God of Jacob*' (Exodus 3:6)? For he is not the God of the dead, but of the living, for all live to him. You are therefore greatly mistaken." When the multitude heard this, they were astonished at his doctrine.

Then some of the scribes answered and said, "Master, you have spoken well." After that they did not ask him any further questions.

When the Pharisees had heard them talking together, and understanding that he had answered them well, that he had put the Sadducees to silence, they gathered together. Then one of them, who was a lawyer, asked him a question, testing him, and saying, "Master, which is the greatest commandment of all?" Jesus answered him, "The greatest of all the commandments is: '*Hear, O Israel, the* LORD *our God is one* LORD; *and you shall love the* LORD your God with all your heart, and with all your soul, and with all your mind, and with all your strength'* (Deuteronomy 6:4). This is the first commandment, and the second is this: *'You shall love your neighbor as yourself* (Leviticus 19:18). There is no other commandment greater than these. On these two commandments hang all the Law and the Prophets."

The lawyer said to him, "Yes, teacher, you have said the truth; for there is but one God and there is no other besides him. And to love him with all the heart, and with all the understanding, and with all the soul, and with all the strength, and to love one's neighbor as oneself is more than all the whole burnt offerings and sacrifices." When Jesus saw that he answered wisely, he said to him, "You are not far from the kingdom of God." After that no one dared to ask him any question.

While the Pharisees were gathered together, Jesus, as he taught in the temple, asked them, saying, "What do you think about the Christ? Whose son is he?" They said to him, "The Son of David." He said to them, "How is it that they say Christ is David's son? For David himself said by the Holy Spirit in the, book of Psalms: *'The* LORD *said to my Lord, sit at my right hand, until I make your enemies your footstool'* (Psalms 110:1). Therefore, if David calls him Lord, how then is he his son?" No one was able to answer him a word, nor did anyone from that day on dare to ask him any more questions. And the common people gladly listened to him.

Then Jesus spoke to the multitude, and to his disciples, saying in his doctrine, "The scribes and the Pharisees sit in the seat of Moses, therefore whatever they tell you to observe, observe and do it, but do not copy them in their works; for they talk, and do not do. They do their works only to be seen by men.

"They make their phylacteries broad, and lengthen the tassels on their garments; they like to walk in long robes, and love the best places at feasts, and the best seats in the synagogues, and greetings in the marketplaces, and to be called, 'Rabbi, Rabbi.'

"But you, do not be called 'Rabbi,' for one is your teacher, even Christ, and you are all brothers. And call no man your father on the earth; for one is your Father, he who is in heaven. Neither be called masters, for one is your Master, the Christ. He who is greatest among you will be your servant. Whoever will exalt himself will be humbled; and he who will humble himself will be exalted.

"Woe to you, scribes and Pharisees, hypocrites! For you shut up the kingdom of heaven against men; for you neither go in yourselves, nor allow those that are entering to go in.

"Woe to you, scribes and Pharisees, hypocrites! For you devour widows' houses, and for a pretense make long prayers, therefore you will receive greater damnation.

"Woe to you, scribes and Pharisees, hypocrites! For you travel over sea and land to make one proselyte, and when he becomes one, you make him twice the child of hell than you are yourselves.

"Woe to you, you blind guides, who say, 'Whoever shall swear by the temple, it is nothing; but whoever shall swear by the gold of the temple, he must fulfill his oath'! You and blind fools! For which is greater, the gold, or the temple that sanctifies the gold? You say, 'Whoever shall swear by the altar, it is nothing; but whoever swears by the gift that is upon it, he must fulfill his oath'! You blind fools! For which is greater, the gift, or the altar that sanctifies the gift? Therefore, whoever swears by the altar, swears by it, and by everything on it. Whoever swears by the temple, swears by it, and by him who dwells in it. He who swears by heaven, swears by the throne of God, and by him who sits on it. You blind guides, who strain out a gnat and swallow a camel."

Jesus sat over against the treasury, and he watched and observed how the people put money into the treasury, and many who were rich put their gifts into the treasury. He also saw a certain poor widow putting two *mites* (which make a *quadrans*) in there. He called his disciples to him and said to them, "Indeed I say to you, that this poor widow has put in more than any of them. For all these have put of their abundance into the offerings to God, but she, out of her extreme poverty, has put in all that she had to live on."

Jesus went out, and departed from the temple. His disciples came to him to show him the buildings of the temple. As some spoke of the temple, one of his disciples said to him, "Master, see what manner of stones and what buildings there are!" How it was all adorned with beautiful stones and gifts. He said, "As for these things which you see—these great buildings? Truly I say to you, the days will come in which there will not be one stone left upon another, that will not be thrown down."

As Jesus sat on the Mount of Olives opposite the temple, Peter and James and John and Andrew asked him privately, saying, "Master, tell us, when will these things be?" What sign will there be when all these things will be fulfilled? What will be the sign of your coming, and of the end of the world?"

Jesus began by saying, "Take care that you are not deceived, for many false prophets will arise and will deceive many. And because wickedness will increase, the love of many will grow cold. Many will come in my name, saying, 'I am the Christ,' and, 'The time draws near,' and will deceive many. Therefore do not follow after them. When you hear of wars and rumors of wars, and commotions, do not be fearful, for these things must first come to pass; but the end is not yet."

Then he said to them, "Nation will rise against nation, and kingdom against kingdom, and great earthquakes will be in various places, and famines, and troubles, and pestilences; and will there be fearful sights and great signs from heaven. All these things are but the beginnings of sorrows. Take heed to yourselves for many will be offended, and will betray one another, and will hate one another. But before all these things they will lay their hands on you, and persecute you, delivering you up to councils, and in the synagogues you will be beaten. They shall deliver you into prisons, and bring you before kings and rulers for my name's sake.

"It will turn out to be for a testimony against them. Therefore, when they will lead you away and deliver you up, settle it in your hearts not to meditate beforehand what you will answer; for I will give you a mouth and wisdom in that hour, which all your adversaries will not be able to repudiate nor resist, for it will not be you who speaks, but the Holy Spirit; whatever will be given you, that speak.

"You will be betrayed by parents, and brothers, and relatives, and friends; and children will rise up against their parents and will cause them to be put to death. Some of you they will put to death, and you will be hated by all for my name's sake; but not one hair of your head will perish. In your patience you will possess your souls; he who will endure to the end, the same will be saved. And this gospel of the kingdom will be preached in all the world for a witness to all nations; and then will the end come."

"When you see Jerusalem surrounded by armies, then you know that its destruction is near. Then let those who are in Judea flee to the mountains; and let those who are in the city leave; and do not let those who are in the surrounding regions enter. For these are the days of vengeance, that all things which are written may be fulfilled. Woe to those who are pregnant, and to those who are nursing babies in those days. For there will be great distress in the land and wrath upon this people. They will fall by the edge of the sword, and will be led away captive into all nations; and Jerusalem will be trodden down by the Gentiles until the times of the Gentiles are fulfilled."

"Therefore, when you see the abomination of desolation spoken of by Daniel the prophet, standing in the holy place where it should not be (let the reader understand), then let those who are in Judea flee into the mountains. Pray that your flight will not be in the winter, nor on the Sabbath day; for in those days there will be great tribulation, such as never was since the beginning of the creation of the world to this time, no, nor ever will be. Except that the LORD had shortened those days, there would be no flesh saved; but for the elect's sake, whom he has chosen, he will shorten those days.

"If anyone will say to you, 'Look, here is Christ,' or, 'Look, there he is,' do not believe him. For false Christs and false prophets will arise and will work great signs and wonders that, if it were possible, they would deceive the very elect. Look, I have told you all things beforehand. Therefore, if they will say to you, 'Behold, he is in the desert,' do not go out. If they say, 'Look, he is inside the rooms,' do not believe it. For as lightning comes from the east and flashes to the west, so also will the coming of the Son of Man be."

"Immediately after the tribulation of those days there will be signs in the sun, and in the moon, the sun will be darkened and the moon will not give its light, and the stars will fall from heaven; and on earth distress of nations, with perplexity; the sea and the waves roaring. Men's hearts failing for fear, for looking at the things that are coming upon the earth; for the powers of heaven will be shaken. "Then will the sign of the Son of Man appear in heaven; they will see the Son of Man coming in the clouds of heaven with power and great glory. Then all the tribes of the earth will mourn. He will send his angels with a great sound of a trumpet, and they will gather together his elect from the four winds, from the uttermost part of the earth to the uttermost part of heaven. When these things begin to come to pass, then look up, and lift up your heads, for your redemption draws near."

Then Jesus spoke a parable to them: "Observe the fig tree, and all the trees. When you see them shooting forth buds, you see and know yourselves that summer is near at hand, even at the door. Just so, when you see these things come to pass, you know that the kingdom of God is near at hand. Truly I say to you, this generation will not pass away until everything is fulfilled. Heaven and earth will pass away, but my words will not pass away. However, no one knows the day and hour, no, not the angels that are in heaven, nor the Son, but only my Father."

"Take heed to yourselves, watch and pray, because you do not know when that time is, lest at any time your hearts be weighed down with carousing and drunkenness and the cares of this life, so that the day comes upon you unawares. Pay attention, for the Son of Man is like a man taking a long journey, who left his house and gave authority to his servants, and to everyone his work, and commanded the doorkeeper to watch. Watch therefore, for you do not know when the master of the house will come. It may be in the evening, or at midnight, or when the cock crows, or in the morning; lest coming suddenly he finds you sleeping. For like a trap it will come on all those who dwell on the face of the whole earth. Watch therefore, and always pray that you may be counted worthy to escape all these things that will come to pass, and to stand before the Son of Man. What I say to you I say to everyone: 'Watch!'"

"Then again, the kingdom of heaven can be likened to ten virgins who took their lamps and went out to meet the bridegroom. Five of them were wise, and five were foolish. Those who were foolish took their lamps, but took no oil

with them, but the wise took oil in their vessels with their lamps.

"While the bridegroom was delayed, they all slumbered and slept. At midnight there was a cry: 'Look, the bridegroom is coming, go out to meet him!' Then all the virgins got up and trimmed their lamps. The foolish said to the wise, 'Give us some of your oil, for our lamps have gone out.' The wise answered, saying, 'No, lest there not be enough for both us and you, but you go instead to those that sell, and buy for yourselves.' While they went to buy, the bridegroom came, and those who were ready went in with him to the wedding; and the door was shut. Afterwards the other virgins also came, saying, 'Lord, Lord, open to us.' He answered and said, 'Truly I say to you, I do not know you.' Watch therefore, for you do not know either the day or the hour when the Son of Man will come."

"The kingdom of heaven is like a man traveling into a distant country, who called his servants and delivered to them his goods. To one he gave five talents, to another two, and to another one, to each man according to his ability; and immediately went on his journey.

"Then he who had received the five talents went and traded with them and made another five talents. Likewise he who had received two, he also gained another two. But he that had received one went and dug in the earth, and hid his lord's money.

"After a long time the lord of those servants came, and reckoned with them. Now he who had received five talents came and brought another five talents, saying, 'Lord, you delivered to me five talents, look, with them I have gained five more talents.' His lord said to him, 'Well done, you good and faithful servant; you have been faithful over a few things, I will make you ruler over many things; enter into the joy of your lord.'

"He also who had received two talents came and said, 'Lord, you delivered to me two talents, look, I have gained two other talents with them.' His lord said to him, 'Well done, good and faithful servant; you have been faithful over a few things, I will make you ruler over many things; enter into the joy of your lord.'

"Then he who had received the one talent came and said, 'Lord, I knew that you are a hard man, reaping where you have not sown, and gathering where you have not scattered; and I was afraid, and went and hid your talent in the earth, see, there you have what is yours.' His lord answered and said to him, 'You wicked and lazy servant, you knew that I reap where I did not sow, and gather where I have not scattered; you should therefore to have put my money with the bankers, and then at my coming I would have received my own back with interest. Therefore take the talent away from him, and give it to him who has ten talents. For to everyone that has more will be given, and he will have abundance; but from him who has not will be taken away even that which he has. And cast the unprofitable servant into outer darkness; there will be weeping and gnashing of teeth.'"

"When the Son of Man comes in his glory, and all the holy angels with him, then he will sit upon the throne of his glory. Before him will be gathered all nations; and he will separate them one from another, as a shepherd separates his sheep from the goats; and he will set the sheep on his right hand, and the goats on the left.

"Then the King will say to those on his right hand, 'Come, you blessed of my Father, inherit the kingdom prepared for you from the foundation of the world; for I was hungry, and you gave me food; I was thirsty, and you gave me drink; I was a stranger, and you took me in; naked, and you clothed me; I was sick, and you visited me; I was in prison, and you came to me.'

"Then the righteous will answer him, saying, 'Lord, when did we see you hungry, and fed you? Or thirsty, and gave you drink? When did we see you a stranger, and took you in? Or naked, and clothed you? Or when did we see you sick, or in prison, and came to you? The King will answer and say to them, 'Truly I say to you, inasmuch as you have done it to one of the least of my brothers, you have done it to me.'

"Then he will also say to those on the left hand, 'Depart from me, you cursed, into the everlasting fire prepared for the devil and his angels; for I was hungry, and you gave me no food; I was thirsty, and you gave me no drink; I was a stranger, and you did not take me in; naked, and you did not clothe me; sick, and in prison, and you did not visit me.'

"Then they will answer him, saying, 'Lord, when did we see you hungry, or thirsty, or a stranger, or naked, or sick, or in prison, and did not minister to you?' Then he will answer them, saying, 'Truly I say to you, inasmuch as you did not do it to one of the least of these, you did not do it to me.' These will go away to everlasting punishment, but the righteous to life eternal."

No Other NAME

During the day he was teaching in the temple, and at night he went out and stayed on the mount that is called the Mount of Olives. All the people came early in the morning to him in the temple to hear him. It came about, when Jesus had finished teaching, he said to his disciples, "You know that after two days is the Passover and the Feast of Unleavened Bread, and the Son of Man will be handed over to be crucified."

Then the chief priests, and the scribes, and the elders of the people assembled together in the palace of the high priest, who was called Caiaphas, and consulted together that they might take Jesus by deceit and put him to death. But they said, "Not during the feast lest there be an uproar among the people."

Then Satan entered into Judas, surnamed Iscariot, who was one of the twelve. He went and talked with the chief priests and captains, how he might betray him to them. He said to them, "What will you give me so that I will deliver him to you?" They were glad when they heard it, and agreed to give him money—thirty pieces of silver. He promised, and from that time on looked for an opportunity how he might conveniently betray Jesus to them in the absence of the multitude.

Then came the first day of the feast of unleavened bread, when the Passover must be killed. Jesus sent Peter and John, saying, "Go and prepare for us the Passover, that we may eat." They said to him, "Where will you have it that we prepare for you to eat the Passover?" He said to them, "Notice, when you have entered into the city, there a man will meet you carrying a pitcher of water, follow him into the house he enters. You shall say to the master of the house, 'The Master says to you, my time is at hand, where is the guest room at your house where I will eat the Passover with my disciples?' He will show you a large, furnished upper room; there make it ready." They went out, and came into the city and found it just as he had said to them; and they made the Passover ready.

Before the feast of the Passover, when Jesus knew that his hour had come that he would leave this world and go to the Father, having loved his own who were in the world, he loved them to the end. When the hour had come, he sat down and the twelve apostles with him, they sat and ate. As they were eating, he said to them, "With desire I have desired to eat this Passover with you before I suffer; for I say to you, I will no more eat of it until it is fulfilled in the kingdom of God. Jesus took the cup, and gave thanks, and said, "Take this, and divide it among yourselves." I say to you, I will not drink again of the fruit of the vine, until that day when I drink it new with you when the kingdom of God has come."

He took bread, and gave thanks, and broke it, and gave it to them, saying, "This is my body which is given for you; this do in remembrance of me." Likewise also the cup after supper, saying, "This cup is the new testament in my blood, which is shed for many for the remission of sins," and they all drank of it—the blood of the new testament.

When Jesus had said this, he was troubled in spirit, and testified, and said, "Indeed, I say to you, that one of you who eats with me will betray me; the hand of him who betrays me is with me on the table. Then the disciples looked at one another, and they were exceedingly sorrowful, not knowing of whom he spoke. They questioned among themselves which of them would do this thing. Every one of them began to say to him, "Lord, is it I?" He answered and said, "He that dips his hand with me in the dish will betray me. The Son of Man goes as it is written of him, but woe to that man by whom the Son of Man is betrayed. It would have been better for that man if he had not been born."

Now there was reclining against Jesus' chest one of his disciples, whom Jesus loved. Therefore Simon Peter gestured to him that he should ask who it was of whom he spoke. The one leaning against Jesus said to him, "Lord, who is it?" Jesus answered, "It is he to whom I will give a piece of bread when I have dipped it." When he had dipped the bread he gave it to Judas Iscariot, the son of Simon. Then Judas, who betrayed him, said, "Master, is it I?" Jesus said to him, "You have said it."

After Judas received the piece of bread Satan entered into him. Then Jesus said to him, "What you do, do quickly." No one at the table knew why he said this to him. For some of them thought, because Judas had the bag, that Jesus had said to him, "Buy the things we have need of for the feast, or, that he should give something to the poor." Immediately after having received the piece of bread, Judas went out; and it was night.

Supper being ended, the devil having already put it into the heart of Judas Iscariot, Simon's son, to betray him, Jesus, knowing that the Father had given all things into his hands, and that he had come from God and was going back to God, rose from supper, laid aside his garments, and took a towel and wrapped it around himself. After that he poured water into a basin and began to wash the disciples' feet, and to wipe them with the towel with which he had girded himself.

Then Jesus comes to Simon Peter, and Peter said to him, "Lord, are you washing my feet?" Jesus answered and said to him, "What I do you do not understand now, but later you will understand. Peter said to him, "You shall never wash my feet." Jesus answered him, "If I do not wash you, you have no part with me." Simon Peter said to him, "Lord, not only my feet, but also my hands and my head." Jesus said to him, "He who is bathed need only wash his feet and is completely clean; and you are clean, but not all of you." For he knew who would betray him, therefore he said, "You are not all clean."

So after he had washed their feet, and had taken up his garments and had sat down again, he said to them, "Do you know what I have done to you? You call me Master and Lord, and you say correctly, for so I am. If I then, your Lord and Master, have washed your feet, you should also wash one another's feet. For I have given you an example, that you should do as I have done to you.

"Indeed, I say to you, a servant is not greater than his lord, nor is he who is sent greater than he who sent him. If you know these things, blessed are you if you do them. I do not speak of you all, I know whom I have chosen, but so that the Scripture may be fulfilled: '*He who eats bread with me has lifted up his heel against me*' (Psalms 41:9).

Now I tell you before it happens, that when it comes to pass you may believe that I am he. Indeed, I say to you, he who receives whomever I send receives me, and he who receives me receives him who sent me."

Therefore, after Judas had gone out, Jesus said, "Now is the Son of Man glorified, and God is glorified in him. If God is glorified in him, God will also glorify him in himself, and will immediately glorify him. Little children, only a little while longer am I with you. You will look for me, and, as I said to the Jews, where I go you cannot come. So now I say to you, a new commandment I give to you, that you love one another. As I have loved you, you should also love one another. By this everyone will know that you are my disciples, if you have love one for another." Simon Peter said to him, "Lord, where are you going?" Jesus answered him, "Where I go, you cannot follow me now, but you will follow me afterwards." Peter said to him, "Lord, why can I not follow you now? I will lay down my life for your sake."

Then Jesus said to them, "All of you will stumble this night because of me, for it is written: '*I will strike the shepherd, and the sheep will be scattered*' (Zechariah 13:7). After I have risen again, I will go ahead of you into Galilee." Peter answered and said to him, "Though all men will stumble because of you, yet I will never stumble."

Jesus answered him, "Will you lay down your life for my sake? Indeed, I tell you, Peter, that this day, even this night, before the cock crows twice, you will have denied me three times." But he spoke all the more vehemently, "If I should die with you, I will not in any way deny you." All the disciples also said the same thing.

The Lord said, "Simon, Simon, indeed, Satan has desired to have you, that he may sift you as wheat; but I have prayed for you, that your faith will not fail, and when you have turned back again, strengthen your brothers."

There was a contention among them, about which of them would be counted as the greatest. Jesus said to them, "The kings of the Gentiles exercise lordship over them, and those who exercise authority over them are called benefactors. However, with you it will not be, he who is greatest among you let him be as the youngest, and he who leads, as he who serves. For who is the greater, he who sits at the table, or he who serves? Is it not he who sits at the table? But I am among you as one who serves.

"You are those who have continued with me in my trials. I appoint to you a kingdom, even as my Father has appointed one to me, that you may eat and drink at my table in my kingdom, and sit on thrones judging the twelve tribes of Israel."

"When I sent you without purse, or bag, or sandals, did you lack anything?" They said, "Nothing." Then he said to them, "But now, he who has a purse, let him take it, and also his bag, and he who has no sword, let him sell his cloak and buy one. For I say to you, that what is written of me must yet be fulfilled: '*And he was reckoned among the transgressors*' (Isaiah 53:12). For the things concerning me have an end." They said, "Lord, look, here are two swords." He said to them, "It is enough."

"*Do not let* your heart be troubled; you believe in God, believe also in me. In my Father's house are many rooms; if it were not so, I would have told you. I go to prepare a place for you. If I go and prepare a place for you, I will come again and receive you to myself; that where I am, there you may be also. Where I go you know, and the way you know." Thomas said to him, "Lord, we do not know where you go, so how can we know the way?" Jesus said to him, "I am the way, the truth, and the life; no man comes to the Father, except through me.[23]

"If you had known me, you would have known my Father also; and from now on you know him, and have seen him." Philip said to him, "Lord, show us the Father, and it will be enough for us." Jesus said to him, "Have I been with you for so long a time and still you have not known me, Philip?[24] He who has seen me has seen the Father, how then can you say, show us the Father? Do you not believe that I am in the Father, and the Father is in me? The words that I speak to you I do not speak from myself; but the Father who abides in me, he does the works. Believe me that I am in the Father and the Father is in me, or else believe me for the sake of the very works.

"Indeed, I say to you, he who believes in me, the works that I do he will also do, and greater works than these will he do because I go to my Father. Whatever you will ask in my name, I will do it, that the Father may be glorified in the Son. If you ask anything in my name, I will do it.

"If you love me, keep my commandments. I will ask the Father, and he will give you another Advocate, that he may abide with you forever, even the Spirit of truth, whom the world cannot receive, because it neither sees him, nor knows him; but you know him; for he abides with you, and will be in you. I will not leave you as orphans; I will come to you.

"After a little while, the world will see me no more, but you will see me; because I live, you will live also. At that day you will know that I am in my Father, and you in me, and I in you.

"He who has my commandments, and keeps them, it is he who loves me; and he who loves me will be loved by my Father, and I will love him, and will reveal myself to him." Judas (not Iscariot) said to him, "Lord, how is it that you will reveal yourself to us, and not to the world?" Jesus answered and said to him, "If a man loves me, he will keep my word; and my Father will love him, and we will come to him and make our home with him. He who does not love me does not keep my word, and the word that you hear is not mine, but the Father's who sent me.

"These things I have spoken to you, still being present with you. The Advocate, which is the Holy Spirit, whom the Father will send in my name, he will teach you all things, and bring whatever I have said to you to your remembrance.

"Peace I leave with you, my peace I give to you, not as the world gives do I give to you. Do not let your heart be troubled, nor let it be afraid. You have heard how I said to you, I go away, and come again to you. If you loved me, you would rejoice, because I said, I go to the Father; for my Father is greater than I. So I have told you before it comes to pass, that when it comes to pass you may believe. After this I will not talk much with you because the ruler of this world is coming and he has nothing in me. But that the world may know that I love the Father, and as the Father commanded me, that I do. Arise! Let us go from here."

"*I am the* true vine, and my Father is the vine-dresser. Every branch in me that does not bear fruit he takes away, and every branch that bears fruit, he prunes so that it may bear even more fruit. You are clean through the word that I have spoken to you. Abide in me, and I in you. As the branch cannot bear fruit of itself, except it abide in the vine; neither can you, except you abide in me. I am the vine, you are the branches; he who abides in me, and I in him, the same bears much fruit; for without me you can do nothing.

"If a man does not abide in me he is thrown out as a branch and withers, and men gather them up and cast them into the fire, and they are burned. If you abide in me and my words abide in you, you will ask what you will and it shall be done for you. In this is my Father glorified, that you bear much fruit, so you will be my disciples. As the Father has loved me, so have I loved you; continue in my love. If you keep my commandments, you will abide in my love, even as I have kept my Father's commandments and abide in his love.

"These things I have spoken to you that my joy may remain in you, and that your joy may be full. This is my commandment, that you love one another as I have loved you. Greater love has no man than this, that a man lays down his life for his friends. You are my friends if you do whatever I command you. After this I will not call you servants, for the servant does not know what his lord does; but I have called you friends, for all things that I heard from my Father I have made known to you. You did not choose me, but I have chosen you and appointed you, that you should go and bear fruit, and that your fruit should remain; that whatever you will ask from the Father in my name,²⁵ he may give it to you. These things I command you, that you love one another.

"If the world hates you, you know that it hated me before it hated you. If you were of the world, the world would love its own, but because you are not of the world, but I have chosen you out of the world, the world hates you. Remember the word that I said to you, 'The servant is not greater than his lord.' If they have persecuted me, they will also persecute you; if they have kept my sayings, they will also keep yours. All these things they will do to you for my name's sake, because they do not know him who sent me. If I had not come and spoken to them, they would not have sin, but now they have no cover for their sin. He who hates me also hates my Father. If I had not done the works which no other man did among them, they would not have had sin; but now they have seen and hated both me and my Father. But this comes to pass that the word may be fulfilled that is written in their law: '*They hated me without a cause*' (Psalms 35:19). When the Advocate has come, whom I will send to you from the Father, even the Spirit of truth who proceeds from the Father, he shall testify of me. You will also bear witness, because you have been with me from the beginning.

"These things I have spoken to you, that you should not stumble. They will put you out of the synagogues; yes, the time is coming that whoever kills you will think that he does a service to God. These things they will do to you, because they have not known the Father, nor me. I have told you these things that when the time comes, you may remember that I told you of them. These things I did not say to you at the beginning, because I was with you."

"Now I will go to him who sent me, and none of you asks me, 'Where are you going?' But because I have said these things to you, your hearts are filled with sorrow. However, I tell you the truth, it is better for you that I go away, for if I do not go away, the Advocate will not come to you, but if I depart, I will send him to you. When he has come, he will convict the world of sin, and of righteousness, and of judgment. Of sin, because they do not believe in me. Of righteousness, because I go to my Father, and you see me no more. Of judgment, because the ruler of this world has been judged.

"I have still many things to say to you, but you cannot bear them now. When he, the Spirit of truth, has come, he will guide you into all truth, for he will not speak from himself, but whatever he will hear, that he will speak; and he will show you things to come. He will glorify me, for he will take of mine and will show it to you. All things that the Father has are mine, therefore I said that he will take of mine, and will declare it to you."

"A little while, and you will not see me; and again, a little while, and you will see me, because I go to the Father." Then some of his disciples said among themselves, "What is this that he said to us, 'A little while, and you will not see me; and again, a little while, and you will see me'; and, 'because I go to the Father'?" Therefore they said, "What is this that he said, 'A little while'? We do not understand what he says." Jesus knew that they were wanting to ask him, and said to them, "Do you question among yourselves that I said, 'A little while, and you will not see me; and again, a little while, and you will see me'? Indeed, I say to you, that you will weep and wail, but the world will rejoice; and you will be sorrowful, but your sorrow will be turned to joy. A woman when she is in labor has sorrow, because her time has come; but as soon as she is delivered of the child she no more remembers the suffering for the joy that a child is born into the world. You presently have sorrow; but I will see you again, and your heart will rejoice; and your joy no one can take from you."

"In that day you will ask me nothing. Indeed, I say to you, whatever you will ask the Father in my name, he will give it to you.[25] Until now you have asked nothing in my name; ask, and you will receive it, that your joy may be full. These things I have spoken to you in riddles; but the time comes when I will no longer speak to you in riddles, but I will plainly show you from the Father. At that day you will ask in my name;[25] and I do not say to you that I will ask the Father for you; for the Father himself loves you because you have loved me and have believed that I came from God. I came from the Father and have come into the world; again, I will leave the world and go to the Father." His disciples said to him, "See, now you speak plainly, and speak no riddle. Now are we sure that you know all things, and no one need ask you; by this we believe that you came from God." Jesus answered them, "Do you now believe? Indeed, the hour comes, yes, it has now come, that you will be scattered, each to his own and will leave me alone; but I am not alone, because the Father is with me. These things

I have spoken to you, that in me you may have peace. In the world you will have tribulation; but be happy, I have overcome the world."

***Jesus spoke** these* words, and, lifting his eyes to heaven, said, "Father, the hour has come; glorify your Son, that your Son may also glorify you. As you have given him power over all flesh, that he should give eternal life to as many as you have given him. This is eternal life, that they may know you the only true God, and Jesus Christ, whom you have sent. I have glorified you on the earth; I have finished the work that you gave me to do. Now, O Father, glorify me with your own self with the glory which I had with you before the world existed. I have manifested your name to those whom you gave me out of the world; yours they were, and you gave them to me, and they have kept your word. They know that everything you have given me is from you. For I have given to them the words which you gave me, and they have received them, and know surely that I came from you, and they have believed that you sent me.

"I pray for them; I do not pray for the world, but for those whom you have given me, for they are yours. All mine are yours, and yours are mine, and I am glorified in them. I am no longer in the world, but these are in the world, and I come to you. Holy Father, keep through your own name those whom you have given me, that they may be one, as we are one. While I was with them in the world, I kept them in your name; those whom you gave me I have kept and not one of them is lost, except the son of perdition, that the Scripture may be fulfilled.

"I come to you, and these things I speak in the world that they may have my joy fulfilled in themselves. I have given them your word, and the world has hated them, because they are not of the world, even as I am not of the world. I do not ask that you would take them out of the world, but that you would keep them from the evil one. They are not of the world, even as I am not of the world. Sanctify them through your truth; your word is truth. As you have sent me into the world, even so I have also sent them into the world. For their sakes I sanctify myself, that they might also be sanctified through the truth.

"Neither do I ask for these alone, but also for those who will believe in me through their word, that they may all be one, as you, Father, are in me, and I in you; that they may also be one in us, that the world may believe that you have sent me. The glory which you gave me I have given to them, that they may be one, even as we are one; I in them, and you in me, that they may be made perfect in one, and that the world may know that you have sent me, and have loved them as you have loved me.

"Father, I also want that those, whom you have given me, be with me where I am, that they may see my glory, which you have given me; for you loved me before the foundation of the world. O righteous Father, the world has not known you; but I have known you, and these have known that you have sent me. I have declared to them your name, and will declare it; that the love with which you have loved me may be in them, and I in them."

When Jesus had spoken these words, and when they had sung a hymn, he went out with his disciples over the brook Kidron, to the mount of Olives, where there was a garden called Gethsemane, into which he entered, and his disciples followed him. When he was at the place, he said to them, "Sit here while I go and pray over there, and pray that you do not enter into temptation."

He took with him Peter and the two sons of Zebedee, James and John, and began to be sorrowful and very distressed. Then he said to them, "My soul is extremely sorrowful, even to death; wait here and watch with me." He withdrew from them about a stone's throw, knelt down and fell on his face and prayed, saying, "O Abba, my Father, if it be possible, let this hour pass from me. If you are willing, remove this cup from me; nevertheless, not my will, but yours be done." There appeared an angel from heaven strengthening him. Being in agony he prayed more earnestly; and his sweat was as it were great drops of blood falling down to the ground. When he arose from prayer and came to his disciples, he found them sleeping from sorrow, and said to Peter, "What, could you not watch with me one hour? Arise and pray, that you do not enter into temptation; indeed the spirit is willing, but the flesh is weak."

He went away again the second time, and prayed, saying, "O my Father, if this cup will not pass from me unless I drink it, your will be done." He came to the disciples and found them asleep again, for their eyes were heavy; and they did not know what to answer. He left them, and went away again, and prayed the third time, saying the same words. Then he came to his disciples, and finding them asleep for the third time, said, "Sleep on now and take your rest; it is enough. The time has arrived and the Son of Man is being betrayed into the hands of sinners. Arise, let us be going, look, he who betrays me is here."

Judas also, who betrayed Jesus, knew the place, for Jesus often met there with his disciples. So Judas, having gotten a great cohort of soldiers and officers from the chief priests and Pharisees, came there with lanterns and torches, swords and clubs, and other weapons.

He who betrayed him had given them a sign, saying, "Whomever I kiss, that is the one, take him, hold him securely, and lead him away safely." As soon as he came he went straight away to him, and said, "Master, Master," and kissed him. Jesus said to him, "Judas, will you betray the Son of Man with a kiss?"

Jesus, knowing everything that would come upon him, went forward and said to them, "Whom do you seek?" They answered him, "Jesus of Nazareth." Jesus said to them, "I am he." Judas also, who betrayed him, stood with them. As soon as he had said to them, "I am[26] he," they pulled back and fell to the ground.

Then he asked them again, "Whom do you seek?" They said, "Jesus of Nazareth." Jesus answered, "I have told you that I am he, therefore, if you seek me, let these go their way"; that the saying which he spoke might be fulfilled: "Of those whom you gave me I have lost none."

Then Jesus said to the chief priests, and captains of the temple, and the elders, who had come to him, "You have come out as against a thief, with swords and clubs? When I was with you in the temple every day, you did not stretch out your hands against me; but this is your hour, and the power of darkness." All this was done, that the Scriptures of the Prophets might be fulfilled.

When those who were with Jesus saw what would follow, they said to him, "Lord, should we strike with the sword?" Then Simon Peter, having a sword drew it, and struck the high priest's servant and cut off his right ear—the servant's name was Malchus. Then Jesus said to Peter, "Put away your sword into its sheath, for all those who take the sword will perish by the sword; shall I not drink the cup that my Father has given me?" Jesus then said, "Enough, allow even this. Do you think that I cannot ask my Father, and he will quickly send me more than twelve legions of angels?" He touched his ear, and healed him.

Then the soldiers and the captain and officers of the Jews took Jesus, and bound him; then all the disciples abandoned him and ran away. A certain young man followed him, having a linen cloth wrapped around his naked body, and young men seized him; and he left the linen cloth and ran away naked.

They led Jesus away to Annas first, for he was father-in-law to Caiaphas, who was the high priest that year. It was Caiaphas who counseled the Jews that it was expedient that one man should die for all the people.

Simon Peter followed Jesus, and so did another disciple. Now that disciple was known to the high priest, and went in with Jesus into the palace of the high priest. Peter stood outside at the door. Then the other disciple, who was known to the high priest, went out and spoke to her who kept the door, and brought Peter in.

Then the servant girl who kept the door said to Peter, "Are you not one of this man's disciples also?" He said, "I neither know nor understand what you are saying," and a cock crowed.

The servants and officers stood there; they had made a fire of coals for it was cold, and they warmed themselves; and Peter stood with them and warmed himself. The high priest then asked Jesus about his disciples, and about his doctrine. Jesus answered him, "I spoke openly to the world. I always taught in the synagogues, and in the temple, where the Jews always come together; I have said nothing in secret. Why ask me? Ask those who heard me what I have said to them. Indeed, they know what I said." When he had said this, one of the officers who stood by struck Jesus with the palm of his hand, saying, "Is that how you answer the high priest?" Jesus answered him, "If I have spoken wrong, bear witness of the wrong, but if well, why did you strike me?" Then Annas sent him bound to Caiaphas the high priest.

Then those who had seized Jesus took him, and, leading him, brought him to Caiaphas, into the high priest's house, where the scribes and the elders were assembled.

Now the chief priests, and elders, and all the council, sought false testimony against Jesus in order to put him to death, but found none. Many false witnesses came forward, yet they found none, for even though many bore false witness against him, their testimonies did not agree one with another. At last two false witnesses came, and said, "This man said, 'I am able to destroy the temple of God that is made with hands, and within three days I will build another made without hands." But neither did their testimonies agree with each other.

The high priest arose and said to him, "Do you answer nothing? What is it that these testify against you?" Jesus held his peace and answered nothing. The high priest said to him, "I adjure you by the living God, that you tell us whether you are the Christ, the Son of God." Jesus said to him, "You have said it. Nevertheless, I say to you, 'From now on you will see the Son of Man sitting at the right hand of the Power, and coming on the clouds of heaven.' "

Then the high priest tore his clothes, saying, "He has spoken blasphemy, what further need do we have for witnesses? See, now you have heard his blasphemy. What do you think?" They all condemned him and said, "He is guilty of death!" Then they spat in his face, and they beat him with their fists, and others struck him with the palms of their hands. When they had blindfolded him, they struck him on the face and asked him, saying, "Prophesy to us Christ, who was it that struck you?" And many other blasphemous things they spoke against him.

As Peter was below in the palace courtyard warming himself, a certain maid saw Peter and intently looked at him, and said, "This man was also with Jesus of Nazareth." He denied it with an oath, saying, "Woman, I do not know him." In about an hour, one of the servants of the high priest, being a relation of him whose ear Peter had cut off, said, "Did I not see you in the garden with him?" He then confidently affirmed it, saying, "Indeed this man was with Jesus, for he is a Galilean and your speech betrays you." Peter began to curse and to swear, saying, "I do not know this man of whom you speak. I do not know what you are saying." Immediately, while he still spoke, the cock crowed the second time. The Lord turned and looked at Peter. And Peter remembered the word of the Lord, how he had said to him, "Before the cock crows twice, you will deny me three times." When Peter thought about it he went out and wept bitterly.

When morning had come, as soon as it was day, all the chief priests and elders of the people immediately held a consultation and took counsel against Jesus to put him to death. They came together and led him away into their council, saying, "Are you the Christ? Tell us."

Jesus said to them, "If I tell you, you will not believe me. If I ask you, you will not answer me, nor let me go. From now on you will see the Son of Man seated at the right hand of the power of God."

Then Judas, who had betrayed Jesus, when he saw that he had been condemned, repented, and brought back the thirty pieces of silver to the chief priests and elders, saying, "I have sinned. I have betrayed innocent blood." They said, "What concern is that to us? You deal with it." He threw down the pieces of silver in the temple, and left, and went and hanged himself. The chief priests took the silver pieces, and said, "It is not lawful for us to put them into the treasury, because it is the price of blood." They took counsel, and bought the potter's field with them, to bury strangers in. Therefore the field was called, "The Field of Blood," to this day.

Then was fulfilled that which was spoken by Jeremiah the prophet, saying:

They took the thirty pieces of silver, the value of him who was priced, whom those of the children of Israel set a value, and gave them for the potter's field, as the LORD *appointed me* (Zechariah 11:12-13).

The whole multitude of them arose and led Jesus from Caiaphas to the Praetorium and delivered him to Pilate. It was early; and they themselves did not enter into the Praetorium, lest they should be defiled, but that they might eat the Passover.

Pilate then went out to them, and said, "What accusation do you bring against this man?" They answered and said to him, "If he were not a criminal, we would not have brought him before you." Then Pilate said to them, "Take him yourselves and judge him according to your law." Therefore they said to him, "It is not lawful for us to put anyone to death," that the word of Jesus might be fulfilled, which he spoke signifying what death he would die.

Then Pilate entered into the Praetorium again, and called Jesus, and he stood before Pilate the governor. The Jews began to accuse him, saying, "We found this man perverting the nation, forbidding to give tax-tribute to Caesar, and saying that he himself is Christ, a King." When he was accused by the chief priests and elders, he answered nothing. Then Pilate said to him, "Do you not hear how many things they testify against you?" But he never answered him a word, so that Pilate the governor greatly marveled.

Pilate said to him, "Are you the King of the Jews?" Jesus answered him, "Do you say this on your own, or did others tell you about me?" Pilate answered, "Am I a

Jew? Your own nation and the chief priests have brought you to me; what have you done?" Jesus answered, "My kingdom is not of this world, if my kingdom were of this world, then my servants would fight, so that I should not be delivered to the Jews; but now my kingdom is not from here." Therefore Pilate said to him, "Are you a king then?" Jesus answered, "You say correctly that I am a king. To this end was I born, and for this cause I came into the world, that I should testify to the truth. Everyone who is of the truth hears my voice." Pilate said to him, "What is truth?" When he had said this, he went out again to the Jews, and said to them, "I find no fault in this man at all. They were all the more insistent, saying, "He stirs up the people, teaching throughout all Judea, beginning from Galilee to this place."

When Pilate heard Galilee, he asked whether the man were a Galilean. As soon as he knew that he belonged to Herod's jurisdiction, he sent him to Herod, who also was in Jerusalem at that time.

When Herod saw Jesus he was very happy, for he had wanted to see him for a long time, because he had heard many things about him, and he hoped to see some miracle performed by him.

Then he questioned him with many words, but he answered him nothing. The chief priests and scribes stood by and vehemently accused him.

Herod with his men of war treated him with contempt, and mocked him, and clothed him in a gorgeous robe, and sent him back again to Pilate. That same day Pilate and Herod became friends, because before they had hostility between themselves.

Pilate, when he had called the chief priests and the rulers and the people together, said to them, "You have brought this man to me, as one that misleads the people, and, see, I have examined him and have found no fault in this man concerning those things of which you accuse him; no, neither did Herod, for I sent you to him and, see, he has done nothing worthy of death. Therefore, I will flog him and release him."

Now at that feast the governor was obliged to release to the people one prisoner, whom they desired. Crying loudly the crowd began to demand him to do as he had always done for them. And they then had a notorious prisoner called Barabbas. Now Barabbas was a robber who was chained in prison along with those who had made a violent, seditious uprising with him, and who had committed murder during the uprising.

Therefore, when they were all gathered together, Pilate said to them, "Whom do you want me to release to you? Barabbas, or Jesus who is called Christ, the King of the Jews?" For he knew that they had delivered him up because of envy. Then they all cried out again, saying, "Not this man, but Barabbas."

When Pilate had sat down on the judgment seat, his wife sent to him, saying, "Have nothing to do with that righteous man; I have suffered many things in a dream today because of him." However, the chief priests and elders persuaded the crowd that they should ask for Barabbas, and destroy Jesus. The governor answered and said to them, "Which of the two do you want me to release to you?" They said, "Barabbas!"

Therefore Pilate, wanting to release Jesus, said to them, "What then will I do with Jesus who is called Christ?" They all say to him, "Let him be crucified." The governor said to them the third time, "Why, what evil has he done?" But they cried out all the more vehemently, saying, "Crucify him! Crucify him!" And their voices, and those of the chief priests, prevailed.

Then Pilate, wanting to placate the people, saw that he could accomplish nothing, but rather an uproar was beginning, pronounced sentence that it should be as they required; and he gave Jesus up to their will. Pilate took water, and washed his hands before the crowd, saying, "I am innocent of the blood of this righteous person, you see to it." Then all the people answered, and said, "His blood be on us, and on our children." Then he released Barabbas to them.

Then Pilate took Jesus and had him flogged. The soldiers twisted together a crown of thorns and put it on his head. On him they also put a purple robe, and said, "Hail, King of the Jews!" And they struck him with their hands.

Pilate went out to them again, and said, "Here, I bring him out to you, that you may know that I find no fault in him."

Then Jesus came out wearing the crown of thorns, and the purple robe. Pilate said to them, "Behold the man!" When the chief priests and officers saw him, they cried out, saying, "Crucify him! Crucify him!" Pilate said to them, "You take him and crucify him; I find no fault in him." The Jews answered him, "We have a law, and by our law he ought to die, because he made himself out to be the Son of God."

When Pilate heard those words, he was even more afraid, and went again into the Praetorium and said to Jesus, "Where are you from?" But Jesus gave him no answer. Then Pilate said to him, "Will you not speak to me? Do you not know that I have power to crucify you, and have power to set you free?" Jesus answered, "You could have no power at all against me unless it were given to you from above; therefore he who delivered me over to you has the greater sin."

From that time Pilate tried to release him, but the Jews cried out, saying, "If you let this man go, you are not Caesar's friend; whoever makes himself a king stands in opposition to Caesar." Therefore, when Pilate heard that, he brought Jesus out, and sat down in the Praetorium in a place that is called the Pavement, but in the Hebrew, Gabbatha. It was the preparation day for the Passover, and about the sixth hour. He said to the Jews, "Behold your King!"

They cried out, "Away with him! Away with him! Crucify him!" Pilate said to them, "Shall I crucify your King?" The chief priest answered, "We have no king except Caesar." Then he gave Jesus to them to be crucified.

Then the soldiers of the governor took Jesus into the common hall, called the Praetorium; and gathered together to him the whole cohort of soldiers. They put a reed in his right hand, and bowing down before him, began to salute him, mockingly worshiped him, saying, "Hail, King of the Jews!" They spat on him, and then took the reed and struck him on the head with it.

After they had mocked him, they took the robe off of him, and put his own clothes on him, and then led him away to crucify him. Bearing his cross he set out to a place called the Place of a Skull, which is called in Hebrew, *Golgotha*.

As they led him away, they laid hold of a certain man, Simon, a Cyrenian, the father of Alexander and Rufus, coming from the country, and on him they laid the cross, compelling him to bear it after Jesus. There followed him a great crowd of people, and of women, who also mourned and lamented him.

Turning to them Jesus said, "Daughters of Jerusalem, weep not for me, but weep for yourselves and for your children. For indeed, the days are coming, in which they will say, "Blessed are the barren, and the wombs that never bore, and the breasts that never nursed. Then they will begin to say to the mountains, *'Fall on us,' and to the hills, 'Cover us'* (Hosea 10:8). For if they do these things to the green tree, what will be done to the dry?"

There were also two others, thieves, led away with him to be put to death. When they had come to the place that is called Calvary, they gave him wine mingled with myrrh to drink; and when he had tasted it, he would not drink it.

There they crucified him, and the two thieves with him, one on the right hand, and the other on the left, with Jesus in the middle. And the Scripture was fulfilled, that said: "*He was numbered with the transgressors*" (Isaiah 53:12). It was the third hour. Then Jesus said, "Father, forgive them, for they do not know what they are doing."

Then the soldiers, when they had crucified Jesus, took his garments, and divided them into four parts, a part to each soldier, and also his tunic; now the tunic was without a seam, woven as a single piece from the top down. Therefore they said among themselves, "Let us not tear it, but cast lots for it, whose it shall be"; that the Scripture might be fulfilled, which said: *"They divided my garments among them, and for my clothing they cast lots"* (Psalms 22:18). These things the soldiers did.

The people stood watching him. Those that passed by reviled him, shaking their heads and saying, "You who destroyed the temple, and rebuilt it in three days, save yourself." Likewise the chief priests also mocked him, along with the scribes and elders, saying, "He saved others, but himself he cannot save. If he is the King of Israel, let him come down from the cross now and we will believe him. He trusted in God; let him deliver him now, if he will have him; for he said, I am the Son of God." The people with them also derided him, saying, "He saved others, let him save himself if he is Christ, the chosen of God. If you are the Son of God, come down from the cross!" The soldiers also mocked him, coming to him and offering him vinegar, and saying, "If you are the king of the Jews, save yourself."

One of the thieves who were hanged railed at him, saying, "If you are Christ, save yourself and us." The other, answering, rebuked him, saying, "Do you not fear God, seeing that you are under the same condemnation? And we indeed rightly, for we are receiving the just reward for our deeds; but this man has done nothing wrong." He said to Jesus, "Lord, remember me when you come into your kingdom." Jesus said to him, "Truly, I say to you today,[27] you will be with me in Paradise."

Pilate wrote a title, a superscription of the accusation, and put it over his head on the cross. The writing was: "This is Jesus of Nazareth the King of the Jews," and it was written in Hebrew, Greek, and Latin. Then the chief priests of the Jews said to Pilate, "Do not write, 'The King of the Jews,' but that he said, 'I am King of the Jews.'"

Pilate answered, "What I have written I have written." Then many of the Jews read this title, because the place where Jesus was crucified was near to the city.

There stood by the cross of Jesus his mother, and his mother's sister, Mary the wife of Clopas, and Mary Magdalene. When Jesus saw his mother, and the disciple whom he loved standing near, he said to his mother, "Woman, observe your son!" Then he said to the disciple, "Observe your mother!" From that time that disciple took her into his own home.

It was about the sixth hour, and there was darkness over all the earth until the ninth hour. About the ninth hour Jesus cried out with a loud voice, saying, "*Eli, Eli, lama sabachthani?*" That, being interpreted, is to say, "My God, my God, why have you forsaken me?"

When they heard that, some of those who stood there, said, "This man calls for Elijah!" After this, Jesus knowing that everything was now accomplished, said, that the Scripture might be fulfilled, "*I thirst!*" Now sitting there was a vessel full of vinegar, and immediately one of them ran, took a sponge, filled it with vinegar, and putting it on a reed, he put it to his mouth to drink. The rest said,

"Leave it alone, let us see whether Elijah will come to save him, to take him down."

Therefore, when Jesus had received the vinegar, he said, "It is finished!" When Jesus had cried out with a loud voice, he said, "Father, into your hands I commit my spirit"; and after having said this, he bowed his head, and gave up the Spirit.

The sun was darkened, and the veil of the temple was torn in two, in the middle, from the top to the bottom. The earth shook, and the rocks split; and graves came open and many bodies of the saints who slept were raised, and after his resurrection came out of their graves and went into the holy city, appearing to many.

When the centurion, who stood facing him, heard him cry out and give up his Spirit, and all those who were with him guarding Jesus saw the earthquake and the things that were done, they were exceedingly fearful and glorified God, saying, "Certainly this was a truly righteous man! This man was the Son of God!"

All the people who had come together to watch that sight, seeing the things that were done, returned home beating their breasts. All his acquaintances, and the women that followed him from Galilee, stood a short distance away watching these things, among whom was Mary Magdalene, and Mary the mother of James the less and of Joses, and Salome, and the mother of Zebedee's children. Many other women, who followed Jesus from Galilee and ministered to his needs were there, watching from a distance.

The Jews, because it was the preparation day, so that the bodies would not remain on the cross on the Sabbath (for that Sabbath day was a high day), asked Pilate that their legs might be broken, so that they might be taken away.

Then the soldiers came and broke the legs of the first, and then of the other thief who was crucified with him. But when they came to Jesus and saw that he was already dead, they did not break his legs.

One of the soldiers with a spear pierced his side, and immediately there came out blood and water. He who saw this bears witness, and his testimony is true; and he knows that he is telling the truth, that you may believe.

For these things were done that the Scripture should be fulfilled: "*Not a bone of him will be broken*" (Psalms 34:20). Again another Scripture says: "*They will look upon him whom they have pierced*" (Zechariah 12:10).

After this came a rich man named Joseph—from Arimathea, a city of the Jews—an honorable counselor, and he was a good man and righteous, who himself also waited for the kingdom of God. He had not consented to the deed of those of the counsel.

Joseph, being a disciple of Jesus, but secretly for fear of the Jews, went boldly in to Pilate and asked that he might take away the body of Jesus. Pilate marveled that he was already dead; and calling the centurion he asked him whether he had been dead for a while. When he ascertained it from the centurion, Pilate ordered the body to be handed over. Therefore Joseph came and took the body of Jesus.

He bought fine linen, and took Jesus down and wrapped him in a clean linen cloth. Also Nicodemus came, who had at first come to Jesus at night, and he brought a mixture of myrrh and aloes, about a hundred pounds in weight. Then they took the body of Jesus, and wound it in linen cloths with the spices, as is the customary burial manner of the Jews.

Now in the place where he was crucified there was a garden, and in the garden Joseph had hewn out of the rock his own tomb, where no man was ever laid before. There they laid Jesus because of the Jews' preparation day, because the tomb was near at hand, and they rolled a great stone over the door of the tomb and left. And the Sabbath drew near.

The women also, Mary Magdalene and Mary the mother of Joses, who came with him from Galilee, followed behind. Sitting over against the tomb, watched how his body was laid. They returned home and prepared spices and ointments, and rested on the Sabbath day according to the commandment.

The next day, which followed the day of the preparation, the chief priests and Pharisees came to Pilate together, saying, "Sir, we remember that the deceiver said, while he was still alive, after three days I will rise again. Therefore, order that the tomb be made secure until the third day, lest his disciples come at night and steal him away, and say to the people he has risen from the dead; so that the last deceit will be worse than the first one."

Pilate said to them, "You have guards, go and make it as secure as you can." So they went and made the tomb secure, sealing the stone and setting a watch.

When the Sabbath was past, very early in the morning as it began to dawn toward the first day of the week, suddenly there was a great earthquake and the angel of the Lord descended from heaven, and came and rolled back the stone from the door, and sat upon it. His face shone like lightning, and his clothing was as white as snow. The guards shook with fear of him, and became as dead men.

Mary Magdalene, and Mary the mother of James the less, and Salome, came to the tomb early, while it was still dark, at the rising of the sun, bringing the spices that they and certain others with them had prepared, that they might come and anoint him.

They said among themselves, "Who will roll away the stone from the door of the tomb for us?" When they looked, they found that the stone was already rolled away; and it was a very great stone. They entered in, and did not find the body of the Lord Jesus.

It came to pass, as they were much puzzled about it, suddenly they saw a young man sitting on the right side, clothed in a long white, shining garment. They were afraid and bowed their faces down to the earth. He said to them, "Do not be frightened, you seek Jesus of Nazareth, who was crucified. Why do you look for the living among the dead? He is not here, but has risen as he said. Come, see the place where they laid him. Remember how he spoke to you when he was still in Galilee, saying, 'The Son of Man must be delivered into the hands of sinful men and be crucified, and the third day rise again from the dead.'" And they remembered his words.

He said to them, "Go your way, tell his disciples and Peter that he goes before you into Galilee; there you will see him, like he said to you." They went out quickly, and ran from the tomb, for they were trembling with amazement, neither did they say anything to anyone, because they were afraid.

Then Mary Magdalene ran, and returned from the tomb, and told all these things to the eleven, and to all the rest. It was Mary Magdalene, and Joanna, and Mary the mother of James, and other women that were with them, who told these things to the apostles. Their words seemed to them like idle tales, and they did not believe them.

Mary Magdalene came to Simon Peter, and to the other disciple, whom Jesus loved, and said to them, "They have taken away the Lord out of the tomb, and we do not know where they have laid him." Therefore Peter arose and ran out, and the other disciple also, and came to the tomb. They both ran together, and the other disciple outran Peter and came first to the tomb. He, stooping down and looking in, saw the linen cloths lying there, but he did not enter in.

Then came Simon Peter after him, and went into the tomb and sees the linen cloths laid by themselves, and the napkin that was around his head not with the linen cloths, but wrapped up together in a place by itself. Peter wondered within himself at that which had come to pass.

Then the other disciple, who came first to the tomb, went in also, and he saw, and believed. For as yet they did not know the Scripture, that he must rise again from the dead. Then the disciples left again and went to their own homes.

After Jesus was risen early on the first day of the week, he appeared first to Mary Magdalene, out of whom he had cast seven demons.

Mary was standing outside the tomb weeping, and as she wept she stooped down and looked into the tomb. She saw two angels clothed in white, sitting one at the head, and the other at the feet, where the body of Jesus had lain. They say to her, "Woman, why do you weep?" She said to them, "Because they have taken away my Lord, and I do not know where they have laid him." When she had said that, she turned around and saw Jesus standing there, and did not know that it was Jesus.

Jesus said to her, "Woman, why do you weep? Whom do you seek?" She, supposing him to be the gardener, said to him, "Sir, if you have taken him from here, tell me where you have laid him and I will take him away."

Jesus said to her, "Mary." She turned and said to him, "Rabboni!" Which means "Teacher!" Jesus said to her, "Do not touch me, for I have not yet ascended to my Father; but go to my brothers and say to them, I ascend to my Father, and your Father, and to my God, and your God." Mary Magdalene came and told the disciples as they mourned and wept that she had seen the Lord, and that he had spoken these things to her. They, when they had heard that he was alive and had been seen by her, did not believe it.

Other women, as they went to tell his disciples, Jesus suddenly met them, saying, "Rejoice!" And they came and held him by the feet, and worshiped him. Then Jesus said to them, "Do not be afraid, but go and tell my brothers that they should go into Galilee, and there they will see me."

As they were going, some of the guards came into the city and explained to the chief priests all the things that had taken place. When they were assembled together with the elders, and had taken advice, they gave large sums of money to the soldiers, saying, "Tell them his disciples came at night, and took him away while we slept. If the governor comes to hear of this, we will persuade him, and protect you." So they took the money and did as they were told; and this saying is commonly reported among the Jews until this day.

After that Jesus appeared in another form to two of them, as they walked, and went into the country.

Two of them went that day to a village called Emmaus, which was about seven miles from Jerusalem. They talked together about all these things that had happened. It came to pass, that, while they talked together and debated, Jesus himself drew near, and went along with them. But their eyes were restrained so that they should not recognize him. Jesus said to them, "What manner of conversation is this that you have one with another as you walk, and are so sad?"

One of them, whose name was Clopas, answering, said to Jesus, "Are you only a stranger in Jerusalem, and do not know the things that have come to pass within the past few days?"

He said to them, "What things?" They said to him, "Concerning Jesus of Nazareth, who was a prophet mighty in deed and word before God and all the people; and how the chief priests and our rulers delivered him up to be condemned to death, and have crucified him.

"We trusted that it was he who would redeem Israel; and besides this, today is the third day since these things were done. Yes, and certain women of our company, who were at the tomb early, also made us astonished. When they did not find his body, they came saying that they had also seen a vision of angels, who said that he was alive. Some of those who were with us went to the tomb and found it just as the women had said; but him they did not see."

Then Jesus said to them, "O foolish ones, and slow of heart to believe all that the prophets have spoken. It was necessary for Christ to have suffered these things, and to enter into his glory!" And beginning with Moses and all the Prophets, he expounded to them in all the Scriptures the things concerning himself.

They drew near to the village where they were going, and he made as though he would have gone further. They persuaded him, saying, "Stay with us, for it is near evening, and the day is almost gone." He went in to stay with them.

It came to pass, as he sat at a table with them, he took bread, and blessed it, and broke it, and gave it to them. Their eyes were opened, and they knew him; and he vanished from their sight. They said one to another, "Did not our hearts burn within us, when he talked with us on the way, and when he opened the Scriptures to us?"

They immediately rose up and returned to Jerusalem, and found the eleven gathered together, and with those who were with them, saying, "The Lord has indeed risen, and has appeared to Simon." They told of the things that were done on the way, and how he was made known to them in the breaking of the bread. The others did not believe them either.

In the evening of that same day, it being the first day of the week, the doors being shut where the disciples were assembled for fear of the Jews, Jesus himself came and stood in their midst as they said these things, and said to them, "Peace be to you." He rebuked them for their unbelief and hardness of heart, because they did not believe those who had seen him after he was risen.

They were terrified and frightened, and supposed they had seen a spirit. He said to them, "Why are you troubled? Why do doubts arise in your hearts? See my hands and my feet, that it is I myself; feel me and see, for a spirit does not have flesh and bones, as you see I have." When he had said that, he showed them his hands and his side. Then when they had seen the Lord the disciples were glad.

While they still did not believe for joy and wonder, he said to them, "Have you any food here?" They gave him a piece of a broiled fish, and some honeycomb. He took it and ate it in front of them.

Then Jesus said to them again, "Peace be to you!" As my Father has sent me, even so I send you. When he had said this, he breathed on them, and said to them, "Receive the Holy Spirit. Whoever's sins you forgive, they are forgiven, and whoever's sins you retain, they are retained."

Thomas, also called Didymus, one of the twelve, was not with them when Jesus came. Therefore the other disciples said to him, "We have seen the Lord!" He said to them, "Unless I see the scars from the nails in his hands, and put my finger into the scars from the nails, and put my hand into his side, I will not believe."

After eight days his disciples were again inside, and Thomas was with them. Then Jesus came in, the doors being shut, and stood in their midst, and said, "Peace be to you!" Then he said to Thomas, "Reach here with your finger, and see my hands; and reach here with your hand, and put it into my side, and do not be faithless, but believing." Thomas answered and said to him, "My Lord and my God!"

Jesus said to him, "Thomas, because you have seen me, you have believed; blessed are those who have not seen, and still have believed." And many other signs Jesus did in the presence of his disciples that are not written in this book. These are written that you may believe that Jesus is the Christ, the Son of God; and through believing you may have life in his name.

After these things Jesus showed himself again to the disciples at the Sea of Tiberias, and in this manner he showed himself:

There were together Simon Peter, and Thomas called Didymus, and Nathanael of Cana in Galilee, and the sons of Zebedee, and two other disciples. Simon Peter said to them, "I am going fishing." They say to him, "We will also go with you." They immediately went out and got into a boat, but that night they caught nothing.

When the morning had come, Jesus stood on the shore, but the disciples did not know that it was Jesus. Then Jesus said to them, "Children, have you any fish?"

They answered him, "No." He said to them, "Cast the net on the right side of the boat, and you will find fish." They threw out the net, and then they were unable to pull it in for the quantity of fish.

Therefore the disciple whom Jesus loved said to Peter, "It is the Lord!" When Simon Peter heard that it was the Lord, he put on his outer garment (for he had shed it for working), and leapt into the sea.

The other disciples came in a small boat (for they were not far from land, about three hundred feet) dragging the net with the fish. As soon as they came to land, they saw a fire of coals there, and fish laid on it, and bread. Jesus said to them, "Bring some of the fish that you have just caught."

Simon Peter went and pulled the net full of large fish to land—a hundred and fifty-three; and even though there were so many, the net was still unbroken. Jesus said to them, "Come and eat." None of the disciples dared ask him, "Who are you?" They knew that it was the Lord. Jesus then comes and takes bread, and gives it to them, and also the fish. This is now the third time that Jesus had showed himself to his disciples after he had risen from the dead.

So when they had eaten, Jesus said to Simon Peter, "Simon, son of Jonah, do you love me more than these do?" He said to him, "Lord, you know that I care for you." He said to him, "Feed my lambs." He said to him again the second time, "Simon, son of Jonah, do you love me?" He said to him, "Lord, you know that I care for you." He said to him, "Feed my sheep." Jesus said to him the third time, Simon, son of Jonah, do you care for me?" Peter was upset because he said to him the third time, "Do you care for me?" He said to him, "Lord, you know all things, you know that I care for you."²⁸ Jesus said to him, "Feed my sheep. Indeed, I say to you, when you were young you dressed yourself and walked where you wanted, but when you will be older, you will stretch out your hands, and another will dress you and take you where you would not choose." This he said to signify by what death he would glorify God. When he had spoken this, he said to him, "Follow me."

Then Peter, turning around, sees the disciple whom Jesus loved following, who also leaned on his breast at supper, and said, "Lord, who is it that betrays you?" Peter, seeing him, said to Jesus, "Lord, and what will this man do?" Jesus said to him, "If I wish that he remain until I come, what is that to you? You follow me."

Then this saying went around among the brethren, that the disciple would not die, but Jesus did not say to him, "He will not die," but, "If I wish that he remain until I come, what is that to you?" This is the disciple who testifies of these things, and wrote these things; and we know that his testimony is true.

Then the eleven disciples went away into Galilee, to a mountain which Jesus had appointed for them. When they saw him, they worshiped him; but some doubted.²⁹

Jesus came and spoke to them, saying, "All power is given to me in heaven and in earth. Go therefore into all the world and preach the gospel to every creature, and teach all nations, baptizing them in the name of the Father, and of the Son, and of the Holy Spirit; teaching them to observe everything that I have commanded you.

"He who believes and is baptized will be saved, but he who does not believe will be condemned. These signs will follow those who believe: In my name they will cast out demons; they will speak with new tongues; they will take up snakes; and if they drink any deadly thing, it will not hurt them; they will lay hands on the sick, and they will recover, and, surely, I am with you always, even to the end of the age."

Jesus said to them, "These are the words that I spoke to you while I was still with you, that all things must be fulfilled which are written in the Law of Moses, and in the Prophets, and in the Psalms, concerning me."

Then he opened their understanding, that they might comprehend the Scriptures, and said to them, "Thus it is written, and thus it was necessary for Christ to suffer, and to rise from the dead on the third day; and that repentance and forgiveness of sins should be preached in his name among all nations, beginning at Jerusalem. You are witnesses of these things. Indeed, I will send the promise of my Father upon you, but remain in the city of Jerusalem, until you are clothed with power from on high."

He led them out as far as to Bethany, and he lifted up his hands and blessed them. And so it was, as he blessed them that he was parted from them, and was carried up into heaven and was seated at the right hand of God. They worshiped him, and returned to Jerusalem with great joy; and were continually in the temple, praising and blessing God.

They went out, and preached everywhere, the Lord working with them, and confirming the word with signs following.

The world is too small to contain all that could be written about Jesus. There are many other things that Jesus did also, which, if every one should be written down, I suppose that even the world itself could not contain the books that would be written. Amen.

Quote to ponder upon:

> *I am the resurrection, and the life: he that believes in me, though he may die, yet shall he live. Whoever lives and believes in me shall never die. Do you believe this?* (John 11:25–26).

1 *IN THE BEGINNING was **the Word** and **the Word** was with God, and **the Word was God*** (John 1:1). Turning to Genesis 1:1 we read: *In the beginning God....* We now have two beginnings—the beginning of creation and the beginning of *the grace of God*. The whole of Genesis 1:1 is: *In the beginning God created the heavens and the earth*—period.

Following on from that: *Then **GOD SAID**, "**Let there be a firmament** (expanse) in the midst of the waters, and let it divide the waters from the waters* (Genesis 1:6). And we read: **AND IT WAS SO**. Of a consequence God separated the heavens from the seas **by His Word**, by speaking. This is confirmed in the New Testament: *the earth was formed out of water and through water **BY THE WORD OF GOD*** (2Peter 3:5).

Jumping back to Genesis 1:3 we read: *Then **GOD SAID**, "**Let there be light**"; **AND THERE WAS** light.* Here we see that God **spoke the Word** into the darkness and light came forth. Now, the best man has ever been able to do is to shine light **INTO** darkness, but God brought light **OUT OF** darkness— *God ... gives life to the dead and **calls into existence the things that do not exist*** (Romans 4:17), there had never been light before God called it into being. God created light on the **FIRST DAY**, the sun and moon were not made until the **FOURTH DAY**.

*Then **GOD SAID**, "Let ... **AND IT WAS SO*** (Genesis 1:9).
*Then **GOD SAID**, "Let ... **AND IT WAS SO*** (Genesis 1:11).
*Then **God said**, "Let ... **AND IT WAS SO*** (Genesis 1:14).
*Then **GOD SAID**, "Let ....* (Genesis 1:20).
*Then **GOD SAID**, "Let ... **AND IT WAS SO*** (Genesis 1:24).
*Then **GOD SAID**, "Let ...* (Genesis 1:26.

Time and time again God spoke and things came into being—everything is subject to the voice of God.

Then we have the staggering statement: *And **the Word became flesh and dwelt among us**, and we beheld His glory, the glory as of the only begotten of the Father, full of grace and truth* (John 1:14). This is speaking of Jesus, God's Son—he is **the Word** of God and John goes on to tell us that **the Word WAS God** .... *Everything was MADE THROUGH HIM, AND APART FROM HIM NOTHING WAS MADE THAT WAS MADE* (John 1:1-3). As I stated on page 8: "Jesus was God incarnate. He was God acting like God in the body of a Man." Some hold to a belief that Jesus tried to hide his identity, but this nonsense. At least fifty percent of the time Jesus stated who he was, i.e. to the woman at the well in Samaria:

> *The woman said to him, "I know that **Messiah will come, who is called Christ**; when he has come, he will tell us all things." Jesus said to her, "**I who am speaking to you am he**"* (John 4:25-26).

Jesus could not have been more clear that he is the Christ. Others hold to the belief that Jesus is not God. In due course, as we proceed through the gospels, I will further dispel those beliefs.

As we have seen, we have two beginnings—the beginning of creation and the beginning of *the grace of God*. Jesus himself is the answer to the enigmas of both time and eternity.

2 **IT IS WORTH** noting the difference between the reaction of Zacharias and that of Mary to the visitations of the angel Gabriel. According to the angel Zacharias had prayed for his wife Elizabeth to have a child. Yet, when the angel Gabriel tells Zacharias that his prayer had been heard and that Elizabeth would bear a child, he is dumbfounded and unbelieving, saying that both he and his wife were old so how could this be possible? (Many Christians also pray but do not believe in their hearts that what they pray for will actually happen.) The angel's reaction to the unbelief expressed by Zacharias is one of displeasure:

> *I am Gabriel and I stand in the presence of God. I came to bring you good news, but seeing as you do not believe my words you shall be mute until these things come to pass!* (Luke 1:19–20).

Mary's reaction was totally different. A young, godly woman, probably around sixteen years of age, engaged to be married to a man named Joseph. Mary must have been fully aware of how children are conceived and of the consequences for giving birth out of wedlock—Jewish Law called for girls to be stoned to death for such transgressions—yet her only question of the angel Gabriel was: *How will this be, seeing I do not know a man?*, meaning that she had never been intimate with a man. After Gabriel explained that the Holy Spirit will come upon her and impregnate her she says: *"See the handmaid of the* LORD; *let it be to me according to your word."* What an incredible response to such an incredible edict.

Mary was truly a woman of God, few could equal her and her spontaneous song of praise in Elizabeth's house is so very powerful and moving. It is understandable why God chose this young, obviously pure and holy woman to bear the greatest gift the human race has ever received. The angel Gabriel was so right when he said to Mary: *blessed are you among women* (Luke 1:28). Mary's cousin Elizabeth was filled with the Holy Spirit when Mary stepped into her house and also loudly proclaims: *Blessed are you among women and blessed is the fruit of your womb* (Luke 1:42). It was an understatement. Elizabeth also says: *Blessed is she who believed...* (Luke 1:45), which was in direct contrast to Zacharias who did not believe and was mute for more than nine months as a consequence. Nevertheless, while Mary should be honored as a pure, holy woman of God and the mother of Jesus according to the flesh, it is wrong to worship her.

It is interesting to note that in the priestly divisions recorded in 1Chronicles 24:10-11 that: "*the eighth [lot went] to Abijah, the ninth to Jeshua* (Yeshua, Jesus—see Footnotes **3a/3b**) who became Israel's High Priest. And of course the angel Gabriel came first to Zacharias of the division of *Abijah*, then to Mary who brought forth *Jesus*, who is now our *High Priest*.

Going back to Mary's statement to the angel: *I do not know a man* (Luke 1:34), which means in her case that she had never been sexually intimate with a man, has far reaching effects for Christians, not in a sexual way, but in an intimate, personal way with the Lord Jesus. In a biblical context "to know" means to be intimate with someone:

> **Adam knew Eve** *his wife, and she conceived and bore Cain* (Genesis 4:1).

Cain knew his wife, and she conceived and bore Enoch (Genesis 4:17).

Adam knew his wife again, and she bore a son and named him Seth (Genesis 4:25).

As it was in the days of Genesis so it was in the days of Jesus. Mary was engaged to Joseph, but did not *know* a man prior to giving birth to Jesus. Let us now see the ramification of the word *know* as used by Jesus. One example is the parable of the ten virgins (ten virgins represent ten followers of Jesus) five of whom were wise, and five were foolish. They were all waiting for the bridegroom (Jesus), but only the wise virgins took oil along with their lamps and were ready for him:

> *While the bridegroom was delayed, they all slumbered and slept. At midnight there was a cry: "Look, the bridegroom is coming, go out to meet him!" Then all the virgins got up and trimmed their lamps. The foolish said to the wise, "Give us some of your oil, for our lamps have gone out." The wise answered, saying, "No, lest there not be enough for both us and you, but you go instead to those that sell, and buy for yourselves." While they went to buy, the bridegroom came, and **those who were ready** went in with him to the wedding; and the door was shut. Afterwards the other virgins also came, saying, "Lord, Lord, open to us." He answered and said, "Truly I say to you,* **I do not KNOW you**" (Matthew 25:5–12).

Only those who had an intimate, personal relationship with Jesus and were ready to meet him, went in with the "*bridegroom*" to the *marriage supper of the Lamb*. The moral of the parable is, be prepared and be ready for his sudden coming.

In another example we have followers of Jesus who were busy, but not in God ordained work, and who did not have a personal, intimate relationship with Jesus:

> *Not everyone who says to me, "Lord, Lord," will enter the kingdom of heaven, only he who does the will of my Father who is in heaven. Many will say to me in that day, "Lord, Lord, have we not prophesied in your name? And in your name have cast out demons? And in your name done many wonderful works?" Then will I announce to them, "**I never KNEW you**. Depart from me, you who work wickedness"*
> (Matthew 7:21–23).

Only by having a personal, intimate relationship with Jesus, and the keeping of his commandments will get us into his kingdom. No one can enter by simply being involved in church work or by hanging onto the coattails of a godly spouse or parent; it is a very personal issue.

3a/3b *ON PAGE 19* we see that the angel Gabriel said to Mary that she would: *bring forth a son, and will call his name Jesus* (Luke 1:31); Gabriel also said that Jesus would *be called the Son of God* (Luke 1:35).

We know that Jesus is *the only begotten Son of God* (John 3:16) and that he was called *the Son of God* many times, and that he also referred to himself as *the Son of God* eight times. It is generally believed that the name "Jesus" means "Salvation," but it means so much more than that.

In Hebrew the word for "salvation" is ישועה (*yeshuah*), but the name "Jesus" is spelled ישוע (*Yeshua*)—without the ה at the end (Hebrew is read from right to left). On the eighth day, at the circumcision and naming of John the Baptist, his father's tongue was loosed and Zacharias prophesied and said: *Blessed is the Lord God of Israel, for he has visited and **redeemed** his people. He has raised up a horn of **salvation** for us in the house of his servant David....* (Luke 1:68-69). Under the power of the Holy Spirit Zacharias was foretelling the birth of Jesus and gave us the two significant aspects of the name—*Redemption* and *Salvation*. We have seen that the Hebrew name of Jesus ישוע (*Yeshua*) is near to ישועה (*yeshuah*) the word for "salvation" and therefore can be taken to mean that. However, we can go back several thousand years to a ceremony called "**The Redemption of the Firstborn Son,**" which in Hebrew is, and I quote from R. Alcalay's renowned *Complete Hebrew Dictionary* (again reading from right to left), ישוע הבן. We see that the word ישוע (*yeshua*) here means "Redemption." And that is not the end of the matter. The ceremony is the redemption of the firstborn son (Numbers 3:46-51) and God tells us that Israel, as a nation, is His firstborn son:

> *Then you shall say to Pharaoh, "Thus says the* LORD, ***Israel is my firstborn son**, and I say to you, 'Let my son go that he may serve me.' If you refuse to let him go, surely, **I will kill your firstborn son**."*
> (Exodus 4:22-23).

Thus we see that Jesus—ישוע (*Yeshua*)—is first and foremost the redeemer of the nation of Israel. And that is still not the end of the matter. The name יֵשׁוּעַ (*Yeshua*) occurs some twenty-nine times in the Bible: one time in 1Chronicles, one time in 2Chronicles, eleven times in Ezra, and sixteen times in Nehemiah; and each time they are speaking of the same person—יֵשׁוּעַ (*Yeshua*) the priest who came back from the Babylonian exile and who later became High Priest. Therefore יֵשׁוּעַ (*Yeshua*) became the High Priest following the captivity, which is significant. Jesus— יֵשׁוּעַ (*Yeshua*)—became our High Priest following the captivity to sin and after he ascended to heaven sits at the right hand of *God Almighty* (Hebrews 8:1).

Sometimes, translations of the Hebrew Scriptures almost completely kill the import of what is being said to us by God. Almost across the board, English translations have rendered יֵשׁוּעַ (*Yeshua*) as "Jeshua." There is no letter J in Hebrew. Apart from a few instances of the name "Jeshua" the NIV appears confused and renders the name mainly as "Joshua." In Hebrew "Joshua" is יְהוֹשֻׁעַ (*Yehoshua*) and only in Haggai is יְהוֹשֻׁעַ (*Yehoshua*) given as the name of the High Priest.

Born-again believers in Jesus, both Jew and Gentile, *are a chosen people, a royal priesthood, a holy nation* (1Peter 2:9).We are a kingdom of priests, and Jesus—יֵשׁוּעַ (*Yeshua*)—is our High Priest. Jesus—יֵשׁוּעַ (*Yeshua*) paid our redemption price on the cross at Golgotha. Nearing the end of his dreadful ordeal he said: *It is finished!* (John 19:30). It was the last word in the redemption of mankind. All a person need do is accept God's redemption by believing in Jesus. The reason that it is so easy for man to receive salvation is because it cost God so much.

4 *IT HAS BEEN* said that no two passages of Scripture have produced more difficulties than the genealogy of Jesus. Both Luke and Matthew give genealogies of Jesus, but on many points they differ, and it was a headache blending them accurately into a single list. The genealogies provide names not even found in the biblical lists, plus they also diverge and converge. And, as it says in 1Chronicles 4:22: *the records are ancient*, which tells us that even thousands of years ago the scribes had difficulty following the genealogical lines. Add to this the complications that would arrive from such as the following:

> *Now the sons of Reuben the firstborn of Israel—he was indeed the firstborn, but because he defiled his father's bed, his birthright was given to the sons of Joseph, the son of Israel, so that the genealogy is not listed according to the birthright* (1Chronicles 5:1).

And 1Chronicles 3:17 lists *Shealtiel* as the son of *Jeconiah*, but Luke lists him as the son of *Neri* (Luke 3:27).

Some Bible commentators believe that Matthew provides the genealogy of Joseph, while Luke gives that of Mary; however, while this may be true, Mary's name does not appear or get alluded to in the genealogy contained in Luke; and she is only mentioned in Matthew as the wife of Joseph, *of whom was born Jesus who is called Christ*. Both Joseph and Mary were descended from king David, but via different lines. Joseph was not the biological father of Jesus; Mary provided both the lineage and the biological seed in order for Jesus to be born as both the *Son of David* as well as the *Son of God*.

Luke gives the genealogy from Adam right through to Joseph, but he diverges and follows king David's line through Nathan, Solomon's brother. Luke shows himself to be something of a historian, but Matthew is clearly a Jew writing to Jews; he deliberately drops many names from his genealogical list in order to establish three blocks of fourteen generations, which would have been simpler for Jews to memorize.

The answer to the vexing questions raised by the genealogies is as follows: Jewish law mandated that if a man died without producing children then his brother was duty bound to raise up children to him by taking his widow as wife, and any offspring from that union was recognized as the deceased's legal children (Deuteronomy 25:5-7). Heli died without children and Jacob married his widow and produced Joseph, the husband of Mary, who gave birth to Jesus—this was also the opinion of the early Church fathers. Joseph was Heli's legal son and heir and was recognized as such and therefore the two genealogical lines converge.

We have an example of a deceased husband's widow being married in order to raise up an heir to the deceased in the story of *Ruth*, a Moabite, whose Israelite husband *Mahlon* had died without leaving children. Ruth's deceased husband's redeemer, Boaz, purchased the deceased's property and then says to the elders sitting in the city's gate:

> *Moreover, Ruth the Moabitess, the widow of Mahlon, I have acquired as my wife, to perpetuate the name of the dead through his inheritance, that the name of the dead may not be cut off from among his brethren*

and from his position at the gate. You are witnesses this day (Ruth 4:10).

I reversed the genealogical order provided by Luke in chapter 3:23-38 solely to maintain conformity. Instead of beginning the genealogical record of Jesus with Joseph and working back to the creation of Adam, as it is given in Luke's gospel, I began with God's creation of Adam and then progressed through to Joseph. This gives uniformity to the entire genealogy and blends in Matthew's list, thus providing a complete whole.

5 *THE GOSPELS MAKE* mention of "*the Jews*" and this has been interpreted by some as being anti-Semitic. However, that is far from the truth and no one among the writers of the gospels intended their readers to gain that impression. Jesus himself spoke this phrase both to his disciples (John 13:33), and also to Pontius Pilate (John 18:36).

Israel was under Roman military occupation, but the leaders of Israel (apart from the king) were religious leaders and were it not for the Romans they would have held almost absolute power. There were tens of thousands of these religious leaders who were usually divided into their own groups, but not always so. In Matthew 22:34-35 we can see that a *Lawyer* was also a *Pharisee,* and 2Chronicles 34:13 informs us that some of the Levites were Scribes.

At the top of the religious pyramid was the *High Priest* who wielded very considerable power, and he was the head of all other *Priests*, including the approximately two hundred *Chief Priests*. Also subject to the High Priest were the *Levites, Pharisees, Sadducees, Lawyers, Scribes,* and *Elders.*

Lawyers formulated laws that were anchored on "*the Jews*" interpretation of the *Torah* (the five books of Moses)—they were experts on the Law of Moses.

Scribes not only copied the scrolls of the Law and the Prophets, but they also acted as secretaries of state and drew up the decrees of the king and high officials.

Pharisees were an ultra-religious school of Jewish thought and had both political and religious power.

Sadducees were another school of Jewish thought; they held to different interpretations of the Law of Moses than did the Pharisees. They did not always see eye-to-eye politically with the Pharisees who were more popular with the common people. Sadducees were aristocrats, usually wealthy, and held the majority of seats in the *Sanhedrin* (the Jewish Council) and therefore wielded more power that the Pharisees.

Levites were on the lowest rung of the religious ladder and thousands of them served in Temple duties.

Altogether, "*the Jews,*" as the religious leaders, controlled the common people and we see in John 9:22 that the parents of the man born blind and who was given sight by Jesus: *feared the Jews, for the Jews had already agreed that if anyone confessed that Jesus was the Christ, he would be put out of the synagogue.* Also, many of "*the Jews* despised the common people and looked upon them as little more than uneducated rabble. This attitude is clearly depicted in John 7:49 when "*the Jews*" say of the common people: *this crowd that does not know the law is accursed.*

(This view is probably still held by the majority of ultra-religious Jews living in Israel and the diaspora today.)

These groups of religious leaders are referred to as *"the Jews"* because they were the *Rulers* and *Elders* of the common people and virtually controlled all aspects of their lives. The writers of the gospels were unanimous in differentiating between *"the Jews"* and the common people, but occasionally when *"the Jews"* are mentioned it was a mixed throng of both the religious and the common people. It is interesting to note that the term *"the Jews"* in a religious connection only appears one time in both Matthew and Luke and not at all in Mark's gospel, but it appears fifty-six times in John's narrative. Why John uses the expression so often is not known. He obviously mixed with the religious because after the arrest of Jesus we read: *Since that disciple [John] was known to the high priest, he entered with Jesus into the courtyard of the high priest* (John 18:15). Perhaps John purposely used the term to mark them out because it was usually the members of the religious groups who confronted Jesus at every turn (and continue to do so today, almost two thousand years later).

Jesus was clearly not enchanted with the majority of the religious of his day. John makes a point in differentiating them from the common people, while Matthew rages fire and brimstone against them. In Matthew's gospel Jesus refers to them as *"hypocrites"* thirteen times and as *blind fools!* two times, *Brood of vipers* four times, *offspring of vipers*, *Serpents*, and *whitewashed tombs full of dead men's bones*. Before Jesus is recorded as denigrating *"the Jews"* John the Baptist had called the Pharisees and Sadducees who came to his baptism a *"generation of vipers"* (Matthew 3:7). But if we really want to understand the frustration that Jesus felt with the religious and their traditions we need but read:

> *Woe to you, scribes and Pharisees,* **hypocrites!** *For you travel over sea and land to make one proselyte, and when you have one,* **you make him twice the child from hell than you are yourselves**
> (Matthew 23:15)

6 **"Son of Man"** was the favorite term Jesus would refer to himself as, and in Matthew's gospel alone Jesus uses that description of himself thirty-one times. In all there are seventy-nine references to the *Son of Man* in the gospels. There are some that hold to the belief that Jesus tried to hide his identity, but that is absolute nonsense. We saw earlier that Jesus referred to himself as *"the Son of God"* eight times and even stated outright that he and God were one and the same (John 10:30). Here Jesus uses a phrase that some believe he uses to show his identification with man, but again, that is ridiculous nonsense.

In the use of *"Son of Man"* Jesus is borrowing from Daniel 7:13, but in order to comprehend properly we need begin at Daniel 7:9-10:

> *I watched till thrones were put in place,*
> *And the Ancient of Days was seated;*
> *His garment was white as snow,*
> *And the hair of His head was like pure wool.*
> *His throne was a fiery flame,*
> *Its wheels a burning fire;*

> *A fiery stream issued*
> *And came forth from before Him.*
> *A thousand thousands ministered to Him;*
> *Ten thousand times ten thousand stood before Him.*
> *The court was seated,*
> *And the books were opened.*

We see that *thrones*, plural, were put in place and *God Almighty* was seated on one of them. Another is reserved for Jesus to sit on at Gods right hand following his ascension:

> *Therefore being* **exalted to the right hand of God**, *and having received from the Father the promise of the Holy Spirit, He poured out this which you now see and hear.*
> *For David did not ascend into the heavens, but he says himself:*
> *"The* Lord *said to my Lord,*
> **'Sit at My right hand'"** (Acts 2:33–34).

Continuing on in Daniel chapter 7 we read:

> *I was watching in the night visions,*
> *And behold, One like the Son of Man,*
> *Coming with the clouds of heaven!*
> *He came to the Ancient of Days,*
> *And they brought Him near before Him.*
> *Then to Him was given dominion and glory and a kingdom,*
> *That all peoples, nations, and languages should serve Him.*

> *His dominion is an everlasting dominion,*
> *Which shall not pass away,*
> *And His kingdom the one*
> *Which shall not be destroyed* (Daniel 7:13–14).

This passage is clearly speaking of Jesus and the Church. In a religious Jewish commentary on the book of Daniel published in 1979, even Jewish sages like the great Rashi said that the Man brought to *God Almighty* (Hebrew שׁדי אל – *El-Shaddai*) is "King Messiah." Jewish commentators go on to say that the Messiah has two comings: "a poor man and riding upon as ass (Zechariah 9:9) and if they merit it he will come with the clouds." That commentary most certainly speaks of Jesus entering Jerusalem on Palm Sunday and again in his Second Coming for his Church.

The gospels are full of allusions to the "*Son of Man*" and the passage in the Book of Daniel. Here are just a few:

> *Then the sign of the Son of Man will appear in heaven, and then all the tribes of the earth will mourn, and they will see the **Son of Man coming on the clouds of heaven** with power and great glory* (Matthew 24:30).

> *I say to you, hereafter you will see the **Son of Man sitting at the right hand of the Power, and coming on the clouds of heaven*** (Matthew 26:64).

> *Then they will see **the Son of Man coming in the clouds** with great power and glory* (Mark 13:26).

> *And you will see **the Son of Man sitting at the right hand of the Power, and coming with the clouds** of heaven"* (Mark 14:62).

the Son of Man will sit on the right hand of the power of God (Luke 22:69).

No one has ascended to heaven but He who came down from heaven, that is, the Son of Man who is in heaven (John 3:13).

What if you should see the Son of Man ascend where He was before? (John 6:62).

And I, if I am lifted up from the earth, will draw all peoples to Myself." This He said, signifying by what death He would die. The people answered Him, "We have heard from the Law that **the Christ remains forever**; *so how can You say, 'The Son of Man must be lifted up'?* **Who is this Son of Man?**"
(John 12:32–34).

It is worth noting that in verse 13 of Daniel's vision it says "*one* **like** *the son of man*." Jesus was a man according to the flesh, but he was God incarnate, therefore he was only *like* a man:

who, being in the **form** *of God, did not consider it robbery to be equal with God, but made himself of no reputation, taking the* **form** *of a bondservant, and coming* **in the likeness of men** (Philippians 2:6–7).

Daniel's vision goes on to tells us:

Then to Him was given dominion and glory and a kingdom (7:14).

The Aramaic word (the first few chapters—2:4b–7:28—of Daniel are in Aramaic) is שׁלטן (*shultan*), from which the world Sultan comes. *Shultan* means "sovereign" or "absolute" power and in Matthew 28:18 we see Jesus saying to his disciples: "***All authority** has been given to Me in heaven and on earth.*" Daniel 7:14 also says that the one like the *Son of Man* was given *a kingdom*. In Luke 22:29 Jesus says to his disciples: "*I bestow upon you **a kingdom, just as My Father bestowed one upon Me**.*" And of course the angel Gabriel told Mary about the child she would bear:

> *He will be great, and will be called the Son of the Most High, and the* Lord *God will give him the throne of his father David, and he will reign over the house of Jacob forever; and **of his kingdom there will be no end*** (Luke 1:32–33).

The significance of the expression "*Son of Man*" was not lost to the people; they rightly equated it to the Messiah, but being spiritually obtuse they did not understand that Jesus was the Messiah and that he was to be crucified in order to fulfill prophecy. Rather than trying to hide his true identity Jesus made every effort to publicize it. Jesus did repeatedly charge people they should not tell anyone what was done when he performed a great miracle, but this was not said in order to hide who he was, rather it was in order that he would not be forcibly made a king. This was about to happen following the feeding of the five thousand men plus women and children:

> *Knowing that they were about to come and **take him by force to make him king**, Jesus withdrew again to the mountain by himself* (John 6:15).

7 *WITH THE PARABLES* about *not sewing a piece of a new garment onto an old garment* and *not putting new wine into old wineskins*, Jesus was telling the people that he was not patching up Jewish tradition, but was establishing a new order of conduct. Jesus was in fact challenging the status quo, which had become hypocritical to the extreme and largely driven by the avarice of the ruling religious elite, which the writers of the gospels called "*the Jews.*" This ruling religious elite argued with Jesus, withstood and rejected him because he was challenging its established traditions with his "*new wine*" and they were happy with the religious status quo. Thus Jesus said, "*New wine must be put into new wineskins,*" and directly referencing "*the Jews*" he said "*no one having drunk old wine immediately desires new wine; for he says, 'The old is better.'*" And is that not the way of the Church also? Tradition is paramount— *the old is better*. There are two things stronger than either truth or fact and they are prejudice and tradition.

Jesus made it quite clear that he did not come to abolish the Law of Moses: *Do not think that I came to destroy the Law or the Prophets. I did not come to destroy them but to fulfill them* (Matthew 5:17). Three times Jesus said: *You have heard that it was said to those of old, '***You shall not ...***', but I say to you* (Matthew 5:21-22, 27-28, 33-34). Jesus upheld the Law, he did not question it, *but I say to you* there is more to it than that, there is yet a better way. We see this no more clearly than in John's gospel where Jesus would uphold the Law, but showed there was still room for mercy:

Early in the morning Jesus came into the temple again, and all the people came to him, and he sat down and taught them.

The scribes and Pharisees brought to him a woman taken in adultery; and when they had placed her in the midst, they said to him, "Master, this woman was taken in adultery, in the very act. **In the law Moses commanded us that such women should be stoned, but what do you say?"** *They said this to test him, that they might have something to accuse him of. Jesus stooped down and wrote on the ground with his finger, as though he had not heard them.*

So when they continued asking him, he raised himself up and said to them, "He that is without sin among you, **let him throw the first stone at her."**

He stooped down again and wrote on the ground. Those who heard it, being convicted by their own conscience, went out one by one, beginning at the eldest, down to the youngest; and Jesus was left alone, and the woman standing in the midst.

When Jesus had raised himself up and saw no one except the woman, he said to her, "Woman, where are your accusers? Has no one condemned you?" She said, "No one, Lord." Jesus said to her, **"Neither do I condemn you; go and sin no more"**
(John 8:2–11).

8

***Jesus said: The** hour is coming, and has now already come,* **when the dead will hear the voice of the Son of God; and those who hear will live** (John 5:25).

This saying of Jesus should spur a remarkable change in the way Christians deal with an unsaved world. It may come as a shock to some that *God Almighty* views all non-believers in His *only begotten Son* Jesus as living in a state of being dead. They are **dead spiritually**.

In the Book of Genesis we read:

And the LORD *God formed man of the dust of the ground, and breathed into his nostrils the breath of life; and man became a living being* (Genesis 2:7).

God is Spirit. He *is* Spirit. He is **not a** Spirit:

God is Spirit*, and those who worship Him must worship in spirit and truth* (John 4:24).

Therefore, with God being Spirit, what God breathed into the first man was nothing less than the Holy Spirit. Adam was the first Spirit-filled human being, but Adam sinned, and *the wages of sin is death* (Roman 6:23)—spiritual death. Therefore, unsaved family members, friends and colleagues are all in a perilous position. The statement Jesus made concerning the dead was not an isolated one:

Another of His disciples said to Him, "Lord, let me first go and bury my father." But Jesus said to him, "Follow Me, and **let the dead** *bury their own* **dead***"* (Matthew 8:21–22).

But there is an answer:

> *For if by the one man's offense death reigned through the one,* **much more those who receive** *abundance of grace and of the gift of righteousness* **will reign in life through the One, Jesus Christ** (Romans 5:17).

The answer is the *renewing* again of God's Holy Spirit, which is brought about by belief in Jesus, God's *only begotten Son*:

> *According to His mercy He saved us, through the* **washing of regeneration** *and* RENEWING *of the* **Holy Spirit** (Titus 3:5).

> *And you,* **being dead in your trespasses** *and the uncircumcision of your flesh,* **he has made alive** *together with Him, having forgiven you all trespasses* (Colossians 2:13).

> *For* **the wages of sin is death***, but the gift of God is eternal life in Christ Jesus our Lord* (Romans 6:23).

> *Now there was a man of the Pharisees named Nicodemus, a ruler of the Jews. This man came to Jesus by night and said to him, "Rabbi, we know that you are a teacher come from God, for no one can do these signs that you do unless God is with him." Jesus answered him, "Most assuredly, I say to you,* **unless one is born again he cannot see the kingdom of God***." Nicodemus said to him, "How can a man be born when he is old? Can he enter a second time into his mother's womb and be born?" Jesus answered, "Most assuredly, I say to you, unless one is* **born of**

water and the Spirit, he cannot enter the kingdom of God. That which is born of the flesh is flesh, and that which is born of the Spirit is spirit. Do not marvel that I said to you, '**You must be born again**.' The wind blows where it wishes, and you hear its sound, but you do not know where it comes from or where it goes. So it is with everyone who is born of the Spirit"
(John 3:1–8).

Those who are not born again of the Spirit are dead in their sins. Only those who respond to Jesus, to God's own gospel, who truly believe and trust in Jesus *will live*, not only eternally but will also live in the here and now on earth and not simply exist.

9 **SPEAKING OF HIMSELF** as the "*Son of Man*" Jesus says:

the hour is coming in which **all who are in the graves will hear his voice and will come out** (John 5:28–29).

This statement by the "*Son of Man*" is one of the most earth-shattering statements found in the gospels. Can the reader really imagine Jesus speaking a word and every grave containing a person's bodily remains opening up and the body resurrecting? Some would no doubt deride such a belief, but I, for one, believe it implicitly. I will tell of what contributed to my very strong belief.

I used to travel widely and in 1988, while in China for ministry, I purchased, for the equivalent of US$1.00, an unusually large cup, a coffee mug, that had a lid to keep the contents hot. It was a very tall and ornate hand-painted, black ceramic cup with a myriad of small, multicolored flowers covering the outside and the lid. I carried it throughout my days of ministry in China, and also halfway around the world for six months, before reaching home. That cup became the cup I used exclusively at home in Jerusalem, I took it up and down—to and from—my office for several years.

One day, in June 1996, I was going up to my office with my beloved cup in hand when I tripped on the stone stairs. I tried to protect the cup, which was full of coffee, by falling onto my arms, but despite the cuts and bruises I sustained, the cup still smacked down hard onto the stonework, spilling much of its contents. The cup only partially survived, it was cracked from the top almost to bottom, and some of the glazed finish and flowers were missing along the length of the crack. Later, when I was rinsing the mug, my wife saw the damage and knew that I was upset over it. She attempted to console me by saying, "It could last for years like that."

As the weeks and months passed by I continued to use and rinse the cup, but the now dark coffee-stained crack seemed to mock me. Then one day, as I was rinsing the cup, I did not notice the crack and put it down to distraction or imagination. A week later I examined the mug thoroughly—there was no crack! No crack, no chipped black glaze finish, and no missing flowers. I called my wife into the kitchen and said, "God has healed my cup!" We then got a magnifying glass and we both very carefully examined the cup, it was perfect! My wife said, "How did He do that?"

We still have the "miracle" cup, but have stopped using it in case we break it absolutely. It is kept in a glass display cabinet; it is a constant reminder that our God can do anything.

Speaking to Martha, the sister of Lazarus, four days after he had died, Jesus said:

> *I am the resurrection and the life; he that believes in me, even though he dies he will yet live* (John 11:25).

Martha went back to the house of mourning in Bethany and called the grieving Mary to come to Jesus; and she came and fell at his feet, weeping.

> *When Jesus saw her weeping, and the Jews who came with her weeping, he groaned in the spirit and was troubled. Then he said, "Where have you laid him?" They said to him, "Lord, come and see." Jesus wept, and the Jews said, "See how He loved him!" Some of them said, "Could not this Man, who opened the eyes of the blind, also have kept this man from dying?"*
>
> *Then Jesus, again groaning in Himself, came to the tomb. It was a cave, and a stone lay against it. Jesus said, "Take away the stone." Martha, the sister of him who was dead, said to him, "Lord, by this time there is a stench, for he has been dead four days."*
>
> *Jesus said to her, "Did I not say to you that if you would believe you would see the glory of God?" Then they took away the stone from the place where the dead man was lying. And Jesus lifted up his eyes to heaven and said, "Father, I thank you that you have heard me. I know that you always hear me, but because of the people who are standing around I said this, that they may believe that you sent me." When*

He had said these things, he called out with a loud voice, "Lazarus, come forth!" And he who had died came out bound hand and foot with grave linens, and his face was wrapped with a cloth. Jesus said to them, "Loose him, and let him go" (John 11:33-44).

This is probably one of the best known passages in the New Testament. Lazarus, the friend of Jesus, had died (see also Endnote **18**) and his body lay in a tomb for four days before Jesus called him out. Jesus called Lazarus by name because if he had not all the dead would have risen:

*the hour is coming in which **all who are in the graves will hear his voice and will come out*** (John 5:28-29).

For Jesus, calling the remains of human bodies out of their graves will be child's-play, he has already done that in a limited way, but *the hour is coming....*

10

At that time it came to pass, on the second Sabbath after the first, that he went through the grainfields...
(Luke 6:1).

AT THAT TIME. Luke fixes the time—he says that it was the *second Sabbath after the first*. To understand this, it is first necessary to understand that the Jewish *Feast of the Passover* was observed during the month of *Nisan*, roughly corresponding to the last part of March and the early part of April. The *Feast of the Passover* was held for seven days, commencing on the fourteenth day of the month (Exodus 12:1-28), which was the second day of the *Feast of the Passover*. God's law required that a sheaf of barley should be offered up as the first fruits of the harvest (Leviticus 23:10-11). From this second day of the *Passover* seven weeks were counted (Leviticus 23:15-16), bringing us to what we know as *Pentecost* (Acts 2:1, 20:16; 1Corinthians 16:8. *Pentecost* was originally known as the *Feast of Weeks* (Exodus 34:22; Deuteronomy 16:10). This second day in the *Passover*—also called, in both the Old and New Testaments, the *Feast of Unleavened Bread* (Exodus 12:17; Luke 22:1) This was the beginning of the reckoning, from there the sabbaths were counted down to *Pentecost*. The sabbath in the week following the second day of the Passover would be the second sabbath after this first one, in the reckoning of the seven sabbaths. This was the time when Jesus went through the grainfields.

11

YOU ARE THE salt of the earth, but if the salt has lost its flavor, with what will it be salted? It is good for nothing, except to be thrown out and trodden under foot (Matthew 5:13).

The above passage is one of the most misunderstood in any of the Gospels. There is a measure of truth in saying that born-again Christians add flavor to this world, but that is far from what Jesus is saying here.

Salt has the capacity to make things burn—it is a catalyst. The problem of correctly understanding what Jesus is saying lies with the word "earth." A consensus of opinion of very learned Protestant and Catholic scholars is that the gospel of Matthew was originally written in Hebrew, not Greek. In Hebrew the word for "earth" or "land" is אֶרֶץ (*aretz*), but Jesus was not speaking about "earth" or "land" he was speaking about the oven in common use at the time for baking bread. Jesus often used Aramaic phrases and some are recorded in the gospels, i.e:

> *Then He took the child by the hand, and said to her,* **"Talitha, cumi,"** *which is translated, "Little girl, I say to you, arise"* (Mark 5:41).

Somehow the Aramaic word ארע meaning "oven" arrived into the Hebrew as ארץ, meaning "earth" or "land." Only the last letter of the words (reading from right to left) is different, but that makes all the difference in the world to what Jesus actually said.

The oven in use at the time of Jesus were made of earth. The lower section of the oven was for the fire. Above the fire area there was a grating, mid-way in the oven, on which a thick layer of ashes were laid. On top of the ashes was a layer of salt, and on top of the salt was a layer of pebbles. It took approximately twelve minutes to bake pita bread in the oven. If a tourist is fortunate enough today, he or she can still find Arab women baking bread in such ovens around Hebron.

As said earlier, salt has the capacity to burn, it is a catalyst. The salt draws the fire and greatly accelerates and increases the heat in the upper baking area. In fourteen or fifteen days the salt loses its catalyzing effect and is replaced, the old is thrown away. An Arab tests the salt for effectiveness simply by tasting it, when it has lost its taste it is useful for nothing. This is what Jesus was telling us. We need now to put the passage into perspective by using another of the teachings of Jesus:

*I came to cast **fire on the earth**, and how I wish that it were already kindled!* (Luke 12:49).

The teachings of Jesus brings salvation and eternal life to the spiritually dead *if* they incline their ear and listen to him. His words are like *fire*. They are so revolutionary that they divide families and set one against another:

a man against his father, a daughter against her mother, and a daughter-in-law against her mother-in-law (Matthew 10:35).

Those who believe in Jesus are *the salt of the oven*, and are meant to act as a catalyst for the fire that Jesus *cast on the earth* by living godly lives and sharing the message of salvation—

***but** if the salt has lost its flavor.... It is good for nothing, except to be thrown out and trodden under foot* (Matthew 5:13).

The passage carries the same message as other passages spoken to the disciples by Jesus:

Every tree that does not bear good fruit is cut down and thrown into the fire (Matthew 7:19).

Every branch in Me that does not bear fruit He takes away; and every branch that bears fruit He prunes, that it may bear more fruit (John 15:2).

These sayings of Jesus ought to make all born-again believers in Jesus—both Gentile and Jew—tremble and rush to dedicate their lives afresh to him. We would do well to remember that Jesus also said:

Not everyone who says to me, 'Lord, Lord,' will enter the kingdom of heaven, but the one who does the will of my Father who is in heaven (Matthew 7:21).

Many of the teachings of Jesus are along these lines—they are radical teachings. There is a price to pay for being a follower of Jesus; but if *the salt loses its flavor **it** is good for nothing, except to be thrown out.*

12

I SAY TO you, unless you eat the flesh of the Son of Man, and drink his blood, you have no life in you (John 6:53).

This teaching of Jesus has absolutely nothing to do with the enormously erroneous doctrine of transubstantiation whereby the Eucharist elements of bread and wine are actually converted into the body and blood of Jesus. We often say that an athlete, for example, "eats, drinks and sleeps athletics." It is that sort of devotion that Jesus expects from his disciples, whereby we eat, drink and sleep Jesus—nothing else matters. Jesus tells us repeatedly that his followers must love him more than they do their parents, brothers, sisters, and even their own life.

The Bible tells us, and Jesus also told the devil, *man shall not live by bread alone; but man lives by every word that proceeds from the mouth of God* (Deuteronomy 8:3; Matthew 4:4). As we have seen previously, Jesus is the *Word*, through which the worlds were made and John 1:1 says: ***the Word** was with God, and **the Word was God***. Then John said: *The Word was **made flesh**, and lived among us* (John 1:14). Now Jesus says:

the bread of God is He who comes down from heaven and gives life to the world (John 6:33).

I am the bread of life (John 6:48).

I am the living bread *which came down from heaven. If anyone eats of this bread, he will live forever; and **the bread that I shall give is My flesh, which I shall give for the life of the world*** (John 6:51).

Jesus is the bread of life; his true followers feed upon him because out of his mouth comes *the words of eternal life* (John 6:68). In addition to this, Jesus makes a rather startling statement:

unless you eat the flesh of the Son of Man, and drink his blood, *you have no life in you* (John 6:53).

Eating or drinking blood was strictly prohibited. When an animal was slaughtered its blood was poured out on the ground:

Only be sure that you do not eat the blood, for the blood is the life; you may not eat the life with the meat. You shall not eat it; you shall pour it on the earth like water (Deuteronomy 12:23-24).

We should be careful that we do not miss what God is telling us here—*the blood is the life* and Jesus says *unless you drink his blood you have no life*, because *eternal life is in him. He that eats my flesh and drinks my blood lives in me, and I live in him* (John 6:56). We must abide continually in Jesus:

> *Abide in Me, and I in you. As the branch cannot bear fruit of itself, unless it abides in the vine, neither can you, unless you abide in Me* (John 15:4).
>
> *If anyone does not abide in Me, he is cast out as a branch and is withered; and they gather them and throw them into the fire, and they are burned*
> (John 15:6).

It should be remembered that the blood of Jesus, our passover lamb, was poured out on the ground: *And he who has seen has borne witness* (John 19:35). His life on earth was poured out for our life in *kingdom of heaven*.

Only those who abide in, and feed upon, Jesus—eat, drink, sleep, and breathe him, will have eternal life. It is very, very clear throughout the four gospels that there is no place in the *kingdom of God* for half-hearted, lukewarm followers of Jesus—it is all or nothing—*because you are, neither hot nor cold, I will vomit you out of my mouth* (Revelation 3:16).

13

> **THE PHARISEES, AND** *all the Jews, unless they wash their hands often, will not eat* (Mark 7:3).

Jesus is about to assail the Pharisees over their traditions that negate God's commandments, but what is of interest to us here is the mention of hand washing. Practicing Jews, even today, do not eat unless they first wash their hands, but hand washing was not just restricted to washing only before eating, it was and is done *often* during the days. It was this ritual of washing their hands *often* that saved the

Jewish people from the deadly Bubonic plague—the Black Death. That terrible disease decimated populations across Europe and London in the seventeenth century. Almost a quarter of London's 460,000 inhabitants died in the 1665 plague, and whole communities across Europe were destroyed, approximately one hundred million people died from the disease.

Many people blamed the Jews for causing the plague because they did not succumb to it like non-Jews. Many Jews were attacked and died at the hands of violent mobs. It was simply their ritual of *often* washing their hands that saved the Jews from the worst ravages of the plagues.

14

*YOU SHALL BE called **Cephas**—which is, by interpretation, "a stone"* (John 1:42).

Cephas is a Syriac word, meaning the same as the Greek word *petros* (Peter), a stone. However, Matthew's gospel records this incident thus: *And I tell you, you are Peter* (Matthew 16:18). John sets the naming event very early in his gospel, in the first chapter. Matthew places it more than half way through his gospel—midway through the sixteenth chapter.

There is no other mention of the name *Cephas* in the gospels, but interestingly the Apostle Paul refers to *Cephas* five times in his epistles. Matthew refers to Peter sixteen times in his gospel following his declaration that Jesus was *the Christ, the Son of the living God.* Perhaps the jostling and rivalry for position and greatness among those closest to Jesus had its share in the noticeable omission of the name *Cephas*. There were disputes between the disciples as to who would be the greatest (Luke 9:46; 22:24), and also James and John tried to pressure Jesus into granting them the two places of honor in the kingdom of God, which apparently upset the rest of the disciples and caused some ill will toward James and John (Mark 10:35-41).

Jesus was making a point that only the Roman Catholic Church appears to have picked up on. *Cephas* is the shortened version of *Caiphas*, who was the High Priest, and Jesus wanted the other disciples to understand that Peter was one of a kind. Jesus obviously recognized Peter's potential leadership qualities and naming him *Cephas* he virtually appointed him leader among those who would take the gospel to the Jews.

Peter was impetuous almost to an extreme and this can be seen in the drawing of his sword and severing the ear of Malchus, the high priest's servant. Peter declared that he would never deny Jesus, yet he did just that three times within the space of a few hours, and those denials were accompanied by cursing and swearing (Matthew 26:74). Yet Peter had inordinate courage and incredible faith. He was being impetuous when he asked Jesus to command him to get out of the boat and walk on the waves (Matthew 14:28), but he was courageous enough to get out of the boat and do it (Matthew 14:29). Over the temple-tax issue Jesus tells Peter: *go to the sea, throw in a hook and take the first fish that comes up, and when you open its mouth you will find a piece of money* (Matthew 17:27)—that took great faith and belief in Jesus!

Endnotes (Page 95)

It was Peter who Satan wanted to sift as wheat and Jesus says to him: *but I have prayed for you, that your faith will not fail, and* **when you have turned back again, strengthen your brothers** (Luke 22:32). It was Peter who was to encourage and uphold the other disciples following the crucifixion and resurrection.

Paul was undeniably the Apostle of the Gentiles and was also foremost in the evangelization of the Gentiles throughout the known world. However, Paul obviously recognized the unique authority bestowed upon Peter by Jesus and therefore Paul mostly referred to Peter as *Cephas*, the name Jesus had given him.

What Jesus said following Simon Peter's declaration that he was *the Christ, the Son of the living God* was:

> *Blessed are you, Simon Bar-Jonah, for flesh and blood has not revealed this to you, but My Father who is in heaven.*
>
> *Jesus looked at him and said, "You shall be called Cephas"(which is, by interpretation, "a stone"). And I also say to you that you are [Cephas],* **and on this rock I will build My church....** (Matthew 16:17).

There is absolutely nothing in the words of Jesus that can be construed as meaning that he would build his Church upon a brash, impetuous Peter (*Cephas*). It was on the foundation of Jesus being **the Christ, the Son of the living God** that the Church was to be built. Both the Greek and the Syriac names *petros—Cephas* and *Peter*—mean "a stone," something a little larger than a pebble. Jesus did not say that on this *petros*, this "stone" I will build my

Church, but *on this **petra** "Rock" I will build my Church*. There is a famous city in Jordan called **Petra**, it is an entire city chiseled entirely out of a vertical wall of red *petra*. It was this type of rock Jesus was referring to, an unshakable foundation, a Church built upon himself as *the Christ, the Son of the living God*.

15

PETER CAME TO *Jesus and said, "Lord, how often shall my brother sin against me, and I forgive him? Up to seven times?" Jesus said to him, "I will not say to you, up to seven times, but, until seventy times seven. Pay attention to yourselves, if your brother sins against you, rebuke him, and if he repents, forgive him. If he sins against you seven times in a day, and seven times in a day returns to you, saying, 'I repent,' you shall forgive him* (Matthew 18:21–22).

In Matthew 18:15 Jesus implies that it is the duty of his followers to go to a brother or sister when that person has offended us, implying that it is our duty to forgive him or her; this led Peter to ask how often this was to be done.

To forgive is to treat as though the offense was never committed—to declare that we will not harbor malice toward that person, or treat him or her unkindly, that the matter will be buried and forgotten.

Until seven times? "*The Jews*" taught that a man was to forgive a brother three times, but not a fourth time. Peter's question to Jesus therefore, more than doubled this number, asking whether forgiveness was to be shown to such a large extent.

Until seventy times seven. This means that we are not to limit our forgiveness to any fixed number of times. As often as a brother or sister injures us, and asks forgiveness, we are to forgive that person. It is the other person's duty to ask forgiveness (see Luke 17:3-4). If that person does this it is our duty to declare that we forgive them, and to treat them accordingly. If they do not ask us to forgive them we are never to follow up with revenge or malice, we are to treat them kindly, and to do them good. And it is at our peril that we ignore a divine edict related to the above:

> *For if you forgive men their trespasses, your heavenly Father will also forgive you. But **if you do not forgive** men their trespasses, **neither will your Father forgive** your trespasses* (Matthew 6:14–15).

16

Your father Abraham rejoiced to see my day, and he saw it and was glad (John 8:56).

Jesus was here referencing Abraham's prophetic actions much of which are lost to almost the entire Church of the firstborn. What Abraham believed and did is enough to give me goosebumps. We must now travel back in time to Abraham's time in Genesis. Unfortunately, nowhere is there a more glaring mistranslation of words in the original Hebrew text than in the majority of English translations of our passage. It was said earlier in Endnote **3a/3b** that translations of the Hebrew Scriptures often completely obscure what is really being said by God. This is one of those times. The English words that affect this passage for the reader and student are "*provide*" and "*provided.*" The Hebrew word is יראה (*yireh*), which is the future tense of "*see*" and means "*will see*" (Genesis 22:8). The word יראה is used again twice in Genesis 22:14, one time as "*will see*" and one time as "*be seen.*" It is the same word with three different inflections and I have replaced the misleading words with the correct renderings as per the original Hebrew. We see the mix up with the same words again in 1Samuel 16:1 where God tells Samuel that He has rejected Saul as king and: "*I have seen* (ראיתי - *raiti*) *a king for Myself among the sons of Jesse.*" Many English translations have translated ראיתי (*I have seen*) as "*I have provided*".... The NRSV and ESV have "seen," which is correct, and NKJV has a margin note informing that "*seen*" is literally correct.

As we go to the passage the reader should be prepared for several prophetic points that *God Almighty* makes known. Here then is our passage from the NKJV with pertinent words emphasized:

> *Now it came to pass after these things that God tested Abraham, and said to him, "Abraham!" And he said, "Here I am."*
>
> *Then He said, "Take now* **YOUR SON, YOUR ONLY SON** *Isaac, whom you love, and go to the land of* **MORIAH**, *and* **OFFER HIM THERE** *as a burnt offering on one of the mountains of which I shall tell you."*
>
> *So Abraham rose early in the morning and saddled his donkey, and took two of his young men with him, and Isaac his son; and he split the wood*

for the burnt offering, and arose and went to the place of which God had told him. Then **ON THE THIRD DAY** *Abraham lifted his eyes and saw the place afar off. And Abraham said to his young men, "Stay here with the donkey; the lad and I will go yonder and worship, and* **WE WILL COME BACK TO YOU."**

So Abraham took the wood of the burnt offering and laid it on Isaac his son; and he took the fire in his hand, and a knife, and the two of them went together. But Isaac spoke to Abraham his father and said, "My father!" And he said, "Here I am, my son."

Then he said, "Look, the fire and the wood, but where is **THE LAMB** *for a burnt offering?"*

And Abraham said, "My son, God **WILL SEE HIMSELF THE LAMB** *for a burnt offering." So the two of them went together.*

Then they came to the place of which God had told him. And Abraham built an altar there and placed the wood in order; and he **BOUND ISAAC HIS SON AND LAID HIM ON THE ALTAR, UPON THE WOOD. AND ABRAHAM STRETCHED OUT HIS HAND AND TOOK THE KNIFE TO SLAY HIS SON.**

But the Angel of the LORD *called to him from heaven and said, "Abraham, Abraham!" So he said, "Here I am."*

And He said, "Do not lay your hand on the lad, or do anything to him; for now I know that you fear God, since **YOU HAVE NOT WITHHELD YOUR SON, YOUR ONLY SON, FROM ME."**

> *Then Abraham lifted his eyes and looked, and there behind him was a* **RAM** *caught in a thicket by its horns. So Abraham went and took the* **RAM**, *and offered it up for a burnt offering instead of his son. And Abraham called the name of the place,* **THE-LORD-WILL-SEE**; *as it is said to this day,* "**IN THE MOUNT OF THE LORD IT SHALL BE SEEN**"
> (Genesis 22:1-14).

Here again are the salient points. Notice the parallels between Issac and Jesus:

Issac is Abraham's **only son.**
Jesus is God's **only begotten Son.**

Abraham takes Issac to **the land of Moriah.**
Jesus was crucified on **Mount Moriah.**

They came to Mount Moriah **on the third day.**
Jesus was resurrected on the third day—on Mount Moriah.

we will come back to you."
Abraham believed Issac would be resurrected.

where is **the lamb** (שׂה) for an offering?
God **will SEE HIMSELF the lamb** (שׂה).
Jesus was God's **Passover lamb.**

Abraham bound Issac, laid him on the wood, and took the knife to slay his son—**ISSAC WAS AS GOOD AS DEAD AT THAT MOMENT**, but the angel stopped Abraham.

behind him was a **ram** (איל) *caught in a thicket.*
Abraham went and took the **ram** (איל).

It was ***a ram***, not ***a lamb*** that Abraham sacrificed following Issac's reprieve.

Abraham names Moriah, ***The-Lord-Will-See.
In the Mount of the Lord it shall be seen.***
And the death and resurrection of ***the Lamb of God*** was seen on Mount Moriah.

After the ascension of Jesus to the *right hand of God Almighty* (Acts 1:9–11), he isl not to be seen again until he comes for his bride, which is the Church:

> *that He might **present her to Himself a glorious church**, not having spot or wrinkle or any such thing, but that she should be holy and without blemish*
> (Ephesians 5:27).

> *Then one of the seven angels who had the seven bowls filled with the seven last plagues came to me and talked with me, saying, "Come, **I will show you the bride, the Lamb's wife**"* (Revelation 21:9).

> *Then he said to me, "Write: **'Blessed are those who are called to the marriage supper of the Lamb!'** "
> And he said to me, "These are the true sayings of God"* (Revelation 19:9).

Just as Jesus will not be seen until he comes for his bride, so Issac is not heard of again until Rebekah, his bride, comes to him:

> *And Isaac brought Rebekah into his mother Sarah's tent, and took her, and she became his wife*
> (Genesis 24:67).

The passage we have been looking at is divinely prophetic, but its import has been lost to most followers of Jesus probably because the Hebrew did not make a great deal of SENSE to translators. Interestingly enough, the 1611 *Authorized King James Version* is more accurate on this than modern versions that should have translated it more correctly.

17 THROUGHOUT THE GOSPELS "heaven" is synonymous with "God," as in *the kingdom of heaven*, and *the kingdom of God*. In our passage the prodigal son says that he has *sinned against heaven*, meaning, *I have sinned against God*. Ultimately, all sin is against God, even though we actually do it against a person or persons—we must always bear this in mind.

King David sinned against Uriah the Hittite by sleeping with his wife and then having Uriah killed in an attempt to hide his hideous sin. God confronted David through Nathan the prophet, which brought David to repentance. David prayed to the LORD:

Against You, You only, have I sinned, and done this evil in Your sight.... (Psalms 51:4).

This is not an isolated scripture, the Bible is replete with examples of man's sin against God. Here is just one from each of the first four books of the Bible; the fourth example shows restitution is required:

*But the men of Sodom were exceedingly **wicked and sinful against the LORD*** (Genesis 13:13).

Then Pharaoh called for Moses and Aaron in haste, and said, "I have sinned against the LORD your God and against you (Exodus 10:16).

*If a person **sins** and commits a trespass **against the LORD by lying to his neighbor** about what was delivered to him for safekeeping, or about a pledge, or about a robbery, or if he has extorted from his neighbor....* (Leviticus 6:2).

*Then the LORD spoke to Moses, saying, "Speak to the children of Israel: 'When a man or woman commits **any sin that men commit** in unfaithfulness **against the LORD**, and that person is guilty, then he shall confess the sin which he has committed. He shall make restitution for his trespass in full, plus one-fifth of it, and give it to the one he has wronged* (Numbers 5:5–7).

18 THIS PASSAGE IS dealing with a parable exclusive to Luke's gospel (16:19-31) about a rich man and a beggar named Lazarus—a common name in those times. The beggar was covered in sores and had to be carried and placed at the gate of the rich man, in the hope that he may receive some scraps from the rich man's leftovers. The story is about heaven (*Abraham's bosom*) and hell (*the flames of torment*). In time Lazarus dies and is carried to heaven; the rich man also dies and has all the privileges of wealth—he has a burial, but ends up tormented in hell.

The rich man sees Lazarus being comforted and asks Abraham to send Lazarus with a drop of water because it was literally as hot as hell down there. Abraham replies to the effect that those in heaven cannot go to hell and those in hell cannot get into heaven. The rich man is desperate and says:

> *I ask you therefore, father, that you would send him to my father's house, for* **I have five brothers**, *that he may testify to them lest they also come to this place of torment* (Luke 16:28).

Abraham replies:

> ***They have Moses and the Prophets**, let them hear them.*

The rich man said:

> *"No, father Abraham, but **if someone goes to them from the dead, they will repent**.*

Abraham then says to him:

> ***If they do not hear Moses and the Prophets, neither will they be persuaded even though one rose from the dead*** (Luke 16:31).

The parable is not just about heaven and hell, it is also about greed, riches and injustice. It is a story about Israel being a divided nation—the rich religious, and the poor masses. Israel has twelve tribes—the rich man has *five brothers*: the *Priests*, the *Levites*, the *Lawyers*, the *Scribes*, and the *Sadducees*. We also saw in Endnote (**5**) that *Pharisees* and *Sadducees* were a part of the brotherhood of six, who were the religious elite—***they have Moses and the Prophets***. Jesus said to "*the Jews*":

*You search **the Scriptures**, for in them you think you have eternal life; and **these are they which testify of Me*** (John 5:39).

And Jesus delivered the *coup de grâce*:

If they do not hear Moses and the Prophets, neither will they be persuaded even though one rose from the dead (Luke 16:31).

And indeed, relatively few religious Jews have been persuaded to believe throughout the past two millennia; however, hundreds of thousands of Jews have since come to believe the truth about Jesus (Yeshua), their *Messiah*.

19 J*ESUS HERE GIVES* his disciples (and us) an object lesson on death (see also Endnote **9**). Jesus loved Lazarus, Mary and Martha, and when the sisters sent to tell him that his friend was sick, he stayed two more days where he was to ensure Lazarus had more than enough time to die:

When he had heard that Lazarus was sick, he remained another two days in the same place where he was (John 11:5).

When Jesus knew Lazarus was dead he said to his disciples:

Our friend Lazarus sleeps, but I go that I may awaken him out of sleep. ... Jesus spoke of his death.... Then Jesus said to them plainly, "Lazarus is dead."

By the time Jesus reached Bethany, Lazarus had been dead four days, and in the Middle East's hot climate bodies begin to decompose very quickly. Martha goes to meet Jesus and is naturally grief stricken at her brother's death, and she tells Jesus that had he been there Lazarus would not have died. Jesus says to Martha:

> Your brother will rise again. Martha said to him, "I know that he will rise again in the resurrection at the last day." Jesus said to her, "**I am the resurrection and the life; he that believes in me, even though he dies he will yet live**" (John 11:25).

Martha and Mary could believe for a resurrection on the last day, but they had not the faith for an instant resurrection even though Jesus had said *I am the resurrection* and *the life; he that believes in me, even though he dies he will yet live*. Jesus sees everyone around shedding tears and asks where the body had been laid and they say *"Come and see."* And then we have the shortest verse in the Bible—*Jesus wept* (John 11:35); however, Jesus was not shedding tears for the loss of a loved friend, he wept because of everyone's absolute unbelief.

A stone had been rolled across the entrance to the tomb. Jesus said:

> Take away the stone. Martha, the sister of him who was dead, said to him, "Lord, by this time he will stink, for he has been dead four days." Jesus said to her, "Did I not say to you, that **if you would believe you will see the glory of God?**" (John 11:39–40).

Jesus called Lazarus by name and out he came from the tomb, still wrapped in grave linens and cloths. Jesus wanted (and still wants) everyone to know that he is able to call the dead out of their sleep:

ENDNOTES (Page 142)

> *I am the resurrection and the life; he that believes in me, even though he dies he will yet live*
> (John 11:25).

When Jesus referred to Lazarus as being asleep it was not the first time this expression was used in the New Testament, but Jesus clarified it at the time that Lazarus was actually dead. The first time a dead person was referred to as being asleep was in the story of Jairus, whose young daughter was sick, and later, died. Jesus went to Jairus' house and found the mourners weeping and wailing and said to them:

> *"Do not weep, **she is not dead, but sleeping."** And they laughed him to scorn, **knowing that she was dead*** (Luke 8:52–53).

And of course Jesus went into the girls room where she was lying on her bed, took her hand and said in Aramaic: *"Little girl, arise,"* and she immediately got up and walked.

Immediately following the death of Jesus on the cross we read:

> *and graves came open and many bodies of the saints **who slept** were raised, and after his resurrection came out of their graves and went into the holy city, appearing to many* (Matthew 27:52–53).

On three occasions believers in Jesus are said to have *"fallen asleep"* (1Corinthians 15:18, 20; 1Thessalonians 4:13). Falling *asleep* became the usual expression employed in the New Testament to describe the death of believers in Jesus. It indicates the calmness and peace with which they die, like sinking into a gentle sleep. It replicates that of a small child who has played all day and runs to his mother expecting more playtime, but who falls asleep from sheer exhaustion in her loving arms. It also denotes the hope of a resurrection; they sink into sleep with an expectation of awaking again.

20

WERE THERE NOT** ten cleansed? **Where are the other nine? Have none returned to give glory to God save this foreigner? (Luke 17:17–18).

In this simple passage we get a glimpse of God's hurt from man's ingratitude. Jesus is making a point that gratitude and having a thankful heart is important to him. There are few parents who like ungrateful children—God is no different. We take too much for granted and our "giving of thanks" before meals is often more of a Christian rite than of a heartfelt giving of thanks to God for his bountiful provision. In the gospels Jesus "gave thanks" and "blessed" the bread when he broke it for the multitudes, first for five thousand men, plus women and children, and then for four thousand men, plus women and children. The Greek word used in the gospels is *eulogeo*, from which we get our word eulogy, which means to speak well of, to praise something.

The Samaritan man *came back*. Gratitude is *coming back* to say thank you to the One who makes it possible; we must never take something for granted:

ENDNOTES (Page 145)

> *Every good gift and every perfect gift is from above, and comes down from the Father of lights, with whom there is no variation or shadow from turning* (James 1:17).
>
> *all this abundance that we have...is from your own hand and is all your own* 1Chronicles 29:16).

These *good* and *perfect gifts* include the air we breath, the food we eat, the clothes we wear, the roof that is over our heads and the material goods that we possess. God is the One who makes it all possible. When we offer something to God we are merely offering that which rightfully belongs to him. Woe be to us if we try to keep it all for ourselves.

In the Protestant churches we have litany which is called "Praise and Worship." But this phrase is not biblical, there is no such linking together of "praise and worship" in the Hebrew text of the Bible. There are, however, many usages of the phrase *"thanks and praise"* (1Chronicles 16:4, 25:3 and many others), which, reading from right to left in Hebrew is להודת והלל, and *"a sacrifice of thanksgiving"* is used five times in English translations.

At least fifty percent of the renderings *"praise"* (הלל – *halal*) in English translations is wrong. The word in Hebrew is *"thanks"* (תודה – *todah*) and there is a world of difference between *praise* and *thanks*, but church traditions have caused both those that read the Bible and students of it to be blind to this fact.

Below is one English translation that does render the word (תודה – *todah*) correctly in this instance, almost all others render it as *praise*:

*The one who offers **thanksgiving** as his sacrifice glorifies me* (Psalms 50:23 (ESV).

To fully understand the importance to God of a grateful, thankful heart we should look at Psalm 118:19–20):

*Open to me **the gates of righteousness**, that I may enter through them **and give thanks to the** L*ORD*. **This is the gate of the** L*ORD*; the righteous shall enter through it.*

The **gates** *of righteousness* are gratitude and thankfulness. We enter those gates only with hearts overflowing with gratitude and thankfulness to God; only the righteous enter those **gates** and give *thanks* (תודה – *todah*) to the L*ORD*. Then look what the L*ORD* says to us by his Spirit:

This is the gate of the L*ORD*; *the righteous shall enter through **it**.*

We now go from the plural *gates*, to the singular **gate**. Thankfulness **IS** *the gate of the* L*ORD*. In other words, thankfulness and gratitude is the gateway to the heart of God. When we are truly grateful to God for all that he is and all that he has done we have open access to the heart of God. Also, he gives us more of everything because he is assured that we will be grateful and say "thank you" for whatever does for us, and for everything he gives to us.

21 I*NDEED,* T*HE* K*INGDOM* of God is *within us*. It stems from the heart; it is inexpressible peace and joy:

the kingdom of God is not eating and drinking, but righteousness and peace and joy in the Holy Spirit
(Romans 14:17).

> *the joy of [knowing] the* LORD *is your strength*
> (Nehemiah 8:10).

Sadly, there are too many joyless "Christians" today. What they really need is to have a face-to-face encounter with Jesus and really get saved.

22

> TRULY I SAY *to you,* **it is easier** *for a camel to go through a needle's eye,* **than it is for a rich man to enter into the kingdom of God**
> (Matthew 19:24; Mark 10:25; Luke 18:25).

In comparison with the mass of Christianity, there are relatively few rich people who have accepted Jesus Christ and his teachings. However, Jesus did not say it was *impossible* for rich men to enter the kingdom of God, merely that it was *difficult* for them.

There has been a great deal of discussion over our verse above, and some hypotheses teeter between the inane and the absolute ridiculous. The short and simple truth is that in the time of Jesus large cities, such as Jerusalem, had, alongside the main gates, a small, narrow gateway known as the "needle's eye." It was so called because the top of the narrow gateway was reminiscent of a needle. The gateway was only a grown man's height, and from shoulder level upward it grew narrower and was little wider than a man's head. The gate was for travelers to gain entry to the city when the main gates were closed, usually at sunset.

Jesus was pointing out that it was difficult for rich men to get into the kingdom of God, simply because they were rich and had many possessions. The rich young ruler *went away sorrowful* after Jesus said to him:

> *go and sell all that you have and distribute it to the poor, and you will have treasure in heaven; and come, take up your cross and follow me*
> (Matthew 19:21; Mark 10:21; Luke 18:22).

Jesus was saying that like a camel, a rich man would need first to be unloaded, then kneel down and virtually crawl through that narrow gate. It was certainly a difficult, but not an impossible feat. Merchants who arrived at a city after its gates were shut were forced to unload their camels and make them crawl on their knees, scraping their bodies through the narrow gate. This type of entry into the kingdom of God is more than the great majority of rich people are prepared to make; however, there is no alternative, they must:

> **Enter by the narrow gate**.... Because **narrow is the gate and difficult is the way which leads to life**, and there are **few** who **find** it (Matthew 7:13–14).

23

> *I* **AM THE** *way, the truth, and the life. No one comes to the Father except through Me.*

Jesus makes it perfectly clear that there is only one way to salvation and eternal life—and that is through himself. There is no "all roads lead to Rome" when it comes to salvation. Jesus said emphatically:

> *I am the way, the truth, and the life. No one comes to the Father except through Me* (John 14:6).

Today we have large Christian ministries that propagate their belief that God has a different plan of salvation for the Jews. This is overt heresy. There is only one way to gain salvation and eternal life, and that is through Jesus, and him alone; there is no alternative plan for Jews or for anyone who adheres to a different belief. Jesus is the way, the only way.

Jews believe that Judaism is the only true way. They place their faith in *Yom Kippur*, the Day of Atonement, when God is believed to write their names in the book of life—if they have sufficiently repented during the previous ten days of awe. However, addressing the Jews, Jesus said:

> *I said to you that you will die in your sins; for **if you do not believe that I AM, you will die in your sins***
> (John 8:24).

Catholics pray to Mary and the saints and the priests hold the Mass and serve the Eucharist, a small wafer and a little wine, or grape juice, in commemoration of the Last Supper. The wafer and the wine is believed to be transubstantiated into the actual body and blood of Jesus, supposedly giving the recipient salvation and eternal life. However, what Jesus said to the Jews also hold true for Catholics, and all those who are born into Protestant homes:

> *I said to you that you will die in your sins; for **if you do not believe that I AM, you will die in your sins***
> (John 8:24).

As stated previously, there is no "all roads lead to Rome" map when it comes to salvation and eternal life, there is only Jesus—he is the only way:

*I am **the** way, **the** truth, and **the** life. **No one comes to the Father except through Me.***

(See latter half of Endnote **2** on *knowing* Jesus.)

24

PHILIP SAID TO him, *"Lord, show us the Father, and it will be enough for us." Jesus said to him, "Have I been with you for so long a time and still you have not known me, Philip?* (John 14:9).

Jesus is essentially telling us that he himself is *God*. We need to understand a compilation of inferences that Jesus and others make in this regard. At the beginning of these notes (Endnote **1**) we have an emphatic statement: *In the beginning was **the Word** and **the Word** was with God, and **the Word was God*** (John 1:1). Then we are informed that: *Everything was made through him* (John 1:3). Notice that it says **through** *him*, this is because all things were created through speaking—*Then **God said**, "Let there be ... and it was so ...* (Genesis 1:6) and so forth. Then we have a further categorical statement: *The Word was made flesh, and lived among us* (John 1:14). This is an obvious and direct reference to Jesus Christ.

Prior to his saying that was directed at Philip, Jesus had said: *I and My Father are one* (John 10:30), which literally means Jesus and *God Almighty* are ONE ESSENCE. Now, when Philip asks Jesus to show them the Father, Jesus says, *"Have I been with you for so long a time and still YOU HAVE NOT KNOWN ME?* Jesus is saying that those who have seen him have seen the Father because they are essentially one and the same. Then Jesus says:

> *I will ask the Father, and he will give you another Advocate* [other than himself], *that he may abide with you forever, even **the Spirit of truth**, whom the world cannot receive, because it neither sees him, nor knows him; but **you know him; for he abides with you**, and will be in you. I will not leave you as orphans; **I will come to you*** (John 14:16-18).

Jesus has been telling the disciples that he is going away, but will ask the Father to send ANOTHER Advocate, *the **Spirit of truth***, and then goes on to say, *you know him; for **he abides with you**.* It was Jesus who was abiding with them, therefore Jesus is also *the Spirit of truth* who will come from the Father and this is borne out by: *I WILL COME to you.* Then Jesus says: *At that day you will know that I am in my Father, and you in me, and I in you* (John 14:20). Then Jesus drops a bombshell:

> *If a man loves me, he will keep my word; and my Father will love him, and **WE** will come to him and make **OUR** home with him* (John 14:23).

Jesus goes on to say:

> *These things I have spoken to you, still being present with you. The Advocate, **which is the Holy Spirit**, WHOM THE FATHER WILL SEND in my name, he will teach you all things, and bring whatever I have said to you to your remembrance* (John 14:25-26).

Thus we learn that **the Spirit of truth** and **the Holy Spirit** are one and the same. Then Jesus says **the Spirit of truth / Holy Spirit** proceeds **from the Father** (John 15:26) and goes on to say:

> *However, I tell you the truth, it is better for you that I go away, for if I do not go away, the Advocate will not come to you, but if I depart, **I WILL SEND HIM to you*** (John 16:7).

Jesus also says to the disciples:

> ***I WILL GIVE YOU*** *a mouth and wisdom in that hour, which all your adversaries will not be able to repudiate nor resist, for **it will not be you who speaks, BUT THE HOLY SPIRIT*** (Luke 21:15).

Again we see that Jesus is the *Holy Spirit*. Summing up the goings back and forth between Jesus' "*I*" and "*the Father*" (*God Almighty*), it is clear (at least to me) that they are referring to the same person. And in Isaiah's prophecy of chapter 9 we have solid confirmation:

> *For **unto us a CHILD is born**,*
> *Unto us **a SON** is given;*
> *And the government will be upon His shoulder.*
> *And **HIS NAME** will be called*
> *Wonderful, Counselor, **MIGHTY GOD**,*
> ***EVERLASTING FATHER**, Prince of Peace*
> (Isaiah 9:6).

Jesus is *God Almighty* incarnate—God himself living in a man's body who is now our *High Priest* (Hebrews 2:17 etc.) interceding on our behalf. There will come a day when everything has been made subject to Jesus:

> *Now when all things are made subject to him, then the Son himself will also be subject to him who put all things under him, **that God may be all in all***
> (1Corinthians 15:28).

There will eventually be a blending of Jesus (*God's only begotten Son* and our *High Priest*) and *the Father* (*God Almighty*) in order **that God may be all in all**, without the necessity of needing a *mediator between God and man* (1Timothy 2:5). We shall have personal and direct access to *God Almighty* himself.

25

> **WHATEVER YOU WILL** ask from the Father in my name, he may give it to you (John 15:16).
>
> whatever you will ask the Father in my name, he will give it to you (John 16:23).

In the Church the name of Jesus is tacked onto the end of prayers, as a virtual religious talisman. However, this is not at all what Jesus intended when he said "*in my name.*" To fully understand the import of what asking *in the name of Jesus* really means we must go to the book of Exodus.

In Exodus 33:18 Moses asks *God Almighty* to show him his glory:

> And God said, "I will make **all my goodness** pass before you and **will proclaim before you my name** "**Yahveh**" (LORD). I will be gracious to whom I will be gracious, and will show mercy on whom I will show mercy (Exodus 33:19).

(*God Almighty*'s name is *Yahveh*, expressed as "LORD" in most English translations.) After *Yahveh* said he would proclaim his name before Moses, we read in chapter 34:

> Yahveh descended in the cloud and stood with him there, and **proclaimed the name of Yahveh.**

> *Yahveh passed before him and proclaimed, "Yahveh, Yahveh God, merciful and gracious, slow to anger, and abounding in mercy and truth, keeping mercy for thousands, forgiving iniquity and transgression and sin, but will by no means clear the guilty, visiting the iniquity of the fathers on the children and the children's children, to the third and the fourth generation"* (Exodus 34:6–7).

All that *God Almighty* proclaimed before Moses was his **name**. A "*name*" is more than just a simple moniker, a "*name*" encompasses all that a person is. So when a follower of Jesus prays and is a merciful person, a compassionate person, a truthful person, a loving person, a generous person to the poor and to the widow, *abides* in Jesus and makes Jesus the dominating factor in life, then that person is praying *in the name* of Jesus. There is no need to attach the traditional religious talisman "*in Jesus' name*," which seems to be almost a requisite today, in the hope that the prayer will be answered.

26

> JESUS, KNOWING EVERYTHING *that would come upon him, went forward and said to them, "Whom do you seek?" They answered him, "Jesus of Nazareth."* **Jesus said to them, "I AM** *he." Judas also, who betrayed him, stood with them. As soon as he had said to them,* "I AM *he,"* **they pulled back and fell to the ground** (John 18:4–6).

A number of English translations render the response of Jesus as "*I am he,*" but there is no "he" in the Greek text, it is simply "*I AM.*" Jesus says the same thing in John 8:24 and again in John 8:58 when he says, "*Most assuredly, I say to you, before Abraham was, I AM.*"

Jesus here again shows his divinity. When the crowd in the garden of Gethsemane demand *Jesus of Nazareth*, he responds with, "*I AM*" and they go backwards and fall to the ground.

There is too much similarity here to simply pass over it. In Exodus 3:13 *God Almighty* tells Moses that he is sending him to Egypt to bring out the Israelites, but Moses protests:

> *If I go to the people of Israel and tell them, "The God of your ancestors has sent me to you," they will ask me, "What is his name?" Then what should I tell them?*
>
> *And God said to Moses, "I AM WHAT I AM." And He said, "Thus you shall say to the children of Israel, 'I AM has sent me to you'"* (Exodus 3:13–14).

The Hebrew rendered *I AM WHAT I AM* is (reading from right to left: אהיה אשר אהיה, which literally means, "**I will become whatever I want to become and do whatever I want to do whenever I want to do it.**" Such is the sovereignty of *God Almighty*! To make things easier for Moses, God says: "*Thus you shall say to the children of Israel, 'I AM [*אהיה*] has sent me to you.* And in the gospel of John we have Jesus saying thrice that he was: "*I AM.*" Coincidence? I think not (See Endnote **23**).

27

> **LORD, REMEMBER ME** *when you come into your kingdom." Jesus said to him, "Truly, I say to you today, you will be with me in Paradise"* (Luke 23:43).

The sentence that was spoken by Jesus to the thief has been copiously used to undergird a false belief that both the thief and Jesus entered Paradise that day. This is nonsense. It cannot be. It is the placing of the comma that has led to such a belief, but there is no such comma in the original Greek texts; however, a comma has been placed there in modern Greek texts simply because tradition requires it. Let us look at the facts devoid of fantasies:

> *A wicked and adulterous generation seeks after a sign, and no sign shall be given to it* **except the sign of the prophet Jonah** (Matthew 16:4).

> *For as Jonah* **was three days and three nights in the whale's belly, so will the Son of Man be three days and three nights in the heart of the earth*
> (Matthew 12:40).

Jesus was three days and nights in the heart of the earth, in the netherworld. That, by any stretch of the imagination, cannot be considered as "Paradise." That Jesus was dead and descended into the heart of the earth for three days and nights is one of the foundational truths of Christianity. Jesus did not rise from the dead until the third day:

> *thus it was necessary for Christ to suffer,* **and to rise from the dead on the third day** (Luke 24:46).

> **God raised him up on the third day**, *and showed Him openly* (Acts 10:40).

Jesus said to the repentant thief that he would be **with him** in Paradise, but Jesus went down into the netherworld and did not rise for three days, therefore there has to be a different interpretation to what Jesus really said, because obviously the reformed thief did not go straight to heaven (Paradise).

As with all the dead, the spirit remains alive. Jesus was very much alive in the Spirit when he descended into the netherworld and gave the gospel to its inhabitants:

> *Christ also suffered once for sins, the just for the unjust, that he might bring us to God, being* **put to death in the flesh** *but made* **alive by the Spirit, by whom he also went and preached to the spirits in prison**, *who formerly were disobedient*
> (1Peter 3:18-19).

The thief had repented and had also been accepted by Jesus, but the former thief certainly did not get raised from the grave before Jesus:

> *He (Jesus) is the ...* **firstborn from the dead**
> (Colossians 1:18).
>
> *Jesus Christ, the faithful witness,* **the firstborn from the dead** (Revelation 1:5).

No doubt some will quote the Apostle Paul's desire to be *absent from the body and to be present with the Lord* (2Corinthians 5:8). Paul wrote screeds on this subject and one needs to thoroughly study these writings in their contexts, unfortunately, it would take far too many pages to delve into them here. I am merely presenting scriptural fact, not promoting any doctrine.

Suffice it to say, death (Endnote **18**) is like falling asleep. No one is ever lost. Jesus said to the Sadducees, who did not believe in the resurrection:

> *Now touching that the dead are raised, have you not read in the Book of Moses that which was spoken to you by God, saying,* **"I am the God of Abraham, and the God of Isaac, and the God of Jacob"***? For he is not the God of the dead, but of the living, for all live to him* (Luke 20:37–38).

One of the clearest examples of believing loved ones and small children not being lost is found in the book of Job:

> *There was a man in the land of Uz, whose name was Job; and that man was blameless and upright, and one who feared God and shunned evil. And* **seven sons and three daughters were born to him***. Also, his possessions were* **seven thousand sheep, three thousand camels, five hundred yoke of oxen, five hundred female donkeys** (Job 1:1–3).

Probably the majority of readers know the story of Job. How calamity followed catastrophe, which was followed by disaster until Job had lost everything—possessions, children, even his own health. Fortunately the story does not end there. We skip over forty-one interesting chapters and see that in the end *God Almighty* restored the fortunes of Job:

> *Now the* L*ord* *blessed the latter days of Job more than his beginning; for he had* **fourteen thousand**

> *sheep, six thousand camels, one thousand yoke of oxen, and one thousand female donkeys. He also had **seven sons and three daughters***
>
> (Job 42:12–13).

Job's fortunes were restored. He had twice as many sheep, twice as many camels, twice as many oxen and twice as many female donkeys. But he only had his seven sons and three daughters replaced. Why? Because his original sons and daughters were God-fearing (Job 1:5) and were not lost, they were sleeping in the spirit, waiting for their awakening at the resurrection.

There will be a clarion call from Jesus *on the last day* (John 6:40, 44, 54) and we will be resurrected. It will be like waking from a sound sleep. The fortunate few, like Enoch, Moses and Elijah, bypass the dying process, but those who remain on earth at the time of the Second Coming of Jesus will experience the same upward call as the fortunate few just mentioned:

> *For the Lord Himself will descend from heaven with a shout, with the voice of an archangel, and with the trumpet of God. And the dead in Christ will rise first. Then **we who are alive and remain shall be caught up together with them in the clouds** to meet the Lord in the air. And thus we shall always be with the Lord* (1 Thessalonians 4:16–17).

What a Day that will be! We can but dream.

28

> *Jesus said to Simon Peter, "Simon, son of Jonah,* **do you love me more than these do?**" *He said to him, "Lord,* **you know that I care for you**." *He said to him, "Feed my lambs." He said to him again the second time, "Simon, son of Jonah,* **do you love me?**" *He said to him, "Lord,* **you know that I care for you.**" *He said to him, "Feed my sheep." Jesus said to him the third time, Simon, son of Jonah,* **do you care for me?**" *Peter was upset because he said to him the third time, "***Do you care for me?**" *He said to him, "Lord, you know all things,* **you know that I care for you**" *Jesus said to him, "Feed my sheep."*
> (John 21:15–17).

Every English translation that I have consulted renders the word "*love*" that was spoken by Jesus to Peter the same as that spoken by Peter in response to the question put to him. This is very misleading; translators should know better. The word used by Jesus in his first two questions is ἀγαπᾷς – (*agapao*), which means "to love unreservedly." In contrast, the word Peter uses in all three of his responses to Jesus is, φιλῶ – (*phileo*), which means "to be fond of"; "to have affection for."

Peter had shown himself to have both a measure of courage: *Peter got out of the boat, he walked on the water to go to Jesus* (Matthew 14:29), and also a measure of faith: *go to the sea, throw in a hook and take the first fish that comes up, and when you open its mouth you will find a piece of money; take that and give it to them* (Matthew 17:27), but he had been impetuous and boastful: *I will lay down my life for your sake* (John 13:37), *though all men will stumble because of you, yet I will never stumble* (Matthew 26:33).

Denying Jesus three times took the wind out of Peter's sails. Now Jesus was getting Peter to face up to his himself and his bragging: "Do you love (ἀγαπᾷς) me unreservedly, more than these other disciples do?" Peter does not own to loving (ἀγαπᾷς) Jesus unreservedly, he says, "You know that I care (φιλῶ) for you, that I have affection for you." Jesus reaffirms Peter's leadership: *"Feed my lambs."*

Jesus pushes Peter: "Do you love (ἀγαπᾷς) me unreservedly?" Peter repeats his subdued answer: "You know that I care (φιλῶ) for you, that I have affection for you." Jesus reaffirms Peter again: *"Feed my sheep."* The third time Jesus really pushes Peter: "Simon, do you care (φιλῶ - *phileo*), do you have affection for me? Peter is crestfallen, his sorrow for having repeatedly denied Jesus with curses and swearing has filled him with remorse. And the One whom he denied is the One asking him the questions. Peter repeats that he cares (φιλῶ) and has affection for Jesus, but he will in no way say that he loves (ἀγαπᾷς) Jesus unreservedly, because he now realizes what a human heart is capable of. Boasting and impetuousness has now gone. Jesus says to him again: *"Feed my sheep,"* which was yet another affirmation of Peter's leadership of the twelve.

29

WHEN THEY SAW him, they worshiped him; **but some doubted** (Matthew 28:17).

This is one of the most astonishing passages in the gospels.

These disciples had been with Jesus constantly for three years. They were with him when he fed five thousand men plus countless women and children from five small pita loaves and two small fish and had picked up twelve baskets full of leftovers. They were with him when he repeated that miracle by feeding four thousand men plus women and children from seven small pita loaves and some small fish, and picked up seven baskets full of leftovers. They were with Jesus when he raised people from the dead, including their friend Lazarus, and they saw the lame walking, the sick healed, the blind given sight, the lepers cleansed; they must have also seen hundreds of other miraculous events. They all ran away when Jesus was arrested and crucified, but they saw him many times after his resurrection, they ate and drank with him. Now, when they meet at the place Jesus had appointed in Galilee, some of the disciples **have doubts**. Amazing.

It is only human to have doubts concerning one's own faith in the run up to spiritual maturity, but when doubt arises it must be dealt with or it will grow. We must restate to ourselves what we believe and why. We must feed upon God's Word and talk to him often, throughout every day. We must abide in Jesus and feed our inner man upon him, because in him is life and he came that we might have it *more abundantly* (John 10:10). Jesus nowhere promised us a trouble-free life, in fact he said the opposite, but he throws us a buoyancy aid to keep us afloat in troubled times:

> *In the world you will have tribulation; but **be of good cheer, I have overcome the world*** (John 16:33).

To be in Christ Jesus is to be alive:

> *I have been crucified with Christ; it is no longer I who live, but Christ lives in me; and the life which I now live in the flesh I live by faith in the Son of God, who loved me and gave Himself for me*
> (Galatians 2:20).

Crucified people have said all their goodbyes!

NEWSLETTER

Ramon Bennett, the author of this book, also writes the *Update*, the regular newsletter of the *Arm of Salvation Ministries*. The *Update* keeps readers informed on world events that affect Israel, and also, on the ministry of Ramon Bennett and his wife, Zipporah. An annual donation of $20.00 is requested for the *Update*. The *Update* is available only by e-mail in digital PDF format. Amounts given above the stated amount will be put toward the personal expenses of the Bennetts. Subscriptions to the *Update* and any voluntary donations should be made via *PayPal*: <payments@shekinahbooks.com>.

Arm of Salvation (*AOS*) was founded by Ramon Bennett in 1980 and is an indigenous Israeli ministry dependent upon gifts and the proceeds from its book and music sales to sustain its work in and for Israel and the Jewish people. These are critical times for Israel so financial support is both needful and appreciated.

Copies of **No Other Name** and other books authored by Ramon Bennett (see following pages) are all available from Amazon.com.

Albums of popular Hebrew worship songs composed by Zipporah Bennett, are available by making contact with Zipporah Bennett at the following e-mail address: <usa@shekinahbooks.com>.

Visit our website: http://**www.shekinahbooks.com** to subscribe, and/or donate via *PayPal*.

OTHER  TITLES BY RAMON BENNETT

All titles available from Amazon.com

new 2015 fourth edition

"**WHEN DAY & NIGHT CEASE** is the most comprehensive, factual and informative book on Israel—past, present and future. If you want a true picture of how Israel is falling into Bible prophecy today, look no further. You will want to read this book"

324 pages – Paperback, or Kindle e-book

updated 2016!

PHILISTINE lays bare the Arab mind, Islam, the Koran, the United Nations, the news media, rewritten history, and the Israeli-PLO peace accord. **PHILISTINE** will grip you. **PHILISTINE** will inform you. Philistine will shock you. Until you read **PHILISTINE** you will never understand the Middle East—the world's most volatile region.

364 pages – Paperback, or Kindle e-book

updated 2016 extended

"**They lead My people astray**, saying 'Peace!' when there is no peace, and because, when a flimsy wall is built, they cover it with whitewash" (Ezekiel 13:10).

In **The Wall** Ramon Bennett exposes the peace process for what it is, an attempt to break Israel down "piece" by "piece." This book contains information the mainstream news media, the CIA, the White House, and others would rather you did not know.

367 pages – Paperback, or Kindle e-book

updated 2016 extended

UNDERSTAND the chaos taking place around the world today! **SAGA** shows that Jews died because cruelty and evil and anti-Semitism are not confined to one race or nation but are found everywhere. **SAGA** is about Israel and Israel's God; about war and judgment—past, present, and future. Nations came and went, empires rose and fell; and God is still judging nations today. A "must read" in light of world events today.

284 pages – Paperback, or Kindle e-book

OTHER SHEKINAH TITLES BY RAMON BENNETT

All titles available from Amazon.com

THE WILDERNESS

"VERY INFORMATIVE BOOK FOR THOSE WHO are looking for answers to what is happening in the middle east. Most of what you hear in the news media is such surface stuff and news to steer you away from the truth. God's Word is truth and Ramon Bennett breaks down verses that I've wondered about for years. A very good read, you won't be able to put it down." — William D. Douglas

335 pages – Paperback, or Kindle e-book

GAZA! is an accurate account of the events that led up to, and took place during, Israel's Operation Protective Edge, the 50-day war against Hamas in Gaza in 2014. It is a factual account of what took place, when it took place, why it took place, and the result of it having taken place.

This book gives a proper perspective—differing to what was presented on television screens across the world; it gives a different narrative to that told by Hamas-threatened journalists who covered the third round of this never-ending conflict.

134 pages – Paperback, or Kindle e-book

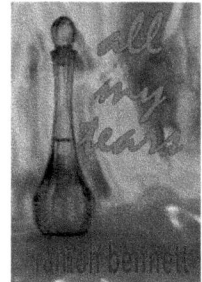

ALL MY TEARS – an autobiography

RAMON BENNETT has been introduced as "someone who has suffered the trials of Job."

Often verging on the unbelievable, ***ALL MY TEARS*** is Ramon's astounding autobiographical testimony; a story of an unwanted, abused child whom God adopted and anointed, and uses for His glory.

448 pages – Paperback, or Kindle e-book

HISTORY, the gospels of Matthew, Mark, Luke, and John blended together into a single uninterrupted narrative. ***HISTORY*** transforms the four individual gospels, each with its own color text, into an edifying read for those interested in the full, uninterrupted story of the nativity, life, death, resurrection, and ascension of Jesus Christ. The **Color Print Edition** shows from where each interpolated piece comes from. Bible Students find this book fascinating. Black Print Edition also available.

184 pages – Paperback, or Kindle e-book

Book & Music Titles By Zipporah Bennett

Return, Daughter of Zion! Zipporah Bennett's testimony and autobiography. Read how Zipporah, a God-hungry Orthodox Jewish girl, found the Reality she longed for. This book, often amusing, will help the reader better understand the way Jewish people think and feel about the "Christian" Jesus.

137 pages – Paperback, or Kindle e-book

Available on Amazon.com

Hebrew worship from one of Israel's foremost composers of Messianic worship songs

Hallelu	Kuma Adonai	Mi Ha'amin?

"Hallelu" – Dual Hebrew–English songs of worship	*"Arise O Lord!"* Songs of warfare and worship	*"Who Hath Believed?"* Hebrew and Aramaic prophecies in song

For a descriptive overview or **to purchase the above CD albums** go to:
http://www.shekinahbooks.com

www.ingramcontent.com/pod-product-compliance
Lightning Source LLC
Chambersburg PA
CBHW060821050426
42453CB00008B/522